Social Analysis for the 21st Century

How Faith Becomes Action

Maria Cimperman

ORBIS BOOKS

Maryknoll, New York 10545

ORBIS BOOKS
Maryknoll, New York 10545

Fathers and Brothers
MARYKNOLL™

Founded in 1970, Orbis Books endeavors to publish works that enlighten the mind, nourish the spirit, and challenge the conscience. The publishing arm of the Maryknoll Fathers and Brothers, Orbis seeks to explore the global dimensions of the Christian faith and mission, to invite dialogue with diverse cultures and religious traditions, and to serve the cause of reconciliation and peace. The books published reflect the views of their authors and do not represent the official position of the Maryknoll Society. To learn more about Maryknoll and Orbis Books, please visit our website at www.maryknollsociety.org.

Library of Congress Cataloging-in-Publication Data

Cimperman, Maria.
  Social analysis for the 21st century : how faith becomes action / Maria Cimperman.
    pages cm
  Includes bibliographical references.
  ISBN 978-1-62698-143-0 (pbk.)
  1. Religion and sociology. 2. Christian sociology. I. Title. II. Title: Social analysis for the twenty-first century.
  BL60.C555 2015
  261.8'3—dc23
                                                    2015009600

*I dedicate this book to Maeve and Sam,
whose capacity to see with love and question injustice at
such a young age reminds me that God is already
in the process of transforming society.
And to their parents, Joe and Nora, who nurture this call
in them by their own example.
May this small contribution support and encourage their
lives and work.*

Contents

Foreword

Social Analysis Revisited

Peter Henriot, SJ

"How we see a problem determines how we respond to it."

These are the opening words of a small book published thirty-five years ago titled *Social Analysis: Linking Faith and Justice*. When Joe Holland, my colleague at the Center of Concern in Washington, DC, and I prepared that text for publication, we had little idea of how popular it would become. Widely printed, widely translated, and widely used, *Social Analysis* introduced a way of seeing a problem that helped determine the response to that problem. In doing so, it contributed to a social justice movement within the Catholic Church that made the call of Vatican II's *Gaudium et Spes* (*The Church in the Modern World*) come alive in so many places for so many causes.

Around the time Joe and I were working on the text of *Social Analysis*, I recall being very much touched by the words of Bishop Dom Helder Camara of Brazil: "When I feed the hungry, I am called a saint; when I ask why they are hungry, I am called a radical, a communist!" To move beyond a charitable response to an issue like hunger toward an effective justice response meant seeing that problem with eyes that uncovered the structural roots of the problem. But to do that required a tool of study, a method of investigation, that probed deeper than mere stories. It required social analysis.

Why did Joe and I get involved in popularizing the social

analysis methodology? Our base at the Center of Concern meant close association with many church and secular movements for justice in the 1970s and 1980s. Joe's academic background was social theology, and he brought experiences of work with immigrant Puerto Ricans and social movements in Chile. My academic background was political science, and I was influenced by racial justice and antiwar involvements and the faith-and-justice emphasis of my religious community, the Jesuits. I would credit Joe particularly with helping me appreciate the structural emphasis in dealing with issues of justice, both domestic and international.

When we wrote *Social Analysis*, the Catholic Church in the United States and wider was still experiencing the spiritual powers released a decade earlier by Vatican II, which meant a theological and pastoral openness to social issues and a motivation for involvement at levels deeper than charitable actions. The implications of Dom Helder Camara's observation rang true for so many committed people of faith. Local, national, and international justice and peace movements held a respected prominence in the church.

Some of the vigor of social commitment of those early years waned with a more conservative turn of church leadership and a more pronounced withdrawal from immediate social action efforts. But interest in social analysis continued in academic settings as well as in practical local efforts for social change. One result was more refinement of the understanding of social analysis and the use of the central apostolic tool that Joe and I had offered in our book: the "pastoral circle."

Just what that refinement meant in practice was explored ten years ago (the twenty-fifth anniversary of *Social Analysis*) in a rich series of essays titled *The Pastoral Circle Revisited: A Critical Quest for Truth and Transformation*. This refinement is hinted at in the titles of some of the essays in that book, for example, "Engendering the Pastoral Cycle," "The Pastoral Circle as Spirituality," "A Cycle Opening to Pluralism," and "Social Discernment and the Pastoral Circle."

Because of the widespread use today of social analysis in many forms, Maria Cimperman's *Social Analysis for the 21st Century* is so very timely and helpful. Based on her experience of teaching courses, conducting workshops, and participating in social movements, Maria has brought together both theory and practice with good examples, realistic methods, and probing challenges.

It's important to recognize that what today we regard as prominent social issues with profound structural dimensions were at the time of the appearance of *Social Analysis* either very modestly considered or simply absent from the agenda of many social justice centers (the Center of Concern included). Many of these issues today reflect the increasing phenomenon of globalization, especially of what Pope Francis has characterized as a "globalization of indifference." This is surely in marked contrast to what Pope John Paul II called a "globalization of solidarity." Creating this globalization of indifference has been an emphasis on the structures of competition, consumerism, comfort, and complacency—all too often numbing us to the everyday suffering of sisters and brothers around our neighborhoods and around our world.

Social analysis, therefore, could be said to be even more necessary for the follower of Jesus's gospel today than when Joe and I explained it in our text thirty-five years ago—necessary both for more profound theological reflection and for more effective social action. Some structures of globalization that need attention because of their growing importance include

- *Ecology*—Global warming with implications for climate change that negatively affects the growth of food all around our world.
- *Inequality*—Growing disparities between rich and poor, with economic structures reinforcing subhuman poverty situations even as rich grow richer.
- *Information technology*—A powerful impact, often negative, on learning, with a reinforcement of stereotypical

descriptions of "others" and circulation of degrading images of humans.

- *Terrorism*—Cooperative and often coordinated efforts among radical religious and social sects that can disrupt peace in various parts of the world.
- *Migration*—Significant movement of peoples, as families or separate individuals, out of situations of poverty and conflict into unwelcome environs of Europe and North America.

Another topic that certainly deserves the focus of good social analysis is feminism. The word "feminism," of course, covers a wide variety of phenomena in a wide variety of places. In simplest terms, feminism emphasizes equal rights for both women and men. Positive contributions of gender equity need to be lifted up as reinforcing structures of authentic development. Negative manifestations of gender bias should be analyzed to show structural links to a range of injustices in society and in our church.

From the experience of twenty-five years in Africa (Zambia and Malawi), I have also seen the contribution that social analysis has made to the development and pastoral work in which my colleagues and I have been engaged. For example, a study of the structures of the external debt crippling the economies of so many African nations demonstrated causes of debt that went well beyond mismanagement and corruption on the part of the African actors. The dominant influence of the World Bank and the IMF and the trade and investment polices of rich nations were exposed in good analytical studies that contributed to the eventually successful call of the Jubilee movement for cancellation of debts.

In addition, analytic studies of the ecclesial structures of small Christian communities (a pastoral priority in the African Catholic Church) also revealed strengths as well as weaknesses in a variety of situations. This has prompted responses at local and national levels—for example, preparation of leaders, testing of innovative sacramental practices, and questioning of seminary training.

With the well-conceived and comprehensive approach that these pages represent, Maria Cimperman has done us all a great favor in giving us a broad overview of the many elements necessary for good social analysis. Since it is so true that "how we see a problem determines how we respond to it," my hope and prayer are that our responses to the many social challenges of today will be made more effective by the way we see these challenges with the help of social analysis.

Peter Henriot, SJ, is a member of the Zambia-Malawi Province of the Society of Jesus. Currently he is helping set up a new "option for the poor" secondary school in Malawi. Previously he worked at the Center of Concern in Washington, DC (1971–1988), and at the Jesuit Centre for Theological Reflection in Lusaka, Zambia (1989–2010).

Acknowledgments

No book is written in a vacuum or a tower, even though writing ultimately needs some solitude for completion. A wide community contributed to this book, and though I will never thank each person completely, I can at least begin.

As with many good ideas, this book began with a conversation and an invitation. Janet Mock, CSJ, then executive director of the Religious Formation Conference (RFC), joined an ongoing conversation between Jim Hug, SJ, and me. The three of us talked about what each was seeing in our ministries—unmet needs we were encountering as well as exciting possibilities that were burgeoning in groups with which we were working. We saw much energy for the transformation of unjust systems and also a desire to find better ways to engage systems. So much seemed possible! How might we galvanize the energy? At the time Janet was also discerning topics for the next set of workshops that the RFC biannually offers its members around a current topic. We asked ourselves: What would it be like to create and offer a process for this millennium that would engage social analysis alongside faith tradition and our deepest Christian values?

Janet looked at us and said, "Do it! Create a series of workshops on social analysis for the twenty-first century and offer it to our members around the country!" So began our examination and implementation of the pastoral spiral—a basic tool of social analysis.

Here I must thank Jim Hug, SJ, a wonderfully wise friend and colleague. It was his insight that we build on the seminal work of Peter Henriot, SJ, and Joe Holland and call the process the *pastoral spiral*. Jim employs a global lens, and his thinking is detailed, a wonderful combination. I am also grateful to the Center of Concern, where at that time Jim was the executive director, and the work the center does on a daily basis to transform structures.

Much gratitude goes to the many groups around the country that engaged the process and applied it to any number of social issues that were of great concern to them: immigration, capital punishment, sustainable energy use, sex trafficking, and more. Each region of the country had different lenses and cases to bring forth, and each helped to fine-tune and hone the process.

Another learning community for me was in the many classes in Catholic social thought I taught during eight years at Oblate School of Theology in San Antonio. In those classes, students not only from the United States but from around the world used the pastoral spiral. Over time I watched them employ the process to make a difference with projects among the people they served in many parts of the world. This was truly an international community, and I am grateful for their ongoing efforts to build the reign of God.

Now I am at yet another international community of learners at the Catholic Theological Union (CTU) in Chicago. Here students have used the process and given suggestions as they look at realities on the South Side of Chicago, Arizona, Rwanda, the Democratic Republic of Congo, and more. We are colleagues in a community that seeks to live justly and creatively and to eliminate gaps so that we are truly one world and one creation. I am grateful for the support of wonderful colleagues in both institutions who have encouraged this work. In the summer of 2014, participants in the Maryknoll Mission Institute, directed by Maria Homberg, MM, offered helpful ideas and suggestions, particularly in practical areas.

There is a more personal set of communities for which I am most grateful. The Ursuline Sisters of Cleveland (OSU) supported this project from its inception, and the Society of the Sacred Heart of Jesus (RSCJ) supported this project to its completion. I am grateful to both communities for their support and encouragement to respond to cries among God's people and Earth.

Friends and mentors are gifts, and I am blessed. I am grateful to friends who walked alongside the initial writing, including Janet Moore, OSU; Joanne Gross, OSU; Mary Charlotte Chandler, RSCJ; Judith Anne Beattie, CSC; and Anita Whitely, OSU.

The RSCJ communities in San Diego and Chicago walked alongside and cheered during the dailiness of rewriting, editing, and revising, whether it was at home or in off-the-beaten track coffee shops. I have a debt of gratitude to each person.

Various friends have also served as invaluable conversation partners as various chapters were in process. They include Katherine Feely, SND; Lisa Buscher, RSCJ; Mary Sharon Riley, RC; and Kristin Matthes, SNDdeN. The book is a better text because of your suggestions, and I am a better person because of the gifts you are in my life. Thank you!

For their love, friendship, and example, I am grateful to my brother Joe, sister-in law Nora, niece Maeve and nephew Sam, who remind me that love and justice go hand in hand, personally and collectively. For embodying love in action, thank you! For reminding me that play is important, thank you also!

Finally, I am indebted to the community at Orbis Books, for they have undoubtedly grown in the virtue of patience in waiting for this book to come to fruition. Susan Perry was the editor of my first manuscript, and I was honored and grateful when she invited me to write this book. Sue's commitment to this project and her willingness to wait as my own life was in transition is a reminder that we are always to be about a service beyond ourselves. Mercy, compassion, and love are necessary companions to perseverance. Sue's life and ministry are a model of such virtues. I am also very grateful to editors Jim Keane and Robert Ellsberg, who understand the pastoral spiral from the inside out. They are amazing persons who live what they believe. I am also grateful to Peter Henriot, SJ, now ministering in Malawi, for the Foreword to this book and even more for his decades of work on social analysis, both from North America and Africa. In addition, the life and work of Dean Brackley, SJ, who engaged spirituality and social analysis, speak to me of the life we are all called to live deeply and fully.

I am indeed grateful to the many who contributed to what this book has become. Any errors are mine.

Finally, and most important, I give thanks with all my being to this good God who is love and who calls all of us forth to discover God's love, reveal God's love, and "love all as God loves."

1

Our Sacred Calling in the World

Rooted in Hope

> Challenges exist to be overcome! Let us be realists, but without losing our joy, our boldness, and our hope-filled commitment.
> —Pope Francis, *The Joy of the Gospel*

This is a book about hope, and a way of hope for the world. But before beginning the work of social analysis, consider the following questions:

- As you look around at the world, what do *you* see? What do *you* hear?
- What are other people seeing and hearing?
- What are the unmet needs in the world today?
- What needs to be done?

SEEING THE WORLD

Two science programs recently offered breathtaking images of the world. The first came from a telescope at the South Pole that detected faint spiral patterns in space; the South Pole telescope team, led by John M. Kovac of the Harvard-Smithsonian Center for Astrophysics, contended that these images were the very beginning of time. These patterns of waves are the "long-sought markers for a theory called inflation, the force that put the bang in the Big Bang: an antigravitational swelling that began a trillionth of a trillionth of a trillionth of a second after the cosmic clock started ticking."[1] We have clues now to what happened a moment after the big bang, showing how energy moved into forms that created our universe and world. The second image came from a television broadcast about a telescope named ALMA that can see parts of the universe that had been otherwise invisible, detecting gases that may be the building blocks of new stars and planet formations and helping us better understand not only how universes form but also what they look like as they are forming.[2] The past and the future are converging into our present, and people are able to see better both near and far.

But when *you* look at the world, what do *you* see? Sometimes what we see is great beauty, accomplishments, breakthroughs on any number of levels. As I looked around the world near and far this year, I saw a Massive Open Online Course (MOOC)[3] in Arabic at a university in Israel; my five-year-old niece learning Mandarin in kindergarten in Cleveland; efforts by Roman Catholic bishops in the Congo to galvanize people against a referendum to change the Constitution that currently mandates term limits for the highest political office; Olympic Games in Sochi, Russia, where politics for a few moments were forgotten as many watched athletes excel in beauty, speed, and grace; a new pope's words, actions, and dispositions beginning to shift polemic rhetoric in the U.S. Catholic Church—and also in global politics—to communal attentiveness of persons economically poor and marginalized; growing numbers of medical school students in Venezuela trained in a community health model that quickly brings them to learn about and respond to needs of those often removed from help; a billionaire planning a $100 million ad campaign during the 2014 mid-term elections to push leaders to take action on climate change after a devastating November 2013 super typhoon in the Philippines.

In the UN's *Millennium Development Goals Report 2013*, a

global survey that examines each country and region, Secretary-General Ban Ki-moon writes,

> The Millennium Development Goals (MDGs) have been the most successful global antipoverty push in history. Significant and substantial progress has been made in meeting many of the targets—including halving the number of people living in extreme poverty and the proportion of people without sustainable access to improved sources of drinking water. The proportion of urban slum dwellers declined significantly. Remarkable gains have been made in the fight against malaria and tuberculosis. There have been visible improvements in all health areas as well as primary education.[4]

But what we see can also be heartrending, unjust, and even violent. This has also been a time of continuing devastation and slaughter in Syria; violent political upheaval in the Ukraine followed by Russian annexation of Crimea after a contested referendum; protests in Brazil about the money spent on preparation for the World Cup in 2014 and the 2016 Summer Olympics when there are great needs for education and civic infrastructure; four hundred young people arrested at the White House while protesting the Keystone XL pipeline; and no end to foreclosures in Chicago, particularly in the most economically challenged neighborhoods. Within the Roman Catholic Church, there is uncertainty about how the structural reform of the Roman Catholic curia will transpire and how Pope Francis's words about a greater role for women in church leadership will materialize.

Again, as the 2015 target date of the MDGs approaches, much remains to be done:

> For example, one in eight people worldwide remain hungry. Too many women die in childbirth when we have the means to save them. More than 2.5 billion people lack improved sanitation facilities, of which one billion

continue to practice open defecation, a major health and environmental hazard. Our resource base is in serious decline, with continuing losses of forests, species, and fish stocks, in a world already experiencing the impacts of climate change.

This report also shows that the achievement of the MDGs has been uneven among and within countries. Children from poor and rural households are much more likely to be out of school than their rich and urban counterparts. Wide gaps remain in basic knowledge about HIV and its prevention among young men and women in sub-Saharan Africa, which has been hardest hit by the epidemic.[5]

Tensions continue all over the world. There are measured dance steps between North Korea and South Korea as reunions of separated family members ensue to ease strained relations and signify possible overtures for better relations. At the same time there are ongoing negotiations between Iran and the UN Security Council to create a framework for nuclear talks that can ease sanctions and reduce threats of military action. In the Middle East, Israeli and Palestinian neighbors continue to take steps to and from the table of dialogue that would lead toward a more lasting peace. Movement in all these areas, and many others, are ongoing.

Many pieces are in flux, in motion, and the work of social analysis must be taken on within the context of such realities and questions as well as the belief that the reign of God is both here, near, and not yet. Graduate students at Chicago's Catholic Theological Union, coming from around the world, describe their own world:

- Rwanda, twenty years after the genocide, has a generation that is a linchpin between a horrific past and a future that sees all as brother and sister.
- The Philippines has high levels of pollution that are destroying the airways of people trying to breathe.

- The gas pipeline between Canada and the United States is a threat to environmental safety.
- Thirst in the United States for the least expensive way to do water treatment damages the future of drinking water.
- The Democratic Republic of Congo is at a critical juncture in the referendum to change the Constitution's mandate of term limits.
- There is much religious and ethnic tension in Bangladesh.
- Capital punishment in the U.S.is barbaric, unjust, and untenable.
- Brazil is struggling to maintain the Amazon even as there are efforts to build thirty new dams in the rain forest for more access to electricity.
- Vietnam must learn to deal with its history of civil war before it can build reconciliation.
- The Democratic and Republican parties in the United States seem unable to work together on immigration reform, although both parties say it is necessary.
- Many in the Roman Catholic Church revel in the joy and hope of Pope Francis's papacy and yet struggle to make the actual economic, political, and personal changes demanded by joy and hope.

These students see the world from around the world. For example, one sees a postgenocide Rwanda and wants to find a way to assist Rwandan youth whose parents are survivors, victims, or perpetrators of the 1994 genocide in order to find a way beyond violence, to incarnate "never again" in another way to live together. Another student who sees Christians in China hungry for the Word of God is trying to find a way to change access to religious education. A student from the Congo fears efforts to change a national constitution that mandates term limits as he works to create a process for education, "conscientization," and socially just action. One person is working to overcome the "economics of impoverishment" in a small region of his country that quietly encourages young, pregnant teenagers to sell their newborns in order to pay for education.

A student from the midwestern United States works to connect very diverse young people in an economically struggling neighborhood in the South Side of Chicago. Another person is searching out the systemic causes and response to high unemployment among young males in gangs who voice little hope for a better future or even a long adult life. Yet others are studying how parishes might adopt a more responsible use of resources and reduce the use of plastics as an act of faith in action. These are but a few examples.

As they seek to respond to situations in their countries of origin, they place their experiences alongside the theology they are learning within a community of faith in the United States. What they learn then flows in and out of all places in the world, hopefully bringing about a world in which the reign of God is more apparent.

When you look at the world, what do *you* see? This question is important—a perspective shapes much of what we understand and do—and where and how we look determine what we see. Both in turn influence greatly how we may respond. We must always remember that there is usually more to a situation than is immediately visible. Much throughout the world is in flux, and the goal of this book is to assist movement to create the world that God invites, the world in which people live to their full human flourishing, and in which all creation is treated as created by God and thus sacred.

WHY IS THIS HAPPENING?
WHAT AM I SUPPOSED TO DO ABOUT IT?

Having taken a quick look at the world near and far, we now must begin to ask questions about why these situations are the way they are. This question is crucial, for it clarifies the important difference between *responding* to symptoms and *seeking out the cause* of a situation. Both need to be addressed, though in different moments.

When we look at a particular issue, we begin to examine

details of particular cases, such as death penalty cases, arrests of persons without documentation, or legislation that allows oil drilling in the Gulf of Mexico in the wake of the BP oil spill. Details will be important in understanding the complexity of the issues that face us. However, examining the larger picture is just as important early on. This entails studying the systems in place and the underlying structures. The details and facts often result from the systems that are in place. So when students strike to protest inadequate funding for education, it would be important to go beneath the externals to determine what funding is actually available and whether it is insufficient. If funding is insufficient, perhaps it would be helpful to explore other possible sources of funding. Questions could then follow about who decides the use of public funds and whether there are some openings for alternative uses of funds or alternative possibilities for education. We would thus gain some understanding of what systems are and are not in place that impact the funding of education. The goal in the end is to understand the larger picture, the systems and structures at play, the outcomes of those systems, who the decisionmakers are, and what other possibilities might exist that could provide more adequate funding for education.

Understanding the bigger picture brings us to globalization and its impact on our lives. The term is defined differently depending on the lens from which you look at an issue (economic, political, technological, etc.), but a good beginning is Robert J. Schreiter's offering. He writes that there is "no one accepted definition of globalization, nor is there consensus on its exact description. Nearly all would agree, however, that it is about the increasingly interconnected character of the political, economic, and social life of the people of this planet."[6] To this we would certainly add the interconnected character of the environmental life of the people and all of creation. Kenneth R. Himes describes globalization as a "braid with distinct yet intertwined strands. Politics, economics, communications, religion, education, environment, fine arts, technology—all are strands forming the braid. Yet each strand has its own distinctive appearance and represents a particular form of globalization."[7] While globalization in itself is neutral, how it impacts people shapes its effect, which is not neutral. Globalization can increase opportunities for solidarity and interconnectedness, from responses to tsunamis to accessibility of the World Wide Web for educational opportunities. However, globalization can also be used by humans to harm people on the margins. Gustavo Gutiérrez reminds us that "to be against globalization as such is like being against electricity. However, this cannot lead us to resign ourselves to the present order of things because globalization as it is now being carried out exacerbates the unjust inequalities among different sectors of humanity and the social, economic, political, and cultural exclusion of a good portion of the world's populations."[8]

People shape and form globalization, and thus can direct it toward good. Johannes Banawiratma writes that

> In our present-day world the Christian community has to be aware of the globalizing process that marginalizes poor people. Imperialistic globalization should be opposed by a counter strategy, a globalization of solidarity or globalization from below, namely, a culture of networking among contextual communities in view of globalization without marginalization, building a worldwide community of justice and peace that recognizes the integrity of creation.[9]

We look at the systems of globalization through many lenses, including economics, politics, the environment, culture, religion, social patterns and traditions, and more. These lenses all inform us of both the complexity of an issue (there is a reason the challenges were not easily or adequately dealt with before) and offer potential hints about where points of leverage or change (transformation) may exist.

These lenses or layers define five important points in dealing with larger issues:

1. It is helpful to understand that problems usually have layers upon layers of complexity that must be considered in order to gain some perspective.
2. At every stage it is important to spend some time exploring, researching, and reflecting on what is actually happening. Humility (seeking truth) and curiosity are most helpful. This step, like every other step in social analysis, requires some reflection instead of immediate action; we must hold back from early action.
3. We need others working with us. In order to see a situation clearly we must be attuned to as many of the layers of interrelationships as we can, and we do this best when working with others.
4. Creating alternatives to a problem requires that we allow new insights to emerge and that we free ourselves to see different patterns.
5. At some point we must act, even as other layers of response probably will emerge as we act.

We often look at the larger pictures and systems because of particular values we hold, such as responding to people made poor and vulnerable or maintaining the integrity of all creation. As we do so, we begin to notice the significant gaps of access for many. Three significant gaps include access to resources, power, and opportunities. Basic resources include the major areas of food, water, shelter. These are primary resources for survival—not thriving but just surviving. So when the BBC reports that 7 million people have died because of polluted resources, it tells of a gap in access needed for basic survival.

Another serious set of gaps includes power. When people are unable to bring about change, whether in systems of government, law, communication, or education, their ability to transform their situation is severely limited. This occurs when governments or groups refuse to allow people to speak publicly, protest nonviolently, or vote as they choose.

A third major gap is access to opportunity. When people do

not have access to education, job training, and employment possibilities due to gender, race, ethnicity/tribe, orientation, or political affiliation, major possibilities for change are stymied. The status quo remains fixed, and the situation seems hopeless as there appears to be no way out of poverty, hunger, or continuing strife.

Once we begin questioning the why and what underneath a problem, another question naturally arises. What am I supposed to do? To begin to answer that, I suggest we first ask: What does the world need? Indeed, the world needs to pay attention to the gaps and to remove the reasons that they exist at all. Further, the world is asking us to create better ways to address some of the needs that underlie the gaps. Asking what the world needs gives us a lens from which to consider our response.

In order to "read" the world we need to go beyond ourselves. More of the world community needs to be invited to participate in naming what the world needs and creating a better world. This is the first answer to the question of "What am I supposed to do?" If I thought I alone had to have the answers to all these problems I would either be foolish or likely to stay hiding in bed all day overwhelmed! Second, as we discuss later on, leadership for social change of any kind usually doesn't happen with one person. Good leadership for change requires a team or a group, and the greater the participation the better. Partnerships that acknowledge the interweaving of our lives are essential for change toward the reign of God. This is one of the great benefits and challenges of social media, which has been used effectively to bring about social change because one can communicate a vision while eliciting responses from others, including those with a similar vision and those with alternative ideas.

A second point to note is that in responding we are seeking to create, from a Christian perspective, a vision of the reign of God (more on this in next section). Our faith calls us to a global perspective, to listen to and hear the cries of our neighbors, of all creation, and to respond, not just by stopping a wrong but by creating a vision of what is possible. In working toward building a people of peace and justice, Pope Francis reminds us of our call to creativity, noting that we need to "give priority to actions which generate new processes in society and engage other persons and groups who can develop them to the point where they bear fruit in significant historical events."[10] Then the lenses from which we see and analyze—economics, politics, culture, religion, environment—flow from a vision of the reign of God. We do not necessarily know where this will lead, however, because asking what the world needs also moves us beyond our own situation and our own needs.

This book explores seeing, analyzing, reflecting, and responding toward the "more" that we sense God wants for the world through the process of what is known as the "pastoral spiral." This process, undertaken communally, in dialogue, is geared toward the transformation of systems and also toward the transformation of individuals and peoples. There is no way to change a system if the persons involved are not also transformed. So it is important to state clearly that the pastoral spiral offers both tools for change and invites the transformation of each person involved. The process offers tools for seeing, assessing, reflecting, responding, and acting. In each of the steps, creativity and the religious imagination will be used in many ways to open up spaces for visions of a better future for the world.

This process offers a method for looking underneath the realities in order to see them with greater clarity. It serves both as a telescope and a microscope, absorbing details and as much of the big picture as we can possibly take in with all of our senses. The process helps us to work together to imagine and allow possible responses to emerge from a vision of God's world, and finally to take action to create this vision. There is much creative potential here. Seeing realities with new eyes through the use of the pastoral spiral offers great energy while it builds capacity and competency.

Essential also is an honest appraisal of our own involvement in some systems we seek to transform for the sake of the common good of the world. At various times it will take both humility to see our role(s) in situations and courage to work together to create another way to respond to issues. This is true in questions about migration-immigration, unjust political policies/practices, and environmental conflicts-impasses, as well as in peacebuilding, living-wage legislation, just international trade policies, and many more. In all, the pastoral spiral offers a way to consider and respond to immediate issues and to the larger invitation to help create the world God invites.

CAN WE MEET THIS CHALLENGE?

If you feel you are aware of some problems, and you sense some of what the world needs, and you are willing to try the pastoral spiral, you may also wonder if it is indeed possible for you (singular or plural) to bring about such transformation. But as was pointed out earlier, this is a book about hope. Throughout, this book understands a world of possibilities. As Christians, we live with hope and we see the hands of God continually at work in us and through us. We know change and transformation are possible because hope sustains us, gives us courage, and allows joy to permeate even amid the challenges we face. Because our hope is rooted in God, it allows us to truly see the world as it is, to imagine more than what we see, and to work for what we sense is possible. Hope compels us to work to meet the world's deep needs.

Hope is also firmly connected to prophetic dialogue, described by Stephen Bevans and Roger Schroeder as "'an attitude of respect and friendship, which permeates or should permeate all those activities constituting the evangelizing mission of the church,' an attitude that can be called 'the spirit of dialogue.'"[11] The focus here is on "a basic attitude . . . that gives direction to each and all of the elements of mission, whether it be the way Christians give witness or proclaim the gospel, celebrate liturgy or pray, do deeds of justice and peacemaking, engage in inculturation or in the process of reconciliation."[12] Bevans and Schroeder also remind us to respond as the prophets did, offering a "vision of what God has in store for people in God's plan of salvation."[13]Prophets speak out when people are not living out God's call. Prophets participate in God's mission, in God's offer of life in abundance for all. Such prophetic dialogue is desperately needed in our world today.

Hope sustains us for prophetic dialogue. Hope sustains us when we see that some of today's challenges were here yesterday and many yesterdays before that, when we realize that the changes called for are immense yet needed, when we realize that we too must change if we expect change to happen. Hope allows us to be continually transformed and to open ourselves to God transforming us and all of creation.

Knowing that the reign of God is here and now also sustains us. During the days of slavery in the United States, Christian slaves were often told to accept their fate and to count on the "world to come" after death as the place they would experience freedom. This was based on an understanding that the reign of God was not yet present. Today, people sometimes still focus on the not-yet and call for patience in the midst of injustice and human-made suffering. Scripture scholar Gerhard Lohfink reminds us that this must not be so by describing the reign of God in terms of time and place.

Lohfink cites texts from Luke and Mark, including verses from the Sermon on the Plain (Luke 6:20–21): "Blessed are you who are poor, for yours is the reign of God! Blessed are you who are hungry now, for you will be filled. Blessed are you who weep now, for you will laugh!" Lohfink notes,

> This is about the poor, the hungry, the weeping in Israel, with whom Jesus was confronted every day. It is about the hopeless, the oppressed, the despairing among the people

of God who followed Jesus. Jesus calls them blessed—not because their weeping, hunger, and poverty were of any value in themselves, but because God's intervention is about to take place and because it is especially the hopeless who will experience God's hope and salvation in a measure beyond all telling.

Jesus is not promising the miserable and the poor a better life after death. . . . Instead he directs their eyes to the eschatological turning point that is now coming that will affect all and change everything. He promises the poor and the beaten down in particular that they will participate in the reign of God.

So Jesus is quite sure: this turning point is at hand. It will gather Israel anew, it will make possible a new society in which the poor have a share in the wealth of the land and the sorrowing participate in the rejoicing of the people of God.[14]

The potential of the reign of God is immense here. All can participate and all will be changed. This message is not simply spoken; it is proclaimed and it has epic implications, as we see now in Mark. In Mark 1:15 the evangelist summarizes Jesus' preaching in this way: "The time is fulfilled and the reign of God has come near; therefore, repent, and believe in the good news!" Powerful to note is that this is a proclamation.

Jesus is not just talking *about* the reign of God. He is announcing it. He proclaims it, and later he has his disciples proclaim it in Israel (Matt. 10:7). A proclamation always has a public character. . . . At the beginning, then, as throughout the Bible, is God's action, not human action. God has taken the initiative. He alone gives the reign of God. It is the business of the people of God to respond. God's action makes human action possible.[15]

Lohfink makes a key point about the reign of God. The reign is here, now, and the people must respond.

It is true that "has come near" contains a "not yet," but it is not about God's action; it is about Israel's response. The people of God, at this moment, has not yet turned back. It is still in the moment of decision for or against the Gospel. Therefore, the Reign of God is near but not yet present. It is being offered to the people of God. It is laid at their feet. They are within reach of it; they can reach out and touch it. But as long as it is not accepted it is only near, and the people must still pray: "Your kingdom come!" (Matt. 6:10).[16]

The proclamation, the invitation, is ours, and the Gospels remind us that while the people at first welcomed this news, then came some doubts and challenges, even as Jesus was preaching, teaching, and healing. Later came the betrayals, the people's inability to say yes to this good news and reality. The reign of God arrived and is here, but the people do not accept it. In other words, the reign of God is here and *not yet*. Lohfink's regret is clear as he writes: "So Jesus' hearers prefer to put everything off into the future, and the story comes to no good end. The reign of God announced by Jesus is not accepted. The 'today' offered by God is denied. And that, that alone, is why 'already' becomes 'not yet.'"[17] Nevertheless, the invitation stands and is continually offered. The time is now. The choice is ours.

Lohfink writes further,

For Jesus, God's "today" was the center of his existence. . . . Jesus knows with the utmost certainty that the promised, longed-for, prayed-for future is here, that the reign of God is breaking forth. That is the only way to understand Jesus' unbending assurance of fulfillment. That is the only way to comprehend his beatitude addressed to his disciples: "Blessed are the eyes that see what you see! For I tell you that many prophets and kings desired to see what you see, but did not see it, and to hear what you hear, but did not hear it" (Luke 10:23–24). And to those in Nazareth and beyond who shook their heads and said that nothing has changed with Jesus there, Jesus answers that something has indeed changed: "If it is by the finger of God that I cast out the demons then the [reign] of God has come to you" (Luke 11:20).[18]

We see "in Jesus' deeds of healing that the 'today' of the reign of God is already visible and tangible."[19] This is an invitation to joy. This joy, however, comes with the cross:

What was contained in Jesus' preaching from the very beginning was fully illuminated by his death: the reign of God demands a change of rulership that human beings must carry out. It demands letting go and self-surrender. The reign of God does not come without pure receiving, and that receiving is also always an acceptance of suffering. In his passion Jesus was by no means far from the reign of God; instead, the reign of God comes precisely in the "hour" in which Jesus himself can do no more but hand himself over and surrender to God's truth. This is the basic thread of John's gospel. . . .

So Jesus' announcement of the reign of God achieves in his death, once again, a final precision and focus: the concept "reign of God" cannot be used from here on unless at the same time one speaks of Jesus' surrender even unto death. For Jesus' disciples this means that they cannot live in the realm where God reigns without obedience to what this reign of God brings with it. And that, in the midst of a resistant society and resistant church, does not happen without suffering, without sacrifice, without passion stories.

Ultimately, Jesus' death lays bare all human self-glorification and thereby also every superficial and presumptuous notion of the reign of God. God's realm can happen only where human beings collide with their own limits, where they do not know how to go on, where they hand themselves over and give space to God alone so that God can act. Only there, in the zone of constant dying and rising, the reign of God begins.[20]

Lohfink summarizes,

[For] Jesus the coming of the reign of God was no longer something in the distant or near future but something that was happening already, now, in the present hour. Rescue, liberation, salvation—for Jesus it has all irrevocably begun. "If it is by the finger of God that I cast out the demons, then the reign of God has come to you" (Luke 11:20). But at the same time Jesus' disciples are supposed to pray daily: "your kingdom come" (Luke 11:2). For the reign of God has not come everywhere, not by a long sight, because it has not yet been accepted everywhere—not even by the disciples themselves, who according to the gospels were still dreaming about their own reign (Mark 9:34).[21]

Lohfink emphasizes that another important dimension of the reign of God is place:

The explosive power of the reign of God is not only defused by pushing it into the distant future or into a time beyond time. It can also be handed over to impotence by being made homeless. For Jesus the reign of God not only has its own time, it also has its own place in which to be made visible and tangible. That place is the people of God.[22]

As the "place" of the reign of God is the people of God, God begins with the individual, "because only the individual is the point where God can build on *change undertaken freely.*"[23] The person is always essential, and change cannot happen without persons saying yes. At the same time, the call is to create a new society, for "redemption, salvation, peace, blessing always have also—and indeed, primarily—a social dimension."[24]

The place of the reign of God is both within the person and visible. The internal nature of the reign of God is noted in Luke 17:20–21: "Once he was asked by the Pharisees when the reign of God was coming, and he answered, 'The reign of God is not coming with things that can be observed; nor will they say 'Look, here it is!' or 'There it is!' For, in fact, the reign of God is [already] among you [*entos hymon*]."[25]

At the same time, the reign of God is intensely visible:

"The blind receive their sight, the lame walk, the lepers are cleansed, the deaf hear, the dead are raised, and the poor have good news brought to them" (Matt. 11:5). All that is happening before everyone's eyes. The reign of God is breaking forth in the midst of the world and not only within people. Every dimension of reality is to be placed within the realm of God: soul and body, health and sickness, wealth and poverty, adults and children, family and society.[26]

The implications are significant for the internal and external dimensions of people's lives: "It is not only individuals and their inner lives that need redeeming but also the situations within which they live—for example, the lack of freedom, the structures of injustice, and the mechanisms of manipulation that have eaten their way into society."[27] The reign of God as present and near gives us the confidence to participate in God's transformation of society.

We must always remember that as Christians *we are Easter people*. How do we manage the reign of God and maintain hope as we realize that the acceptance of the reign of God means affirming joy and accepting that we will deal with suffering? Our hope is in the risen Christ and that we too have this destiny; we are people of the resurrection. From the Upper Room, John reminds us of what the resurrected Christ offers us:

Jesus came and stood in their midst and said to them, "Peace be with you." When he had said this, he showed

them his hands and his side. The disciples rejoiced when
they saw the Lord. Jesus said to them again, "Peace be
with you. As the Father has sent me, so I send you." And
when he had said this, he breathed on them and said to
them, "Receive the holy Spirit." (20:19b–23)

We are offered peace, which is a gift of salvation, oneness
in God. We are also sent, as Jesus was sent. We participate in
the same mission. Just as we are called to open ourselves to
where God sends us, accepting all, we are also sent with the
Spirit. We are called to receive the gift of Godself in the Spirit.
Forgiveness and reconciliation are possible, even in the face
of the reality of suffering and crucifixion. Jesus has modeled
the capacity to love unto death, to forgive, to offer reconciliation, and to create new relationships. He is the source of our
joy and hope.

We can open ourselves to what God invites through *reflection and prayer*. The pastoral spiral asks us to reflect and pray
our way through issues while involving ourselves in ongoing
analysis and engagement. Prayer and reflection are absolutely
essential. This is who we are, and it is also what we offer a
world weary of conflict yet unable to imagine beyond, peoples
carrying heavy loads who need a community to help remove
what is unjust, and our Earth, sickened with pollutants, which
needs the good news to pour in fresh air, clean waters, and
nutrient-rich soils.

Significant innovators are seeing the importance of reflection
in bringing about systemic change and social transformation.
Organizational learning pioneer Peter Senge, for instance,
speaks of reflection as one of the major competencies needed
for leaders in the twenty-first century.[28] He works nationally
and internationally with people in civic and secular organizations to encourage reflection. His work asks for people's
deepest values to come forth in change making. The places
of deepest values are often where we can find common cause
with others from various traditions and among all people of

goodwill. As Christians, our deepest values are named from the gospel and are undergirded in a relationship with God and within a community.

Just as we read that Jesus often went off to pray, we too need to pray often with words, images, the arts, and even with silence. To contemplate is to open ourselves to seeing the realities within and around us that God dearly desires to offer us. In so doing we are reminded that we are not alone but always in God. There is no place where we will reach out to the wounded heart of humanity and the wounded Earth where God is not already present. Work and prayer intersect in life and this is a pattern we must integrate with our practices of prayer, a constant reminder that we are about God's mission and that we rely on grace.

Creativity and religious imagination are inherent in our humanity, our DNA. As people of the risen Christ we see goodness in the world and in humans and thus see possibilities for change. Our religious imagination begins with the good news of Jesus and flows to possibilities for the present time. For example, some read the miracle of the loaves and fishes, or the feeding of the five thousand, as an example of what hospitality can offer. This story may also be seen as community actualizing its capacity for creativity. From hope springs imagination and creativity.

Three brief examples. The first is a story of Jack Andraka, a fifteen-year-old boy who developed a test for detecting early pancreatic cancer, using the Internet to assist him. His experience of a close family friend dying of pancreatic cancer led him to begin research on the disease.[29] The second is the story of Shigeru Ban, who received the 2014 Pritzker Architecture Prize.[30] He has taken the lead in a new way of creating socially conscious architecture, not only using more sustainable resources for building but also going to places of devastation and creating housing with beauty and style. Tom Pritzker proclaimed, "Shigeru Ban's commitment to humanitarian causes through his disaster relief work is an example for all.

Innovation is not limited by building type and compassion is not limited by budget. Shigeru has made our world a better place."[31] Third, a textbook titled *Alleviating Poverty through Profitable Partnerships: Globalization, Markets, and Economic Well-Being* by Patricia H. Werhane, Scott P. Kelley, Laura P. Hartman, and Dennis Moberg, helps businesses see poverty as an opportunity to dramatically improve people's lives.[32] The more students can be exposed to such "opportunity," the better.

Community is extremely important; we work together. Lohfink notes the call of Jesus for community based on the reign of God. The reign of God means people and a changed society. "That is precisely why [Jesus] begins the new thing within a community of disciples whom he orders to quit acting as if they are superior, to forgive one another seventy-seven times a day, and to turn the other cheek when someone strikes them."[33] In order to become this community the disciples will have to be adaptable, following Jesus into ever changing circumstances and situations,[34] and carrying very little, "an *indicative sign* pointing to the eschatological-solidarity mutuality within the people of God that makes Jesus' disciples free and available."[35] To be a disciple "means sharing the fate of Jesus, who had no place to lay his head. It means uncertainty, danger, opposition. It means surrender to the new demands, every day, of the coming of the reign of God. But it also means a new community in Jesus' "new family."[36]

A community of "right relationships" makes what seems impossible possible. A good leader today can only be so within a community—and community also includes the Earth community—so we find ourselves holding up all as valued and important to the reign of God. What one cannot do, others can. Communities give courage and hope and celebrate together. Some issues take a significant amount of time, and community—working together—sustains us. The Eucharist brings us together to give thanks, to be nourished, and then to be sent out to proclaim the good news with our lives. In action and reflection we are ultimately contemplatives in action, reflective persons working together in solidarity to bring about the just world we are offered in peace, hope, and love.

The *capacity for transformation* is already within creation as the cosmos constantly changes. We are constantly changing, growing, and adapting as we encounter each interaction. This is part of our experience each day. Being intentional about the changes we seek is part of living in hope. We have particular hopes, and thus our imagination makes much more possible. Just as creation changes, so do the systems that people create change.[37]

Our Christian tradition speaks of both *metanoia* (change) and *kenosis* (self-emptying) as part of our lives. God took on our human nature to become one of us and thus forever changed our human nature. We are invited to be like God, though not to be God. Our scriptures are replete with examples of change and transformation. Pope Francis reminds us that "if we think that things are not going to change, we need to recall that Jesus Christ has triumphed over sin and death and is now almighty. Jesus Christ truly lives. . . . We are invited to discover this, to experience it. Christ, risen and glorified, is the wellspring of our hope, and he will not deprive us of the help we need to carry out the mission which he has entrusted to us."[38] Our saints' narratives often speak of transformation. Peter changed over the course of his relationship with Jesus. Even after he denied Jesus three times, Jesus sent Peter to "feed my sheep." We read of St. Paul being transformed and of Jesus touching and healing many people and watching their faith directly connect to their transformation.

Narratives of transformation are important, for they remind us of hope. Narratives remind us that nothing is impossible. Pope Francis, elected in 2013, offers people great hope as he points to the gospel vision of justice and peace for all, decrying corrupt systems, merciless policies, and greed-driven corporate practices and people. He invites us to so much more. He writes of this vision in *The Gospel of Joy*, his first apostolic exhortation, and reminds us that the good news is a source of great joy. His own life has been one of great transformation.

I deeply sense that Pope Francis's freedom comes from God's transformative action in his life. He has known great suffering and made mistakes (see his interview in which he describes himself as "a sinner whom the Lord has looked upon"[39]), and he also knows God's love, mercy, and forgiveness. This is the type of person who invites others to the transformation God offers. He is able to offer this same love and forgiveness to others, and he can risk much because the risk comes from knowing God's love. His words and actions also embody prophetic dialogue as he welcomes engagement and challenges a world of great wealth and great suffering. He challenges the church, the people of God: "How I would like a church that is poor and for the poor."[40] Pope Francis's life is one that speaks to personal transformation now also inviting a wider transformation in the church and world today. He sees how much is possible because he has known how much God has made possible in his own life.

Our economic, social, and political systems are all created by persons and thus are capable of being transformed or closed down. Narratives of transformation—wherever they come from—are vital for us. They remind us that CEOs can change, that people who made tragic mistakes can change, that each one of us can change—if we allow ourselves to be open. The stories of transformation that follow remind us that whatever the task, the crisis, or the stakes, bringing about change for the good and creating a new world are possible.

With our eyes on the world, with a sense of how we might look underneath what we are seeing and ask key questions, and with a sense of how we can have such hope to create change and open ourselves to transformation, we turn now to a deeper study of transformation in action.

Notes

[1]Dennis Overbye, "Ripples from the Big Bang," *New York Times*, March 25, 2014, http://www.nytimes.com.

[2]Bob Simon, "Alma: Peering into the Universe's Past," *60 Minutes*, March 9, 2014. See also Miles O'Brien and Jon Baime, "Alma: Seeing the Universe in a Whole New Light," National Science Foundation, December 3, 2012, http://www.nsf.gov.

[3]MOOCs are courses available without charge on the Internet to a large number of people across geographic distances.

[4]United Nations, "Foreword," *Millennium Development Goals Report 2013*, New York, 3. The Eight Millennium Development Goals are: (1) Eradicate extreme poverty and hunger; (2) achieve universal primary education; (3) promote gender equality and empower women; (4) reduce child mortality; (5) improve maternal health; (6) combat HIV/AIDS, malaria, and other diseases; (7) ensure environmental sustainability; and (8) develop a global partnership for development. These can be found, along with their goal indicators, at http://unstats.un.org.

[5]Ibid., 3. The good news, still, is that the Foreword ends with the following: "In more than a decade of experience in working towards the Millennium Development Goals, we have learned that focused global development efforts can make a difference. Through accelerated action, the world can achieve the MDGs and generate momentum for an ambitious and inspiring post-2015 development framework. Now is the time to step up our efforts to build a more just, secure and sustainable future for all" (3). A set of Sustainable Development Goals (SDGs) to build on the MDGs and to converge with the post-2015 development agenda will be voted on in September 2015.

[6]Robert J. Schreiter, *The New Catholicity: Theology between the Global and the Local* (Maryknoll, NY: Orbis Books, 1997), 4–5.

[7]Kenneth R. Himes, *Christianity and the Political Order: Conflict, Cooptation, and Cooperation* (Maryknoll, NY: Orbis Books, 2013), 292.

[8]Gustavo Gutiérrez, "Memory and Prophecy," in *The Option for the Poor in Christian Theology*, ed. Daniel G. Groody (Notre Dame, IN: University of Notre Dame Press, 2007), 32.

[9]Johannes Banawiratma, "The Pastoral Circle as Spirituality," *The Pastoral Circle Revisited: A Critical Quest for Truth and Transformation*, ed. Frans Wijsen, Peter Henriot, and Rodrigo Mejía (Maryknoll, NY: Orbis Books, 2005), 76.

[10]Pope Francis, *The Joy of the Gospel* (Washington, DC: United States Conference of Catholic Bishops, 2013), 223.

[11]Stephen B. Bevans and Roger P. Schroeder, *Prophetic Dialogue: Reflections on Christian Mission Today* (Maryknoll, NY: Orbis Books, 2011), 21.

[12]Ibid., 21–22.

[13]Ibid., 42.

[14]Gehard Lohfink, *Jesus of Nazareth: What He Wanted, Who He Was*, trans. Linda M. Maloney. (Collegeville, MN: Liturgical Press, 2012), 29–30.

[15]Ibid., 30–31.

[16]Ibid., 31.

[17]Ibid., 32.

[18]Ibid., 33.

[19]Ibid., 34.

[20]Ibid., 38.

[21]Ibid., 39.

[22]Ibid., 39–40.

[23]Ibid., 45.

[24]Ibid., 46. "At the very end of the Bible we will find the image of the 'holy city,' the 'new Jerusalem' (Rev. 21)—and the city, the polis, was in antiquity the proper image of society" (46).

[25]Ibid., 50, 51.

[26]Ibid., 51.

[27]Ibid., 52

[28]Peter Senge, MOOC on Leadership for Global Responsibility, at Leadership Competencies for the 21st Century, March 27, 2014.

[29]See also "Boy Wonder: Jack Andraka," *60 Minutes*, October 13, 2013, http://www.cbsnews.com.

[30]Robin Pogrebin, "Pritzker Architecture Prize Goes to Shigeru Ban," *New York Times*, March 25, 2014.

[31]For more on the Pritzker Architecture Prize, see http://www.pritzkerprize.com.

[32]Patricia H. Werhane, Scott P. Kelley, Laura P. Hartman, and Dennis Moberg, *Alleviating Poverty through Profitable Partnerships: Globalization, Markets, and Economic Well-Being* (New York: Routledge, 2009).

[33]Lohfink, *Jesus of Nazareth*, 52.

[34]Ibid., 76.

[35]Ibid., 78.

[36]Ibid., 79.

[37]One theory of change, negative entropy, says that systems tend to have a life cycle and die unless something is done to continue them, illustrating that change and growth are necessary for survival.

[38]Pope Francis, *Joy of the Gospel*, 275.

[39]Antonio Spadaro, SJ, "A Big Heart Open to God," *America*, September 30, 2013, http://www.americamagazine.org.

[40]Joshua McElwee, "Pope Francis: 'I would love a church that is poor,'" *National Catholic Reporter*, March 16, 2013, http://www.ncronline.org.

2

Transformation

Our Call to Love and Serve

I give you a new commandment, that you love one another. Just as I have loved you, you also should love one another. By this everyone will know that you are my disciples, if you have love for one another.

John 13:34–35

An authentic faith—which is never comfortable or completely personal—always involves a deep desire to change the world, to transmit values, to leave this earth somehow better than we found it. We love this magnificent planet on which God has put us, and we love the human family which dwells here, with all its tragedies and struggles, its hopes and aspirations, its strengths and weaknesses. The earth is our common home and all of us are brothers and sisters.

—Pope Francis, *The Joy of the Gospel*

From chapter 1 and from our glimpses of the world around us, we see both immense possibility and immense suffering and challenge. Much good is happening, yet so many more situations are crying for our attention and intervention. Change is needed on both local and global levels. We desire change, yet how is it to come about? Urgent needs compel, yet the call for change may feel daunting. As we look at so many persons and the entire Earth community impacted by poverty, war, and environmental crises, we may wonder if change is even possible. What are we to do? It becomes clear on many levels that on our own, we cannot make any difference.

In this chapter we begin to form a response to these questions as we look at the call for transformation in light of our faith. We consider what transformation demands and situate it in light of a hope that rests in God. We will see how God acts in salvation history to transform all, and we begin with some stories of God's transformative actions in the Old Testament that call forth our participation. We move then to the New Testament and consider Mary's participation in God's transformative action to bring forth new life through Jesus. We see how Jesus incarnates transformation through his life, suffering, death, and resurrection and his invitation to disciples to continue to spread this good news of the reign of God. We then turn to the resources of Catholic social teaching to see what resources might be available to help us. The final part of the chapter considers seven essential characteristics for transformative discipleship in our day.

TRANSFORMATION

We begin with a closer look at transformation. While the words "change" and "transformation" are often considered synonyms, important nuances distinguish them. The word "change" comes from Middle English, from the Anglo-French word *changer*, and the Latin *cambiare*, which means to exchange. I may change my morning routine or change clothes or change the music I listen to. "Transform" also comes from Middle English, from the French word *transformer*, and the Latin *transformare*, a combination of *trans* and *formare*, meaning to form. To transform suggests a major change rather than a cosmetic change. A company may be transformed from prioritizing profits to prioritizing customer service. Personal transformation often happens when someone no longer focuses on self and begins to focus on the needs of others. Something has to change at a deeper level to bring about transformation, because transformation demands much more than external change.

Consider the right to vote, which in the United States became possible for women in 1920 and for black male American citizens in 1870 with the ratification of the Fifteenth Amendment. However, some states still prevented African Americans from voting by resorting to a loophole—the original grandfather clause, which stated that one could not vote unless his grandfather had voted, an impossibility among most blacks. Although the Supreme Court struck down the grandfather clause in 1915, states used a variety of other methods—poll taxes, literacy tests, fraud, and intimidation—to keep African Americans away from the polls. President Lyndon B. Johnson's Voting Rights Act of 1965 empowered the federal government to oversee voter registration and elections in places that had particularly low voter registration or voter turnout in the previous national election.

The laws certainly changed the composition of who could vote, and the number of votes. However, many would challenge whether the character of our country changed with changes in the voting law. Did all people believe that women were equals or that black persons were equals because the voting structure changed? I suggest not. It took longer for people to see the essence of what the laws were promoting. This is, I believe, the heart of transformation: it not only changes the externals, but it forms anew the internals.

Chapter 1 clearly named some of the transformation needed today. Assumptions and questions about who has a right to health care, whether the process of immigration in the United States and internationally needs to be changed, where the right to clean water stands in the midst of desires for more energy resources—all have their roots in a view of the person and Earth.

This is the work of transformation, and it is not easy. Transformation requires hope that a situation can change. As

Christians, we have hope because our hope is in a God who continually transforms us.

What do we mean by "hope"? I mentioned hope briefly in chapter 1, but now, due to its importance to both social analysis and the Christian faith, I give a more detailed description.[1] Hope—deep hope (or hope that is dependent on God)—is not easy. It is neither optimism (for example, I hope the Cleveland Indians will win the World Series this year!) nor idealism (for example, every student will give 100 percent to every class assignment). Although I am still optimistic and have ideals, over the years I've come to a much greater deepening in and praying for the virtue of hope. Hope, the kind that is grounded in God, often goes beyond what we can see. This hope means that, at times, we must close our eyes in order to see the grounding within and around us that is of God. God does move all around us, and the more we enter into the ineffable depth of mystery that is God, the more we will be called to hope in challenging and difficult times.

Hope is the context from which we work toward transformation. If we wanted only modest modifications, we would not necessarily need hope. Optimism or idealism might be enough to keep us moving. However, hope is much more connected to the type of transformation needed to change the situations described in chapter 1.

Hope is not inattentive to the realities around us. In fact, hope must be rooted in reality. Even though it may not be easy to obtain, the transformation of a situation should be within the realm of possible options. I cannot hope for peace in the city of Chicago if I do not realize that within walking distance of where I live is one of the highest rates of gun violence in the country. I need to know why this is so.

We hope only when the answer is not so easy, not so visible. We turn to hope when we cannot see the road in front of us, as if our internal GPS is nonfunctional. Hope is needed when the journey may be long or arduous, and even when we are not sure what the outcome will be. Hope may have a price.

It is not simple or easy. At times it is not even logical. At the same time, we hope for what we think, imagine, or long to be possible. If there is no chance at all, we do not hope.

Hope can cause us to lament because we believe the future could be other than what it is. When we have no hope we simply despair. Nothing says this is going to be easy, or that we will not suffer. It's often a long haul with occasional sparks that indicate something is possible.

Peacebuilding and work toward reconciliation, for example, require great hope. A story is told about Archbishop John Baptist Odama serving in northern Uganda, the region where the Lord's Resistance Army was primarily located. He regularly went into the camps of Joseph Kony, leader of the notorious group, and even spent the night there. When people asked why he did this (he could be killed), he simply answered, "Joseph is a child of God. He is one of my sheep, too." Archbishop Odama has hope and sees possibility.

Transformation rooted in hope will be

- Radical
- Embodied
- Imaginative
- Relational

Transformation rooted in hope is radical. "Radical" in this sense means root. Transformation requires radical dependence on God and radical availability. The only way this can happen is with a deep dependence on God and an openness within ourselves. Availability, perhaps best expressed in the Spanish word *disponibilidad* (or the French word *disponibilité*), means a complete openness of ourselves that goes far beyond "Are you available for a meeting on Tuesday evening?" to "Are you willing to open yourself to what this change might require?"

Second, transformation must be embodied. God asks for our participation in transformation. We are called and invited to be agents of transformation. Our availability must be embodied. To not only change but actually to transform systems requires encounters with others who will stretch us and change us.

Third, transformation is imaginative. Transformation will be beyond what we can even imagine, because hope and transformation are creative. In South Africa the end of apartheid in 1990, followed by democratic elections in 1994, led to what was once unthinkable, the first black president, Nelson Mandela, a man transformed in the most unlikely of places, prison. We are heartened by Isaiah 43:19:

> I am about to do a new thing;
>   now it springs forth, do you not
>   perceive it?
> I will make a way in the wilderness
>   and rivers in the desert.

Fourth, transformation is inherently relational. God's ongoing relationship with us, inviting a response, and our response in relationship with others creates not only the possibilities but also the conditions for transformation.

We find these markers of transformation illuminated in stories of God's interactions in the Old Testament, in God incarnated among us in the New Testament, in the Catholic social tradition's continuing calls for transformation in society, and in our own present call to participate today in God's mission of transformation.

THE OLD TESTAMENT: STORIES OF TRANSFORMATION

A relationship with God is always and continuously transformative. God does not inflict transformation but continually invites it by helping people see, by calling them to be ever more fully who they are created to be, and this fullness transforms.

In the Old Testament the book of Exodus offers a powerful narrative of relationship and transformation. We meet a God who hears the cries of the poor and oppressed, responds by calling forth men and women to articulate in word and action

God's desire for God's people to be free, and creates a covenant with the people that articulates God's continuing fidelity and the responsibilities of the people. Together, the exodus of the Israelites from Egypt and the covenant agreement at Sinai offer us insights about the relationship between God and God's people and how transformation came about.

The Exodus narrative is probably the best-known biblical narrative of liberation from oppressive powers and unjust social structures. Even so, it is "not simply *freedom from* that is important but *freedom for* the formation of a community that lives under the covenant."[2] The Israelites, residing in Egypt and large in number, pose a threat to the pharaoh of Egypt. The pharaoh's response includes enslaving[3] the people and then trying to kill the male children, in effect committing genocide.

God heard their cries of pain and responded,

> I have witnessed the affliction of my people in Egypt and have heard their cry of complaint against their slave drivers, so I know well what they are suffering. Therefore I have come down to rescue them from the hands of the Egyptians and lead them out of that land into a good and spacious land. . . . So indeed the cry of the Israelites has reached me, and I have truly noted that the Egyptians are oppressing them. (Exod. 3:7–9)

God works through the prophet Moses to liberate the people from Egyptian slavery. It is at Mount Sinai, the holy mountain of God, that the Israelites enter into a new relationship of covenant with Yahweh, their God. Scripture scholar Barbara Bowe describes the importance of the covenant: "It was at Sinai that God sealed this relationship and established an everlasting covenant with them. . . . The Hebrew term *berit*—'covenant, binding agreement, fetter, bond'—is a rich term that captures the heart of Israel's religious beliefs."[4]

Theologian Daniel Groody further explains the importance of covenant:

The most significant metaphor Israel uses in describing its relationship to Yahweh, and certainly the most central in understanding the biblical notion of justice, is that of covenant. A covenant (Hebrew *berit*) is a binding agreement between two parties that result in a new relationship. The goal of the covenant is right relationships, which produce life, justice, and peace.[5]

In the Old Testament, two dominant covenant trajectories developed, the first one stemming from Yahweh's covenant with Abraham (Gen. 15:1–18; 17:1–14) and David (2 Sam. 7:1–17), and the second flowing from the Mosaic covenant (Exod. 19–24). The Abrahamic/Davidic covenant is an unbreakable agreement, while the Mosaic covenant can be severed by disobedience. The first covenant stresses God's commitment to Israel, and the second covenant emphasizes Israel's responsibility to God.[6] Biblical scholar Raymond Brown reminds us, "While the covenants of divine commitment gave Israel confidence, the covenants of human responsibility gave Israel a conscience."[7] This beautifully names how covenant is both a gift of relationship and an ensuing call to responsibility.

The Mosaic covenant at Sinai expressed the values of faith that the Israelites believed God revealed to them. Bowe notes,

> First and foremost God called them to be a holy people, as their God was holy (Exod. 19:5–6; Lev. 19:1–2). But holiness must manifest in concrete ethical principles demonstrated in reverent service to God and to neighbor. Covenant stipulations bound them to protect the weak and powerless: the orphan, the widow, strangers, the poor. The Decalogue, or the "Ten Commandments" (Exod. 20:2–17; compare Deut. 5:6–21) as we have come to call them, constitute the heart of covenant, ethical living. These commandments laid down the foundations for communal cohesion and integrity lived in the presence of their God.[8]

God's invitation to relationship thus has transformative implications for relationship with God and also with one another. We hear of God responding to the cries of God's people and offering, through the prophets as agents of transformation, both liberation from oppression and liberation for a new way of being in relationship with God and with all creation. This covenant is of relationship and responsibility, in which the people are *freed from* slavery and *freed for* just relationships, with particular concern for the poor, strangers, widows, and orphans.

God's Concern for the Poor

God's concern for the poor is clear throughout the Bible. What gets debated is not that caring for the poor is important, but what the actual obligation is toward the poor. What does "taking care of" mean? That I give from my excess? That I give not counting the cost? Is care for the poor about making sure basic immediate needs are met? Is it about countering the structures that may enhance, exacerbate, or create poverty in a group or society? Can I be more interested in one way of responding than another? And who exactly are "the poor"?

Noting that the biblical vocabulary for the poor is extensive, biblical scholar John Donahue cites five principal Hebrew terms for the poor:

1. *'ani* (plural *aniyyim*), meaning "bent down" or "afflicted," which the Greek Old Testament most often translates as *ptochos* (beggar or destitute person) and which is the prime New Testament term for "the poor."

2. *anaw* (plural *anawim*), derived from the same root as *'ani* and often confused by copyists, which is most often translated *tapeinos* and *praus* (humble and lowly).

3. *'ebyon* (the term Ebionites derives from this), from the root meaning "lack or need" or "wretched, miserable," used sixty-one times in the Old Testament, especially in the psalms (twenty-three times).

4. *dal*, from the root that means "be bent over, bend down, miserable."
5. *ras*, poor in a derogatory sense with overtones of a lazy person responsible for his or her own poverty, found only in the Wisdom literature (e.g., Prov. 10:4; 13:23; 14:20; 19:7; 28:3).[9]

Donahue then explains the significance of the vocabulary:

The importance of the terminology is twofold. First, it shows that "poverty" was not itself a value. Even etymologically the poor are bent down, wretched, and beggars. While the Bible has great concern for "the poor," poverty itself is an evil. Second, the terminology (as well as actual use) is a caution against misuse of the phrase *spiritually poor*. Though later literature (the Psalms and Dead Sea Scrolls) often equates the poor with the humble or meek, and though the poor are those people open to God in contrast to idolatrous or blind rich people, the prime analogue of the term is an economic condition. When the "poor in spirit" are praised as in Matthew 5:3, it is because in addition to their material poverty they are open to God's presence and love. Certain contemporary usages of "spiritual poverty," which allow it to be used of extremely wealthy people who are unhappy even amid prosperity, are not faithful to the biblical tradition. Nor is an idea of "spiritual poverty" as indifference to riches amid wealth faithful to the Bible. The "poor" in the Bible are almost without exception *powerless* people who experience economic and social deprivation. In both Isaiah and the Psalms the poor are often victims of the injustice of the rich and powerful. Isaiah tells us that the elders and princes "devour" the poor and grind their faces in the dust (3:14–15); they turn aside the needy from injustice to rob the poor of their rights (10:2); wicked people "ruin" the poor with lying words (32:7). In the Psalms the poor, often called "the downtrodden," are contrasted not simply to the rich but to the wicked and the powerful (10:2–10; 72:4, 12–14). Today, poverty is most often not simply an economic issue but arises when one group can exploit or oppress another.[10]

In the Old Testament, as well as in the New Testament and church encyclicals, we see that the type of poverty named is not only not good; it is an evil. As such it needs to be countered in all its manifestations (e.g., hunger, racist oppression) and its roots (e.g., greed, racism, hunger for power and influence). While today we speak of systemic injustice, even in the time of the Old Testament there were understandings that power and wealth were not simply connected to a person or family but to a larger entity or system such as an empire, which could have political and economic power (and in that time often religious power as well).[11] Again the Exodus narrative reminds us that God hears ("I have heard the cry of my people and I see how they are being oppressed" [Exod. 3:9] and responds in word and deed ("Go to Pharaoh and tell him that Yahweh says, 'Let my people go'" [Exod. 8:1]), liberating the people from their bondage and inviting them into a new covenant of relationship with God and one another as a community.

Finally, among groups particularly named in the covenant as concerns of God, and therefore of us, are the stranger, the orphan, and the widow:

- You shall not wrong a stranger or oppress him. You shall not afflict any widow or orphan (Exod. 22:21–22).
- And the sojourner, the fatherless and the widow who are within your house shall come and be filled; that the Lord your God may bless you and all the work of your hands that you do (Deut. 14:29, cf. Deut. 15:7).
- Again Donahue reminds us, "This concern for the defenseless in society is not a command designed simply to promote social harmony, but is rooted in the nature of Yahweh himself who is defender of the oppressed."[12] Thus

we are called upon to act as God acts. When we forget, God calls forth people to remind us of who we should be.

Prophets

Because God works through human means, not inflicting transformation but inviting it, God uses human intermediaries whom we call prophets. Prophets remind the people about who they are called to be in light of God's covenant. When a person or a people forget who they are or whose they are (God's chosen people), forget where they came from (slavery), or forget how they are called to live (in covenant), a prophet emerges to remind people. A prophet is one who listens to the word of God and speaks it.[13] A prophet both names injustice (wrong doing and wrong living) and reminds people of the vision they are called to by God. Thus, a prophet must not only denounce but announce.

When Israel forgets its covenant with Yahweh, the prophets, particularly Amos, Isaiah, and Jeremiah, remind Israel that their part of the covenant must be shown in concern for the poor and oppressed.[14] Donal Dorr reminds us of God's concern for the social issues of Israel's time:

> Through the prophets, God protested in outrage against the social injustice, the bribery, and the arrogance of the rich (e.g., Amos 2:6; 4:1; 5:12; Isa. 3:14–15; 10:1–2; Jer. 22:3). God demanded that the laws of the land would protect and give redress to the poor, the indebted, the widows, the resident foreigners, the animals (domestic or wild), and even the earth itself (e.g., Lev. 19:33; 25:10–16; Exod. 15:12–15; 22:21; 23:11; Deut 23:12; 25:4).[15]

We shall see in subsequent church documents that care for the marginal groups in society will continue to be a scale that weighs or measures the justice of a society.

Prophets were also often connected to a community. We typically have an image of a prophet as a solitary figure, speaking only to God and then retreating into a cave. However, this is not so. They came from a living community and spoke to communities.

Throughout the Old Testament we see God's invitation to new life, to transformation for God's people. In the midst of this we get a sense of God's attributes, actions, and concerns, and how we are invited into right relationship with God, one another, and creation.

THE NEW TESTAMENT: GOD'S INCARNATION

God's relationship with us reaches its fullness in the New Testament. In John 3:16, we read that "God so loved the world" that God became incarnated among us. God became human, among us in flesh, offering us the vision and reality of the fullness of what human life can be. Yet even here God did not come without human participation and human consent in the form of Mary of Nazareth.

Luke 1:26–38, recounting the story of the annunciation of Mary, incorporates some basic characteristics of call—of invitation to participate in enfleshing God's mission:

- The initiative comes from God.
- The call comes in the midst of ordinary, everyday life.
- The call is mission-oriented.
- Objections are given.
- Signs or words of assurance are given.
- Each must respond; each has a choice to make in light of the invitation.
- The call must then be lived out.

That Mary had a choice, a decision to make, is powerfully described in Denise Levertov's beautiful poem "Annunciation." Mary's assent is described not as "meek obedience" but as courageous, free, and "integral to humanness." Mary's story also highlights the importance of community for transformation. Mary immediately visited her cousin Elizabeth to have the companionship of another woman who also said yes to God and who was thus carrying new life within her. God entered our lives so directly because someone else said yes. While never loving us less, God enters only upon our consent, honoring our free choice, our free will. And because of a consent to God's desire to be with us in yet another way, Jesus—Emmanuel, God with us, God in human form—comes among us.

The covenant is no longer a political treaty or a manifesto of the destiny of a people but a new law of love. Love of God and love of neighbor are one. Jesus completely enfleshed this law of love, offering us a vision of God and of what it means to be fully human.

Jesus as the new and everlasting covenant shows us the way, and that way is love—of neighbor and of outward service. Neighbor now expands to include all of God's creation, so that no one and nothing escapes our call and command to love. To be a disciple then is to be what Jesus was. Through his words, presence, and actions he incarnated love and continues to transform humanity by offering us a way to live in love.

The Nature of Love

First, Jesus' words, presence, and action all speak of love. They offer an image of who God is and what it means to be human. The baptism of Jesus, resulting in the pronouncement from above, "This is my beloved Son, in whom I am well pleased," portrays a close and tender relationship. Jesus, the Word made flesh, is beloved. He tells his disciples of his love for them and shows the nature of love in his actions and presence.

John 13:34–35 says it best: "A new command I give you: Love one another. As I have loved you, so you must love one another. By this everyone will know that you are my disciples, if you love one another." This is love without borders or limits. Jesus spent time with those in the mainstream and perhaps more often with those on the margins, which included women and tax collectors. Jesus stopped and engaged any number of groups that others found insignificant or ill-advised for him to spend time with, such as children and those regarded as unclean, including the woman with a hemorrhage.

Jesus' interventions included the woman about to be stoned and persons who suffered with paralysis, demons, leprosy, blindness, and more. He offered healing of every kind, yet in many ways kept calling and inviting people to more, to conversion, to metanoia, to a change of heart. The synoptic writers tell us over and over that "your faith has made you well."[16] No one was exempt from the love of Jesus, even when he was on the cross. Jesus called and invited in many ways. He shared all he could with those he called, teaching people how to pray and setting an example by frequently going off to pray by himself.

The Reign of God

In chapter 1 we considered the reign of God in terms of time and place. Now let us take it a bit further in terms of love and response. Jesus' life and message of love proclaimed the reign of God. Jesus tried to live and proclaim that to live in union with God and with all creation made present the reign of God. This key image is found many times in the New Testament.[17] The reign of God is not only at the end of time; it exists wherever people live out the command to love one another as God loves us. The God of love who abides in us (1 John 4:16) empowers us to love. God's reign is thus present when we love, forgive, reconcile, heal, nurture, and create something new that is good. Jesus used stories and parables in many ways to explain the nature of the reign of God, and often his parables turned upside down what people expected.

John Donahue writes of the impact of God's reign:

This Kingdom is to have effect in the everyday events of life. The Kingdom is the power of God active in the world, transforming it and confronting the powers of the world. It is to find a home among the poor (Matt. 5:3) and the persecuted (Matt. 5:4), and only with difficulty will the rich enter it (Mark 10:23). The person who can summarize the whole Law as love of God and neighbor is not far from the Kingdom of God (Mark 12:34). The exorcisms of Jesus represent Jesus' confrontation with and victory over the power of evil and are signs that "the Kingdom of heaven has come upon you" (Luke 11:20). The Kingdom and therefore the justice of God—his fidelity and his call to fidelity—are to be manifest in history no less than the proclaimer of the Kingdom, Jesus, was incarnate in history.[18]

Because of Jesus' incarnational intersection with humanity, something is forever changed in our lives. And with all of this, the Kingdom of God is also a future reality, an object of hope and prayer: "Thy Kingdom come" (Matt. 6:10).[19] There is more to be done in our time. This gives some sense of the phrase, "the reign of God is here and yet not yet."

Note again that God's reign is an utter gift from a God who offers love, but it is also a commission to be accepted or rejected. We can participate in the reign, but only God's love and power can finally fulfill it. At the same time, we must do our part to participate to make God's gift manifest in the world today. This is our response of gratitude to God's gift of love. Consider the parable of the rich man setting out on a journey who gives his servants money according to their talents and then expects an accounting. How we are using the gifts God has given us to make manifest God's love in creating a world where love, justice, and care for all are the dominant ways of life? How do our daily actions cooperate with God's vision of justice, peace, and the integrity of creation?

Scripture scholar John Meier connects the reign or kingdom of God with Jesus' all-inclusive invitation to relationship, friendship, and table fellowship:

> In the eyes of the stringently pious, Jesus' table fellowship with the ritually or morally unclean communicated uncleanness to Jesus himself. Jesus, of course, saw it the other way round: he was communicating salvation to

religious outcasts. His meals with sinners and the disreputable were celebrations of the lost being found, of God's eschatological mercy reaching out and embracing the prodigal son returning home (see, e.g., Mark 2:13–17; Luke 15:1–32). His banquets with sinful Israelites were a preparation and foretaste of the coming banquet in the kingdom of God—a metaphor that appears in various sayings and parables (see, e.g., Mark 2:19; Luke 13:28–29 par; 14:15–24 par). Thus, the Last Supper does not stand in splendid isolation. It is instead quite literally the "last" of a whole series of meals symbolizing the final feast in the kingdom of God. There is therefore nothing strange about Jesus' holding a special, symbolic meal with his disciples (especially if he sensed his approaching arrest or death) or about his connecting the meal with the coming kingdom of God.[20]

Here again we see the poor, marginalized and powerless—the wounded heart of humanity—expressly included at Jesus' table. The call is clear for us to do likewise. The reign of God is not a place but a *way of life* for both the person and the community. This is the stance we must bring to our work on any social issue.

Cross and Resurrection

Jesus invited his followers to live in love, and yet he did not hide the fact that the price of love might include suffering. His suffering and death for the sake of love (and in opposition to all forces that negate love of God and love of neighbor) offered the greatest embodiment of love. Love, we find, can only love, and so we learn from Jesus both who God is and who we are called to be.

Bowe offers a powerful reflection on Jesus' life poured out in suffering and love and in its transformative potential. In John 19:34, we read that at the moment of Jesus' death, when the soldier pierced Jesus' side, "Blood and water flowed out." Bowe writes that "the multiple layers of symbolism speak of the total outpouring of Jesus' life given in love. . . . This scene in John's passion story suggests images of birth, of the outpouring of sacramental life, and of the everlasting waters that cleanse and give new life. . . . The pierced heart is both an image of suffering and life-giving love poured out to the end."[21]

As Christians, although we know Good Friday very well, we remain Easter people. We know that resurrection carries the day and that Jesus gave his disciples and us the promise that he will remain with us in the Spirit of God (John 14:25; 14:15–17). The Acts of the Apostles continue to tell the stories of ongoing responses to Jesus' call to transform the world as the disciples preached the good news of the reign of God.

CALLS FOR TRANSFORMATION
IN THE CATHOLIC SOCIAL TRADITION

Calls for transformation, including personal transformation and an ever widening emphasis on social transformation, continue in the Catholic social tradition. Persons and groups create the systems that oppress and negate the full flourishing of God's people and creation, so persons must be the locus of transformation. At the same time, because people can transform systems and can create the systems that free, we must remain attentive to systemic injustices, to systems that are unjust, and call for their transformation by both naming the injustice and offering a different vision.

This transformation is in continuation with the markers of biblical justice prescribed in the early covenants, by the prophets and the teachings of Jesus, and in the early church's call to build the reign of God. The Catholic social tradition calls us to make the reign of God present in all areas of the world, transforming oppressive or limiting systems into systems marked by justice and peace. Discipleship commits us to making this manifest, creating a world marked by justice and peace. Thus, the Catholic social tradition flows out of a biblical call to justice to our present time, emphasizing certain themes.

The Importance of Community

First, we walk this journey of transformation as a community led by the Spirit. The opening lines of the Vatican II document *The Constitution of the Church in the Modern World* name specific gospel concerns: "The joys and the hopes, the griefs and the anxieties of the men of this age, especially those who are poor or in any way afflicted, these are the joys and hopes, the griefs and anxieties of the followers of Christ. Indeed, nothing genuinely human fails to raise an echo in their hearts" (1). In response, the church "seeks but a solitary goal: to carry forward the work of Christ under the lead of the befriending Spirit. And Christ entered this world to give witness to the truth, to rescue and not to sit in judgment, to serve and not to be served" (3).[22]

This is a reminder that God does the transforming, the befriending Spirit leads, and that as church we, with all people of goodwill, are to assist in bringing about the reign of God through our witness, service, and love. In no way do we walk alone, whether we are the ones in anguish or the ones called to respond. Whether with suffering or joy, what affects one affects all.

The Need for Solidarity

Solidarity is a hallmark of transformation, rooted in human dignity and the dignity of all creation, focusing particularly on the realities of the poor and vulnerable, the wounded heart of humanity. J. Bryan Hehir beautifully explains that solidarity is "the conviction that we are born into a fabric of relationships, that our humanity ties us to others, that the Gospel consecrates those ties and that the prophets tell us that those ties are the test by which our very holiness will be judged."[23]

As far back as 1963, Pope John XXIII, while not using the

actual term "solidarity," in essence wrote of solidarity in his encyclical *Peace on Earth*:

> National economies are gradually becoming so inter-dependent that a kind of world economy is being born from the simultaneous integration of the economies of individual States.... Each country's social progress, order, security, and peace are necessarily linked with the social progress, order, security, and peace of every other country. ... No State can fittingly pursue its own interests in isolation from the rest, nor, under such circumstances, can it develop itself as it should. The prosperity and progress of any State is in part consequence, and in part cause, of the prosperity and progress of all other States. (130, 131)

His comments about the interdependence of nations to serve the "common good" of the "human family" resonate with what today we name *global solidarity*. John XXIII saw the connections between nation-states and the global vision, and he saw links that went far beyond economics. Today we would add the stewardship of Earth and responsibility for creation as part of our call to global solidarity.

Pope John Paul II first defined *solidarity* in his 1987 encyclical *On Social Concerns*: "[Solidarity] is not a feeling of vague compassion or shallow distress at the misfortunes of so many people, both near and far. On the contrary it is a firm and persevering determination to commit oneself to the common good; to the good of all and each individual, because we are all really responsible for all" (38).

In 1997 the U.S. Catholic bishops published a pastoral letter titled *Call to Global Solidarity: International Challenges for U.S. Parishes*, directing to parishes the call to global solidarity:

> Solidarity is action on behalf of the one human family, calling us to help overcome the divisions in our world. Solidarity binds the rich to the poor. It makes the free zealous for the cause of the oppressed. It drives the

comfortable and secure to take risks for the victims of tyranny and war. It calls those who are strong to care for those who are weak and vulnerable across the spectrum of human life. It opens homes and hearts to those in flight from terror and to migrants whose daily toil supports affluent lifestyles.[24]

Each of these descriptions reminds us of the dignity of each and all.

Pope Benedict XVI and Pope Francis both engage solidarity as they read the signs of their times. In 2009 Pope Benedict XVI wrote his encyclical *Love in Truth* (*Caritas in Veritate*). The context was the global economic crisis of 2008, and he strongly invoked love in order to transform society, particularly declaring that the world's economic system must be changed and that how we look at our relationship with the Earth community must be changed. He named individual as well as structural needs. Let us look at a few of his key points here.

The first of Pope Benedict's key points reminds us that love is first and primary:

Charity is at the heart of the Church's social doctrine. Every responsibility and every commitment spelled out by that doctrine is derived from charity which, accord- ing to the teaching of Jesus, is the synthesis of the entire Law (cf. Matt. 22:36–40). It gives real substance to the personal relationship with God and with neighbor; it is the principle not only of micro-relationships (with friends, family members, or within small groups) but also of macro-relationships (social, economic, and political ones). For the Church, instructed by the Gospel, charity is everything because, as Saint John teaches (cf. 1 John 4:8, 16) and as I recalled in my first Encyclical Letter, *God Is Love* (*Deus Caritas Est*): everything has its origin in God's love, everything is shaped by it, everything is directed towards it. Love is God's greatest gift to human- ity, it is his promise and our hope. (2)

Pope Benedict then lists a variety of challenges, including food insecurity, connecting development with the common good, and the need for greater care of the Earth. On food insecurity, Benedict writes,

> Feed the hungry (cf. Matt. 25:35, 37, 42) is an ethical imperative for the universal Church, as she responds to the teachings of her Founder, the Lord Jesus, concerning solidarity and the sharing of goods. Moreover, the elimination of world hunger has also, in the global era, become a requirement for safeguarding the peace and stability of the planet. Hunger is not so much dependent on lack of material things as on shortage of social resources, the most important of which are institutional. What is missing, in other words, is a network of economic institutions capable of guaranteeing regular access to sufficient food and water for nutritional needs, and also capable of addressing the primary needs and necessities ensuing from genuine food crises, whether due to natural causes or political irresponsibility, nationally and internationally. The problem of food insecurity needs to be addressed within a long-term perspective, eliminating the structural causes that give rise to it and promoting the agricultural development of poorer countries. (27)

Second, on the need to connect political and economic development with the common good, he writes,

> Economic activity cannot solve all social problems through the simple application of commercial logic. This needs to be directed towards the pursuit of the common good, for which the political community in particular must also take responsibility. Therefore, it must be borne in mind that grave imbalances are produced when economic action, conceived merely as an engine for wealth creation, is detached from political action, conceived as a means for pursuing justice through redistribution. (36)

* * *

Development is impossible without upright men and women financiers and politicians whose consciences are finely attuned to the requirements of the common good (71).

Third, in his call for greater care for the Earth so that present and future generations can thrive, Benedict emphasizes that we are called to love and care for God's creation:

Human beings legitimately exercise a responsible stewardship over nature, in order to protect it, to enjoy its fruits, and to cultivate it in new ways, with the assistance of advanced technologies, so that it can worthily accommodate and feed the world's population. On this earth there is room for everyone: here the entire human family must find the resources to live with dignity, through the help of nature itself—God's gift to his children—and through hard work and creativity. At the same time we must recognize our grave duty to hand the earth on to the future generations in such a condition that they too can worthily inhabit it and continue to cultivate it. This means being committed to making joint decisions "after pondering responsibly the road to be taken, decisions aimed at strengthening *that covenant between human beings and the environment*, which should mirror the creative love of God, from whom we come and towards whom we are journeying."[25] (50)

Now let us turn to Pope Francis, a pope from Argentina, a country in the global South whose context gives him a particular purview of the person, economics and other systems, and the call to solidarity and conversion. Even early in his pontificate he is calling for conversion on all levels. Pope Francis praises developments that have enriched lives, and then names the profound gaps in society that diminish humanity:

At the same time, we must also acknowledge that the majority of the men and women of our time continue to live daily in situations of insecurity, with dire consequences. Certain pathologies are increasing, with their psychological consequences; fear and desperation grip the hearts of many people, even in the so-called rich countries; the joy of life is diminishing; indecency and violence are on the rise; poverty is becoming more and more evident. People have to struggle to live and, frequently, to live in an undignified way. One cause of this situation, in my opinion, is in our relationship with money, and our acceptance of its power over ourselves and our society. Consequently the financial crisis which we are experiencing makes us forget that its ultimate origin is to be found in a profound human crisis. In the denial of the primacy of human beings! We have created new idols. The worship of the golden calf of old (cf. Exod. 32:15–34) has found a new and heartless image in the cult of money and the dictatorship of an economy which is faceless and lacking any truly humane goal.[26]

Francis quite directly states that the many "situations of insecurity" are due to a "profound human crisis," and he continues the call of the Catholic social tradition for transformation of persons and systems as they are intimately connected.[27] Articulating the church's role, he says,

For her part, the Church always works for the integral development of every person. In this sense, she reiterates that the common good should not be simply an extra, simply a conceptual scheme of inferior quality tacked onto political programs. The Church encourages those in power to be truly at the service of the common good of their peoples. She urges financial leaders to take account of ethics and solidarity. And why should they not turn to God to draw inspiration from his designs? In this way, a new political and economic mindset would arise that would help to transform the absolute dichotomy between the economic and social spheres into a healthy symbiosis.[28]

Award-winning author and journalist Michael Sean Winters summarizes this statement:

> The Holy Father calls for an economic system that puts the human person at the center of its ethical analysis, not some abstract theories about economic growth. More deeply, he is calling us to conversion, a conversion of heart first and foremost, but also a conversion of lifestyles and attitudes, and, finally, a conversion of our societal systems. His namesake changed the culture of his time when he first kissed a leper. Perhaps our new millennium will be awakened to such new possibilities by Papa Francesco.[29]

Clearly all of these examples from the Catholic social tradition look at human dignity, advocate for poor and those on the margins, and seek transformation of people and society. While Benedict XVI and Pope Francis are contemporary examples, the Catholic social tradition has consistently called economic and human values to converge on the side of full humanity. In 1891, in the first social encyclical, *Concerning the Conditions of Labor*, Pope Leo XIII affirmed the right to private property while rejecting both what we would call communism and unrestricted capitalism. He also supported the right to form labor unions, for "some opportune remedy must be found quickly for the misery and wretchedness pressing so unjustly on the majority of the working class" (3). This concern continues to our time, and it now engages all avenues, including care and respect for all God's creation.

Catholic social teaching offers guidelines for how we are to be in relationship with all as we respond to particular issues and crises (the "signs of the times"), and the gospel vision directs and underscores our acts. The gospel calls forth the gifts of each person and each community to engage together in making the love of God incarnate today in the circumstances and situations we see. These include all areas of society and also all areas within the church, with no exceptions.

In addition to solidarity, human dignity, and the option for the poor and vulnerable, many other themes are found in Catholic social teaching, among them being fully human in community, our rights and responsibilities, the promotion of peace and nonviolence, care for God's creation, and an emphasis on the common good. As you engage the pastoral spiral in the chapters ahead, you will be invited to consider these various themes and virtues. Each and all flow out of the ultimate love of God and our call to live this love in justice and peace.

It Is God Who Transforms

A third emphasis of Catholic social teaching is that as disciples we are called to participate in the transformation of systems, but it must be with an awareness that change of heart or metanoia is God's doing. It is God who transforms.

In the section "Kingdom's Coming Depends on an Attitude of Heart" in Pope Paul VI's *On Evangelization in the Modern World*, we read,

> This Kingdom and this salvation, which are the key words of Jesus Christ's evangelization, are available to every human being as grace and mercy. And yet at the same time each individual must gain them by force—they belong to the violent, says the Lord (Matt. 11:12; Luke 16:16), through toil and suffering, through a life lived according to the Gospel, through abnegation and the Cross, through the spirit of the beatitudes. But above all each individual gains them through a total interior renewal which the Gospel calls *metanoia*; it is a radical conversion, a profound change of mind and heart. (10)[30]

Naturally this does not lessen our responsibility; instead, it actually gives us the comfort and assurance of knowing that our work and efforts ultimately are undertaken with confidence in God.

ESSENTIAL CHARACTERISTICS FOR TRANSFORMATIVE DISCIPLESHIP FOR OUR TIME

We have thus far considered God's transformative actions through the Old and New Testament and the continuing calls for transformation in Catholic social teaching. It may be helpful to summarize these themes by considering seven essential characteristics of transformative discipleship for our time.

1. Discipleship is *rooted in a call* whose initiative comes from God. The call is relational and mission-oriented. Each must choose a response to God's call and then live it out daily.

2. Discipleship is *grounded in love*, beginning with God who loves us and who invites us to respond in love to God and all neighbors, near and far.

3. Discipleship is *lived out in community*. Moral theologian Richard Gula describes Christian discipleship as "a way of discipleship involving a personal relationship with Jesus under the power of the Holy Spirit *working in and through the community of believers* to bring about a world marked by justice and peace."[31] We are called to live discipleship with others very intentionally in the world.

4. Discipleship is *incarnated in loving service* as we participate in Jesus' mission. Jesus' mission is a way of life, of love, mercy, forgiveness, and compassion that is continually creative and responsive to the wounded heart of humanity and all creation.

5. Discipleship is *sustained by prayer*, knowing that the road is a way of life that requires regular sustenance. How we pray may vary, but *that we pray* is essential.

6. Discipleship is *risking all for love*, even to the cross. While we do not seek the cross, our love for one another and God

may very well lead us to the cross. Prayer sustains us for this journey.

7. Discipleship is *Easter enfleshed in hope* (1 Pet. 3:15; John 20:17; Luke 24). Easter reminds us of who we are as God's people: Easter people who embody hope.

These seven characteristics of discipleship offer alternatives to fear, despair, and a sense that "this is not possible." Instead, rooted in God, who embodied love and hope, and in community, we have the freedom, courage, and fortitude to be stretched by and transformed by a God-with-us to be agents of transformation into a future full of hope.

Notes

[1] Hope is one of my abiding interests. Some of the material here was presented at the National Vicars Conference in Chicago (March 17, 2013) and is used in Steve Bevans and Cathy Ross, eds., *Mission on the Road to Emmaus* (London: SCM Publishers, 2015). See also Maria Cimperman, *When God's People Have HIV/AIDS: An Approach to Ethics* (Maryknoll, NY: Orbis Books, 2005).

[2] John R. Donahue, SJ, "The Bible and Catholic Social Teaching: Will This Engagement Lead to Marriage?" in Kenneth R. Himes, ed., *Catholic Social Teaching: Commentaries and Interpretations* (Washington, DC: Georgetown University Press, 2005), 18.

[3] This massive forced labor was described by Maimonides (1135–1204 C.E.) as service without limits of time or purpose (ibid., 18, citing n. 48 from Michael Walzer, *Exodus and Revolution* [New York: Basic Books, 1985], 27).

[4] Barbara E. Bowe, *Biblical Foundations of Spirituality: Touching a Finger to the Flame* (Lanham, MD: Rowman & Littlefield, 2003), 70. Further, "Covenants of varying kinds were common in the ancient Near East. Some were made between equal partners; others were made between unequal partners, such as those treaties common among the ancient Hittite peoples made between a sovereign and his vassals. The lord promised to guard and protect the vassals who, in turn, would pledge fealty and obedience to their lord. This type may have provide a model for Israel's covenant theology and shaped its basic elements."

[5] Daniel G. Groody, *Globalization, Spirituality, and Justice: Navigating the Paths to Peace*, Theology in Global Perspective Series (Maryknoll, NY: Orbis Books, 2007), 41: "See however, Ps 89:20-37, where the

Davidic covenant seems to be conditioned upon obedience, but the unconditional steadfast love of Yahweh for David's line is reasserted. In Ps. 89:38ff., Yahweh seems to break off the covenant with David, but here we see in the end of Book III of the Psalms a movement away from a human king to the divine king in Book IV (Psalms 90–106)," citing Walter S. Brueggemann, *Solomon: Israel's Ironic Icon of Human Achievement* (Columbia: University of South Carolina Press, 2005), 58–59, 219.

[6]Groody, *Globalization, Spirituality and Justice*, 41.

[7]Ibid., citing Raymond E. Brown, *The Book of Deuteronomy*, Reading Guide 10 (Collegeville, MN: Liturgical Press, 1965).

[8]Bowe, *Biblical Foundations of Spirituality*, 71–72.

[9]Donahue, "Bible and Catholic Social Teaching," 21.

[10]Ibid., 21–22.

[11]See further examples of this in the work of Old Testament scholar Walter Brueggemann.

[12]See John R. Donahue, SJ, "Biblical Perspective on Justice," *The Faith That Does Justice: Examining the Christian Sources of Social Change*, ed. John C. Haughey, SJ (New York: Paulist Press, 1977), 73.

[13]Donahue, "The Bible and Catholic Social Teaching," 22.

[14]Donahue, "Biblical Perspectives on Justice," 74.

[15]Donal Dorr, "Preferential Option for the Poor," in Judith A. Dwyer, ed., *Dictionary of Catholic Social Thought* (Collegeville, MN: Liturgical Press, 1994), 755.

[16]A woman who was suffering from a hemorrhage for twelve years touched Jesus' cloak and was physically healed:

"But Jesus turning and seeing her said, 'Daughter, take courage; your faith has made you well.' At once the woman was made well" (Matt. 9:22).

"And He [Jesus] said to her, 'Daughter, your faith has made you well; go in peace and be healed of your affliction'" (Mark 5:34).

"And He [Jesus] said to her, 'Daughter, your faith has made you well; go in peace'" (Luke 8:48).

We also read of Jesus approaching Jericho, and a blind beggar named Bartimaeus, the son of Timaeus, begs Jesus for his sight:

"And Jesus said to him [Bartimaeus], 'Go; your faith has made you well.' Immediately he regained his sight and began following Him on the road" (Mark 10:52).

"And Jesus said to him [Bartimaeus], 'Receive your sight; your faith has made you well'" (Luke 18:42).

Also one of the ten men with leprosy whom Jesus had healed returned to thank him, and Jesus asked not only where were the others, but to the one who returned, he said, "Stand up and go; your faith has made you well" (Luke 17:19).

In the story of the woman who washed Jesus' feet and put perfume on them from her alabaster jar, he not only tells her that her sins are forgiven, but that "your faith has saved you; go in peace" (Luke 7:50).

[17]"The term 'Kingdom of God' occurs four times in Matthew (12:28; 19:24; 21:31; 21:43), fourteen times in Mark, thirty-two times in Luke, twice in the Gospel of John (3:3, 5), six times in Acts, eight times in Paul, and once in Revelation (12:10). Matthew actually prefers the term 'Kingdom of heaven,' which he uses over twenty times in his gospel" (www.theopedia.com).

[18]Donahue, "Biblical Perspectives on Justice," 87.

[19]Ibid., 86.

[20]John P. Meier, *A Marginal Jew: Rethinking the Historical Jesus*, vol. 2, *Mentor, Message, and Miracles* (New York: Doubleday, 1994), 303.

[21]"The open heart of Christ invites us to come with our woundedness and find solace and rest. The pierced heart of Christ invites us to come with our woundedness, to be with it, to feel the piercing, invasion, betrayal, discouragement, deep pain of our lives—not in a masochistic way, not to remain there, but to know that in feeling the pain, it can be transformed through love, through grace, through healing waters—of friends, of tears, of inner sources of life—into life. . . . In the midst of our woundedness—our own and that of our world . . . many of us discover that the precise place of our woundedness becomes the place of our call—of our mission, the place not only for our own healing, but the source of our reaching out to others—because we have been there, we have been healed and those healing waters flow through us of their own power to others. Yes, blood and water flow out. . . ." (Barbara Bowe, adapted from *Biblical Foundations of Spirituality*, privately circulated redaction).

[22]Cf. 2 Cor. 5:15.

[23]J. Bryan Hehir, Catholic Relief Services, quoted in Michael Wiest, "Catholic Relief Services and Fordham University: Faith, Justice and Solidarity in the 21st Century," at http://www.crs.org.

[24]Available at http://www.usccb.org.

[25]Benedict XVI, "Message for the 2008 World Day of Peace," *AAS* 100 (2008): 41.

[26]Pope Francis's speech to an audience of new ambassadors, available at en.radiovaticana.va.

[27]Further on in his speech, Pope Francis names even more directly areas in need of systemic conversion and sees them connected to attitudes of greedy consumerism that diminish humanity: "The worldwide financial and economic crisis seems to highlight their distortions and above all the gravely deficient human perspective, which reduces man to one of his needs alone, namely, consumption. Worse yet, human be-

ings themselves are nowadays considered as consumer goods that can be used and thrown away. We have begun a throwaway culture. This tendency is seen on the level of individuals and whole societies, and it is being promoted! In circumstances like these, solidarity, which is the treasure of the poor, is often considered counterproductive, opposed to the logic of finance and the economy. While the income of a minority is increasing exponentially, that of the majority is crumbling. This imbalance results from ideologies that uphold the absolute autonomy of markets and financial speculation, and thus deny the right of control to States, which are themselves charged with providing for the common good. A new, invisible, and at times virtual tyranny is established, one that unilaterally and irremediably imposes its own laws and rules. Moreover, indebtedness and credit distance countries from their real economy and citizens from their real buying power. Added to this, as if it were needed, is widespread corruption and selfish fiscal evasion, which have taken on worldwide dimensions. The will to power and of possession has become limitless."

[28]Available at http://en.radiovaticana.va.

[29]"Pope Francis and the Modern Economy," *National Catholic Reporter*, May 17, 2013, www.ncronline.org.

[30]Available at www.americancatholic.org.

[31]Richard M. Gula, *The Call to Holiness: Embracing a Fully Christian Life* (New York: Paulist Press, 2003), 21 (emphasis added).

3

Getting Started

There were two blind men sitting by the roadside. When they heard that Jesus was passing by, they shouted, "Lord, have mercy on us, Son of David!" The crowd sternly ordered them to be quiet; but they shouted even more loudly, "Have mercy on us, Lord, Son of David!" Jesus stood still and called them, saying, "What do you want me to do for you?" They said to him, "Lord, let our eyes be opened." Moved with compassion, Jesus touched their eyes. Immediately they regained their sight and followed him.

Matthew 20:30–34

The joys and the hopes, the griefs and the anxieties of the men of this age, especially those who are poor or in any way afflicted, these are the joys and hopes, the griefs and anxieties of the followers of Christ.

—*Constitution on the Church in the Modern World*

As noted in chapter 1, when we look at the world around us locally and globally, we see incredible beauty and potential, as well as enormous need and suffering. Even as we are called to be informed people of faith, we know on a practical level that each of us cannot take on all areas of need. We also know that many unmet needs are interconnected—for example, the connection between lack of education and poverty or the connection between joblessness and immigration. When we take a closer look at a few areas of need, we often find ourselves learning about and contributing to related issues.

Yet how do we choose one topic to which to devote time, energy, and resources? Equally important, how does a community (a school, parish, church, faith-in-action group, and so on) choose an issue and begin the process that ultimately moves to responsive action?

EXPERIENCE

We begin with what we know, with our experience. Choosing an issue begins with a conversation among people who see an unmet need or issue of injustice. They could include persons directly and indirectly affected. Experience is an initial step toward the solidarity of walking together toward a just response to a need. The role of disciples, followers of Jesus, when impacted by an injustice is to name it and respond in love to change the unjust situation.

Of particular importance is the experience of those affected by the issue. If we are not directly affected, our choice to respond to a particular injustice must somehow intersect with the experiences of those who are if we are to move together toward a just response. Finding these connections early on is important, because then we are working together and together being transformed. As noted earlier, the life of discipleship, following Jesus, is transformative. It changes us. As we share information and experience, we open ourselves to transformation.

THE BASIC STEPS

Each step in this process must be covered, although the order of the steps can vary. For example, sometimes an issue comes forth very urgently and people want to know how to address it without delay. In that case, the choice of topic or issue is clear, and the group can move more easily to further steps. At other times, a given group needs to choose a topic, so that becomes the necessary first step. Sometimes there may be more than one layer with a group's choice. A small group or committee might do the initial research on a topic, and then a larger group might immerse itself in the process and the final decisionmaking. However, to get started all individuals and groups must

- Choose a topic.
- Make use of narratives and data.
- Limit the topic.
- Give reasons for the choice.
- Name their experience.
- See who is still needed at the table of discussion.

CHOOSE A TOPIC

There are many ways to choose a topic and many influences on that choice. Four such ways include (1) personal experience; (2) social media, including news media outlets and social networking sites; (3) an established group project; and (4) a request from another group or person.

Personal Experience

The particular experience of a person or a group is a powerful resource for choosing a topic to investigate. An issue that affects *us* often stimulates our initial interest and gives us the energy to pursue a project seriously. It is helpful if at least some members of a group have some personal experience to bring to the topic at hand. The experience may be primary—meaning that someone has personally experienced the situation—or the experience may be secondary—that is, someone known to the group may be experiencing a situation. For example, a friend or coworker may be experiencing challenges related to immigration rules and processes. In one case, a large suburban parish experienced the challenges of the immigration process when its choir director found that her work visa was being revoked and that she would need to leave her position and return to her Eastern European country. In yet another case, students at a university in Texas found out that a friend and classmate who had been living in the United States since she was six months old was undocumented. Now, at age twenty-two, she was scheduled to be deported to her country of birth, even though she hadn't lived in that country since she was six months old.

Experiences related to a particular issue, such as water use, can also galvanize action. Several years ago I lived for one summer in Ghana, West Africa. Because of a break in a water pipeline in the remote area where I was living, water use was very limited for several days. During those days, priority was given to water for drinking and for the local medical clinic. For the first time in my life I found myself taking a "shower," including washing my hair, with one eight-ounce glass of water. Much to my surprise, it was possible! I returned to the United States with new insight and a resolve to use water more carefully. However, over the course of a few years, I found myself once again taking long showers.

A second experience finally moved me to learn more and act more in line with my deeper values about caring for all of our God-given creation and resources. I was visiting Melbourne, Australia, when the country was experiencing a great drought. The government appealed to people to use water sparingly, and a local newspaper gave away free three-minute shower timers to help people be aware of their water use. This experience again raised my consciousness. Now, living often in cities that regularly experience periods of drought, I am more aware of water as a limited resource and the need to make more intentional choices about its use.

A good practice is to choose a topic, at least initially, with which you have some experience and involvement. If gardening and the use of land in your urban area are of personal interest, this topic might be good to consider. Someone living in a rural area or a suburban area close to rural farmland might have interest in questions related to farming, rural land use, and legislation related to subsidies. On the other hand, concern about the rising prices of bread and corn in any region could compel people to look at what is behind the prices, locally and globally. This may lead to research about where wheat and corn are grown, how they are distributed, and who has access to these resources. Studying an issue may even lead to unexpected connections. For example, more work is being done with sustainable food, with farm-to-table chefs in cities like Cleveland and Pittsburgh, that changes relationships between urban restaurants and local farms, resulting in greater menu variety and a new web of relationships among chefs, butchers, farmers, millers, bakers, and brewers.[1]

Being attentive to social location is important. As you look around, you may notice that your community has a number of unemployed young people loitering on the streets at night or asking for food and money on street corners during the day. What is the cause of this reality? In 2012 Chicago experienced over five hundred gun-related deaths, most notably on the South Side. Increased police presence was one response, yet not everyone saw this as a solution. What caused so much violence on the South Side, within a few miles of where I live? What is the reality of the community in which you live?

Clearly, a broad number of topics, and topics quite different in nature, could be of interest to any particular group.

News Media and Social Networking

Sometimes an item in the news catches our attention. We might feel compelled to consider an issue because of what we see, hear, or read on television; in a documentary or movie; on the radio; and increasingly over the Internet and social media—on websites, blogs, Twitter, wikis, emails, Facebook, or other social networking sites. Social media can create an understanding of situations that are not part of our personal experience. They can help us to observe and be open to realities in our neighborhood and also those far away.

The 2011 experience of the nonviolent change of government in Egypt is an example of social media galvanizing both local action and international awareness and support. Similarly, in 2012 there was a surge of awareness of the harm done to children abducted to be child soldiers by Ugandan warlord Joseph Kony and his Lord's Resistance Army. A twenty-nine-minute video by the group Invisible Children went viral in four days and generated over 79 million views.[2] In April 2013 the television show *60 Minutes* aired a segment about continuing efforts to find and arrest Kony. The attention generated continues the pressure to stop Kony, and many more people, particularly teens, are aware of what is happening to their peers in a challenging place. We cannot underestimate the importance of social media outlets in our time, for they are expanding our world and deepening our understanding of issues. We return to the use of social media when we consider possible actions in response to issues.

As language through various media shapes thought, so do images. In the 1970s, a popular television commercial about pollution showed the face of a Native American looking at a large expanse of land; as he observes pollution everywhere in the rivers and on the land, a single tear falls from his eye.

Images raise awareness and invite action. Someone might be moved by televised accounts of college students participating in a sit-in on the lawn of city hall to give public support to the DREAM Act, legislation to assist undocumented college students in the United States in gaining citizenship.[3] Similarly, films can have a great impact. The movie *The Visitor* may galvanize one person to look at immigration issues, and *Gasland* may raise concerns about the environmental hazards of drilling for natural gas. Just as *Food, Inc.* has a powerful message about the way our food is produced and transported, *An Inconvenient Truth* raised global awareness of the hazards of climate change.

Sometimes a combination of events converge; if we make a practice of being reflective in our daily lives, we can notice connections in light of our faith and deep values. For example, one semester a colleague invited me to hear a guest speaker in her evening class. The speaker, Matilde, had survived torture in her home country of Guatemala. This riveting and heartrending presentation described her work as a physician among the poor in the midst of a civil war where human rights violations abounded. She was assaulted and tortured, and when she was let go, she clearly understood that if she stayed in Guatemala her life would be in mortal danger. She left Guatemala, came to the United States, and over the course of many years found a home in this country. However, the long-term effects of torture were present along with the beauty that radiated from her eyes. Poignantly, Matilde shared that even at great personal cost she was speaking out and sharing her story because she hoped she would be the last person ever tortured. Sadly, torture continues.

When she had finished, her husband spoke, noting that over half of the Catholics in the United States said that they could see the possibility of using torture to gain information vital to national security. He quoted from the Pew Research Center's Forum on Religious & Public Life survey in 2009 on the use of torture against suspected terrorists, with 51 percent of white, non-Hispanic Catholics saying that use of torture can often (19 percent) or sometimes (32 percent) be used.[4]

Matilde's husband also pointed out that, at the time of their presentation, over 160 prisoners were in the Guantánamo Bay detention camp, a detainment and interrogation facility in the US Guantánamo Bay Naval Center in Cuba. Over half the prisoners there have been cleared for release but have not been released, and some have been detained for many years. In addition, over two-thirds of the prisoners are on a hunger strike to protest their conditions. The response has been force-feeding rather than further efforts to seek their release.

Interestingly, or providentially, a few weeks after he spoke, the news of the condition of the detainees made national and international news. An op-ed article by a detainee was published in the *New York Times*,[5] and letter-writing efforts and calls to congressional representatives have galvanized pressure on President Obama's administration to keep his promise to close Guantánamo. There is also more public discussion and pressure to do something about the situation that goes beyond keeping the prisoners fed and hydrated. At that time I also viewed the documentary *Beneath the Blindfold*,[6] which included the story of Matilde de la Sierra from Guatemala (whom I had met when she shared her story in the class I attended), Blama Massaquoi from Liberia, Hector Aristtizabal from Colombia, and Donald Vance from the United States. Much came together during these weeks, galvanizing my desire to get involved.

I have become much more sensitive to and aware of references to torture, oblique or obvious. At a hotel not long afterward, while surfing channels looking for news, I came upon the drama *NCIS*. I watched it for a few minutes until I heard a reference to Gitmo and the warning from one of the Naval Criminal Investigative Service officials that, if a certain person was sent there, the NCIS team couldn't guarantee his safety. I had watched this show some years earlier because I had found the main characters interesting and some of the political issues intriguing. Perhaps even then I had heard "Gitmo" references, but I didn't "get it." Now I do. In the hotel I immediately turned the television off, stunned by what I had heard and by what I had often failed to hear. How had I missed this? Was this synchronicity? Providence? A call to action? Yes. We must listen to what is around us and attune our hearts. However we are galvanized, most important is *that we are galvanized*.

When a topic starts emerging, you will naturally become more sensitive to hearing and seeing what else relates to that story. You will become more attuned. Whether you have found or are considering a topic, keep a log or listing of various news items related to your topic(s) of interest. If you have not yet decided on your topic for social analysis, you might keep a log for a month or so of various news items or images that have caught your attention before settling on an issue.

Group Projects

In some instances a group might choose a topic. For example, some schools or courses regularly ask students to consider an important contemporary issue. Some schools choose a particular theme for a year grounded on their value-based or faith-based perspective. A parish committee may be commissioned to offer an experience of faith in action on a local or national issue. In one diocese, for example, a parish named for St. Francis of Assisi decided to use St. Francis's love of creation as a lens to examine environmental issues in its region, state, and the world.

Service trips are also important contexts in which groups choose topics. In preparing for a trip to another region or country, do advance research on current issues there. Some groups undertake an initial preparation and analysis and then, upon their return, do more analysis because their experience is now greater and deeper and more questions emerge for action. One very helpful plan with service or mission-based trips is to complete as much of the first two phases (Experience and Social Analysis) as possible before the trip. The trip will enrich and deepen your knowledge of the narratives and hopes of the people. During your stay, you are encouraged to pray and reflect (personally and communally) on what you are experiencing and learning. The subsequent steps will more naturally emerge on your return when you have time to reflect on your experience. In addition, since one of the steps in social analysis includes action, your time among the people of the region may give you some essential dialogue partners for creating an action response that is in solidarity with the people and region you wish to assist.

An Outside Request

Sometimes a larger group, such as a diocese, might ask a smaller group (a parish, a subgroup of staff) to take on a particular topic. A diocese might ask different parishes to analyze a specific subtopic. For example, one year the archdiocese of Minneapolis–St. Paul studied potable water use. Families, schools, and parishes all undertook research and reflection on the topic, considering the question locally and globally. Similarly, a larger church community may appeal to all people of goodwill to consider a particular topic, as is currently the case in a number of churches regarding immigration reform and US healthcare reform. Pope Benedict XVI made a particular appeal to Catholics to consider issues related to economics, the environment (care of creation / integrity of creation), and a range of other social issues in his 2009 encyclical, *Caritas in Veritate* (Charity in Truth). A group may decide to do a careful reading and then have an open discussion to see what ideas on poverty, environment, corporate responsibility, and more would interest the group.

Pope Francis, since his election as pope in March 2013, has often spoken of people who are poor and on the margins and how our call is to respond to and change these realities. Pope Francis has addressed all people in general and then also particular groups—including people in public service, elected officials, and youth—to respond to the cries of the world and the cries of the Earth. Great media attention is making his message available across the globe, and so choosing an area may be a response to his plea to the people of God.

The group making a request also need not be faith-based. For example, many groups are working with the global HIV and AIDS pandemic, from UNAIDS to the Ecumenical Advocacy Alliance (EAA) to various local nongovernmental organizations (NGOs), to civic communities and families affected by the disease. Many of these groups have looked at various social factors related to the spread of HIV, including poverty, gender inequality, and stigma, that are in turn impacted by lack of access to education, health care, and employment, among other factors. Many such groups have asked faith-based groups to use their particular values to undertake some form of analysis and response in this area of great need.

USING NARRATIVES AND DATA

In choosing a topic and limiting it, get an initial sense of the stories and data connected to the topic. We often find a way to connect with others through stories. My research and subsequent efforts in HIV and AIDS were the result of stories bolstered by statistics. During my twenties I found out that someone I knew from grade school had died of AIDS-related pneumonia; he was also in his twenties. Years later, during the summer I lived in Ghana, West Africa, I listened to a woman dying with AIDS share her story, and my doctoral research topic began to focus on AIDS. Around that same time, when I began talking with young people in Ghana about HIV and AIDS, I realized that a better response to the disease was needed than billboard signs warning about the ways HIV is spread. When I returned to the United States and began reading about HIV and AIDS, I saw the need for a theological conversation and response to the disease that was already a pandemic in some regions of the world and that could grow exponentially.

Stories and statistics both moved me to take action, though in different ways, and I am convinced that we need both to offer an effective response.

Narratives grab us, reminding us that real people are involved in the issues at hand. Narratives also remind us that the Earth, too, is part of God's creation and needs people to act in solidarity on her behalf. Narratives, quite frankly, move our hearts, which also can move us to act. Humans have a natural compassion that moves us to respond to the suffering of others, which in part is what compels us to donate when we see and hear people dealing with the impact of a tsunami in Asia, Hurricane Katrina, or a forest fire in California. Stories move us to action.

Data and statistics help us see the larger picture and the seriousness of an issue. Statistics from reputable sources such as UNAIDS, for example, tell us that over 30 million people are infected and millions more affected by HIV and AIDS.

Statistics insist that we see a need more sharply. Data also help us determine whether a system is at work that needs to change. Practically, stories move our hearts while data move our heads, ultimately asking for an integrated response to God's people living with or at risk of HIV and AIDS. In addition, stories and personal connections can keep me moving when the statistics threaten to overwhelm. Conversely, data command attention from others, and stories invite us into realities that may at times be very different from our own.

We need both. Narratives alone may lead us to think that an issue is small and not in need of analysis. If a factory fire in Bangladesh is only an isolated, though tragic, incident, then a personal response to the people in need is sufficient. However, data and statistics let us know that factory safety conditions in such places are not isolated but more commonplace symptoms of a lack of worker rights and safe working environments.

Stories connect us to people and the Earth. They introduce us to what is happening, and then they keep us working when we realize that some of the issues to which we commit may take considerable time and effort. Data give us some indication of the seriousness of an issue and where some movement is happening. Paul Farmer, a medical doctor working on behalf of the poor in many parts of the world, including Haiti, while also teaching at Harvard Medical School led students in researching data to promote efforts on behalf of the poor. Working with him on a paper describing their research, they knew that every statement of fact he made "had to be verified as coming from some authoritative source."[7] As a medical student working for Farmer explained, "when you're doing these things for the poor, amidst arguments that it's not cost-effective to treat them, you have to be perfect or you'll be picked apart."[8]

We go into much more detail on data in next chapter on social analysis, but for now I simply want to highlight the importance of data to confirm a need in a particular area and the role of stories to help a group connect with others.

LIMIT THE TOPIC

After concluding that there is enough interest, data, and energy to take on a topic, the group should consider whether the topic is sufficiently focused and limited. For example, a group might have an interest in the environment. While "the environment" is a particular lens to look through, the topic is still too broad to be manageable. What area or aspect of the environment is of interest in your area? Possible topics could include water, genetically modified food, air pollution, the use of landfills, noise pollution, a need for recycling, wind energy, and solar energy.

Each of these topics may also need to be more narrowly defined. For example, from the broad topic of the environment, your group may have chosen water. Water supplies a direction, but for most groups the topic is still too large to be manageable for analysis, reflection, and action. In deciding what particular aspect of water or water use to pursue, the group should consider unmet needs with a local connection—and perhaps also a global connection. Some questions that may help could include: Is our water supply adequate? Is the water supply contaminated? Is water being used equitably?

Although a group might prefer to choose a global topic, identifying an issue that you or your group can personally take on and become involved with is usually more effective. While understanding how a local issue is connected to the big picture is very important, so is beginning with a manageable topic; otherwise your intended social analysis might quickly end in paralysis. Taking on topics locally helps supply us with beginning points for action. Over time, the larger issues will often enter into the discussions and even any planned action.

If your group, for example, has chosen to take up water, how then do you choose from among a number of options? You could begin with basic research on the topic. Go to the library to see what is written on the general subject or begin an online search for information from reputable sources. Ask the group's members to recount any experiences, positive or negative, with water use that might be related. If your topic is too broad, you will soon discover how many different dimensions it includes. If this is the first time your group has engaged in social analysis, begin with a topic that is not too broad or overwhelming, as you want to be able to plan specific actions and see some results. On the other hand, if a group has some experience or wants to undertake a long-term project, the topic might be broader but still a manageable area for that particular person or group.

Once a group has settled on a topic and determined a need to improve a situation in your neighborhood, city, or region, you could invite a few others with expertise on the topic to join in the conversation, as they may be able to offer needed insight and direction. It may become clear that a particular topic not only presents an important unmet need but that the wider community knows very little about it. You may also find some rich sources of expertise in people with whom you can collaborate.

Another way to look at an issue is to observe the general picture and then determine where a particular unmet need may exist. For example, a faith-based group in the Midwest took time one year to look more closely at the use of the various natural resources for energy (gas, electricity, and so on) and their impact on the environment. The group also began reading newspaper articles related to the possibilities of drilling for natural gas in the area. Then, after watching the documentary *Gasland*, they began to look at the cost both to the environment and the economy in a time when most states were experiencing economic challenges. Because gas drilling was connected to their local reality and to the wider question of natural resources and the environment, they chose this topic for social analysis. When their first layer of research led them to question whether gas drilling was environmentally unsustainable, they began attending civic meetings related to the topic. They did not know where this would take them, but their first order of business was to understand the reality as fully as possible.

GIVE REASONS FOR THE CHOICE

Be clear why, among all the possible topics, you are choosing a particular issue. You can do your analysis on three different levels: an unmet need, a gospel value, and personal reasons.

You should be able to respond on the level of unmet needs by answering a series of questions. Why is this topic important today? Are water use and drought a reality in your region or the world? If you are choosing drilling for gas near water sources, are some problems not being addressed? Is there any controversy related to the issue? In addition, your concern may have an educational dimension. For example, drilling for natural gas is becoming a much debated topic. Are people in your area adequately informed about the pros and cons of such drilling?

Second, what gospel values are at stake? The Christian call to treat all persons with dignity, for example, could be linked to the treatment of immigrants in detention centers and a number of other causes, including such varied topics as the location and use of landfills. The issue of human trafficking speaks to our relationships with one another as beloved of God, relationships in which individuals are not treated as servants or slaves. Oil drilling in the Gulf of Mexico or drilling for natural gas in Wyoming poses the question of how effective we are as stewards in protecting all of God's creation.

NAME YOUR EXPERIENCE

The fourth level of questioning on why a particular topic is chosen asks group members to articulate their personal involvement and to explore a bit more deeply how this topic directly affects them. This leads to the fifth step of choosing a topic: naming your experience. Members of the group who have energy or passion around a topic will be more engaged. Often there is more to a choice than first meets the eye. This level invites you to probe more deeply into your choice, acknowledging that head and heart are both often involved in the choice of an issue.

"The Five Whys," an exercise that Toyota originally developed and used in its training, tries to get at a problem's root causes. Nancy Sylvester, IHM, adapted this exercise to apply to the feeling level of a situation so as to uncover the deeper motivations for the initial response to a situation. After the feeling is identified, the same "why" question is asked five times, with a limited time in between so that the responder does not ponder the question at length but gives a spontaneous reaction.

The Five Whys[1]

When I reflect on the situation of _____
(name the topic/issue) I feel _____
(Write down the emotion.).

1. Why do I feel this way *(the emotion)*? _____

2. And why does that *(answer of #1)* make me feel this way/*(the emotion)*?
_____

3. And why does that *(answer of #2)* make me feel this way *(the emotion)*?
_____

4. And why does that *(answer of #3)* make me feel this way *(the emotion)*?
_____

5. And why does that *(answer of #4)* make me feel this way *(the emotion)*?
_____

Source: *Process adapted from Nancy Sylvester, IHM, Institute for Communal Contemplation and Dialogue, 8531 West McNichols, Detroit, MI 48221; www.iccdinstitute.org.*

An example that applies the Five Whys is helpful here. A parish-based group chose natural gas drilling in the state. One person responded as follows:

When I reflect on the situation of gas drilling, I feel—scared.

1. Why do I feel fear?
I feel this way because I don't know if we know what we are doing when we embark on this venture.

2. Why does that (answer to #1) make me feel scared?
Because we have at times gotten ourselves in a terrible bind when we act before we know all that we are doing— think of the nuclear disaster in Japan and Gulf oil spill.

3. Why does that (answer to #2) make me feel scared?
Because sometimes our greed can move us to not look at all at the important questions, and we tend to lack humility in our care for the earth.

4. Why does that (answer to #3) make me feel scared?
Because when you make some mistakes, you can cause irreparable damage, such as ruining the water, the Earth, food supply chains, and it can become globally impacted, like radioactive water in Japan spreading elsewhere.

5. Why does that (answer to #4) make me feel scared?
Because we have not yet learned how to care for the Earth with a longer-term vision, and I want my children and children's children to be healthy, to have beauty around them, and I don't feel like I am being responsible for this and I don't know how to go about stopping our waste and poor decisionmaking before we make more mistakes. And I don't know if I trust us all to take good care of the Earth when money is at stake.

Note how the layers of responses deepen, revealing both information and emotion. The person responding increasingly sees what is connected to the question of gas drilling and how very much is at stake. Sharing these insights increases the group's understanding and commitment to the topic and to community members gathering around the topic. These insights are helpful as the spiral continues.

SEE WHO IS MISSING FROM THE TABLE

The final section of "Getting Started" invites us to look at whose experiences and voices we are listening to and whether some voices might not be included. As you look around the room when you begin work on your topic, what experiences and gifts are present? What voices, experiences, and gifts are missing? This point can be illustrated by a sociology class in a Catholic boys' high school that chose a project related to domestic violence and women. Their early research indicated that a large percentage of the women in their city were women of a particular age and income bracket. They quickly realized that they could gain much more information and greater understanding of the issue from any of these women who would be willing to share their experiences of domestic violence. As a result, they contacted a women's resource center and interviewed its executive director, who was able to locate a young woman willing to be interviewed by the group and who also spoke at a parish open meeting on domestic violence. The willingness of the woman to share her experience added a new dimension to their study, one that even a skilled group leader could not supply.

A *diversity of viewpoints* needs to be present in some way. One group researching immigration laws had considerable access to immigrants in various stages of migration. Realizing that the immigrants formed only one part of the picture, the group proceeded to interview a representative of the Immigration and Naturalization Service (INS) and a border patrol agent in order to better understand issues related to immigration. Another group investigating immigration issues did not have immediate access to these many voices but instead watched the documentary *Line in the Sand*, which offers various perspectives on the immigration issue on the US-Mexican border.

When another group working on the use of solar energy for church buildings found no one in the group with environmental or engineering expertise, they invited an outside expert on solar energy to participate. Persons invited may be regular members of the group or invited just for a particular phase in the pastoral spiral. Gaining sufficient initial information to confirm the choice of a topic before proceeding to the next step is important.

When choosing a topic, consider the time available. It may take some time to choose a topic that is appropriately limited, serves as an unmet need with a connection to gospel values, and offers sufficient personal interest to a group's members. Some groups may be able to decide on a topic quickly because of an immediate need, while other groups may take a few weeks to get to know one another through discussing various topics of interest. Take the necessary time in making a choice, but at some point the group must choose its focus. Then the in-depth social analysis begins.

Notes

[1] Julia Moskin, "Replanting the Rust Belt," *New York Times*, May 7, 2013.

[2] Claire Suddaith, "Five Reasons the Kony Video Went Viral," *Bloomberg Businessweek Style*, March 16, 2012, http://www.businessweek.com.

[3] The purpose of the Development, Relief and Education of Alien Minors Act (the DREAM Act) is to help individuals who meet certain requirements have an opportunity to enlist in the military or go to college and have a path to citizenship that they otherwise would not have. Supporters of the DREAM Act believe it is vital not only to the people who would benefit from it, but also to the country as a whole. It would give undocumented immigrant students who have been living in the United States since they were young an opportunity to contribute to the country that has given much to them, and it would provide a chance to use their hard-earned education and talents. This legislation was introduced on March 26, 2009, by Senator Richard Durbin and Representative Howard Berman. On December 20, 2009, however, the Senate voted 55-41 to consider the DREAM Act, falling five votes short of the three-fifths majority needed to bring the bill to the floor for a vote.

[4]Amid intense public debate over the use of torture against suspected terrorists, an analysis by the Pew Research Center's Forum on Religion & Public Life of a new survey by the Pew Research Center for the People & the Press illustrates differences in the views of four major religious traditions in the United States about whether torture of suspected terrorists can be justified. Differences in opinion on this issue also are apparent based on frequency of attendance at religious services. However, statistical analysis that simultaneously examines correlations between views on torture, partisanship, ideology, and demographic variables (including religion, education, race, etc.) finds that party and ideology are much better predictors of views on torture than are religion and most other demographic factors (see "The Torture Debate: A Closer Look," at http://www.pewforum.org). Of course, religion itself is known to be a strong factor shaping individuals' partisanship and political ideology. Attitudes about torture are likely to reflect moral judgments as well as political considerations—both of which may be formed in part by religious convictions—about circumstances under which torture may be justified. See http://www.pewforum.org.

[5]Samir Naji al Hasan Moqbel, "Gitmo Is Killing Me," *New York Times*, April 14, 2013. Samir Naji al Hasan Moqbel is identified as a prisoner at Guantanamo Bay since 2002 who told this story, through an Arabic interpreter, to his lawyers at the legal charity Reprieve in an unclassified telephone call.

[6]See http://www.beneaththeblindfold.com.

[7]Found in Tracy Kidder, *Mountains beyond Mountains: The Quest of Dr. Paul Farmer, a Man Who Would Cure the World* (New York: Random House, 2003), 216.

[8]Ibid., 217.

4

Social Analysis

The basic aim of good analysis is to discover the *why* of the *what*—the causes of the occurrences that we have described.

> —Peter Henriot, "Social Discernment and the Pastoral Circle"

Inspired by no earthly ambition, the Church seeks but a solitary goal: to carry forward the work of Christ under the lead of the befriending Spirit. And Christ entered this world to give witness to the truth, to rescue and not to sit in judgment, to serve and not to be served. . . .

To carry out such a task, the Church has always had the duty of scrutinizing the signs of the times and of interpreting them in the light of the Gospel.

> —*Constitution on the Church in the Modern World*

A reflective exercise such as the one described here provides a useful way to enter into the world of social analysis.

1. Gather enough fresh tomatoes (or any other readily available fruit or vegetable) so that each person can see a tomato clearly. Place them where they can be seen and even touched by the group members.
2. Take three or four minutes and ponder the tomato in silence. What do you see? Keep looking. What else do you see? What does it remind you of?

3. Take a few minutes to share with a few others around you what you saw and thought of as you pondered the tomato.
4. Invite the larger group to the same sharing. You may wish to record the insights shared.
5. Next, have someone read the following poem out loud slowly so that all have a chance to visualize the words.

If you are a poet,

you will SEE CLEARLY that there is a cloud
    floating in this tomato.
Without a cloud, there will be no rain;
without rain, the tomato plants cannot
    grow;
and without tomato plants, we can have no
    tomatoes.
The cloud is essential for the tomato to ex-
    ist.

If we look into this tomato even more
    deeply,

we can SEE the sunshine in it.
Without sunshine, the tomato fields cannot
    grow.
And so we know that the sunshine is also in
    this tomato. . . .

And if we continue to look,

we SEE the farm worker who picked the
    tomato and brought it to the trucks to be
    driven to the agribusiness corporations
    who will send it on to processing plants
    and food franchises,

and we will SEE wheat and beans.

The farm worker cannot exist without his
    daily tortillas and beans
and therefore the wheat and beans that be-
    came his meal are also in this tomato.

The farm worker's father and mother, wife
    and children are in it, too.

And we will SEE people marching in the
    streets to proclaim the farm workers'
    rights in a nation torn apart over issues of
    migration—
only one of many wealthy nations as global
    migration flows reach historic levels.

As your contemplative vision deepens, you
    SEE the farm workers and the fields and
    the planet itself threatened by the pesti-
    cides and fertilizers that permeate them.

And you will KNOW in the very fiber of
    your being that the tomatoes, the farm
    workers, the fields, the families, the social
    movements and the planet are all held in

the suffering LOVE OF GOD.[1]

This exercise illustrates the interconnections between and among so much of life. When we take a few moments to look, ponder, and be attentive to what is around us, such connections abound. A reflective vision invites us to observe ever more deeply and widely. Looking at the chairs we sit on (presuming they are wooden chairs), we begin to notice that the chairs come from trees grown in various parts of the world that are cut down and then sold to companies that shape the wood into what we sit on daily. Noting the connections between trees and chairs invites further questions about where the trees came from, who and what were paid for the trees, what kind of tree was cut and how it is connected to any rainforest and the ecosystem, and whether the distribution of profits was equitable. Just as more coffee shops are advertising whether their coffee beans are "fair trade," so, too, are more furniture stores listing the type of wood used to make furniture, where it came from, and whether they are selling sustainably harvested wood products.[2] Making these connections and asking such questions engage us in the analysis of systems.

This chapter focuses on making more connections and seeing more deeply so that both the immediate picture and the larger picture are as clear as possible before starting the process of discerning the direction for movement on social issues. This chapter includes analytical directions, guidelines, and a method for looking at issues that need attention and action. Chapter 1 looked at global and local realities. This chapter helps us to see the local and global connections involved in the realities and topics we encounter each day.

INTRODUCTION TO SOCIAL ANALYSIS AND SYSTEMS

The method called *social analysis* helps us understand the historical and structural issues at work in situations that may need transformation. Social analysis is defined as "the effort to obtain a more complete picture of a social situation by exploring its *historical and structural relationship*."[3] Social analysis is a method by which one looks at an issue in order to see its individual parts and its entirety. "Social analysis asks: What are the structures and dynamics at work creating the situation we are experiencing as it currently exists?"[4]

Social analysis helps us get underneath a problem and find out systemically why the problem exists, historically and structurally. Major structures include economics, politics, culture, the environment, and religion. Analysis also helps us unearth our blind spots or biases so that we see clearly what is happening, why it is happening, and how it relates to our deepest values and beliefs. Our response will come from the results of our analysis—combined with reflection on the problem based on our faith and values, so that our action is directed to where the difficulties and problems are, where something in the system has shifted out of balance, and where we might intervene. Seeing the whole is vital, for we can miss obvious pieces, much like the story of persons who with their eyes closed each touched one part of an elephant and tried to describe and identify it. To proceed effectively, we need a much bigger and fuller picture.

Bias, Values, and Social Analysis

A bias is usually present in social analysis; social analysis is rarely if ever value free. Values are key factors that guide the analysis. As Christians, we say that our values are to bring forth God's kingdom by loving God and loving our neighbors. Anything that does not move toward these ends is not a Christian value. This book's values are to bring forth the values of the reign of God. All human life is valuable and to be protected. We are (1) looking in particular at situations and realities that affect the poor, vulnerable, and marginalized peoples and creation, and (2) seeking ways to respond that are indicative of God's covenant of right relationships among all people.

Naming the key values at play is crucial. This book is value-laden, and the values (as noted in chapter 2) are clearly gospel-oriented—concerned with the dignity of each person and with the Earth community. They hold a preferential option for the poor, vulnerable, and marginalized, the wounded heart of humanity. The common good is important and must be balanced with how it impacts any one group.

We also need to forthrightly name our personal biases, as they will show up at some point. The more we engage the world—analyzing what is happening, reflecting on the reality with our faith, and then responding to the needs—the more we will discover our cultural, political, economic, and religious biases, which is one reason why listening to narratives is important. A cultural bias on immigration reforms may exist because one's grandparents came to this country through legal means, and so one may feel unable to recognize legitimate reasons to migrate through other means today. As another example, because of our own educational background, we may have some predispositions about those who do not have the same academic background. Such awareness is exceedingly helpful. As we learn about a topic, people from a variety of perspectives can dialogue with us and lead us to understand an issue more deeply.

Ten Guidelines for Research

Because social analysis requires research and sifting of information, the following ten guidelines can assist you as you begin to probe an issue or topic.

1. *Research broadly and widely at first on your limited topic.* You may find more general information in popular areas of social media as well as in newspapers and magazines that will indicate how your topic is seen in wider venues. Keep a running account on your computer or in a folder of what you read and keep updating it. You may Google a topic to see what recent books have addressed it. What is a basic history of the issue? For example, when did immigration laws change? When did the term "climate change" enter our lexicon? Begin to note the persons, organizations, or nations involved in this area in general.

2. *Find reliable resources for data.* Government agencies, UN organizations, and studies from universities are good places to begin. What are they saying, and what sources are they using? As you gain more information, you will begin to give more weight to resources that are credible and well-researched or cited by persons with expertise on the topic, rather than those from general and at times more anonymous sources.[5]

3. *Talk to specialists with expertise on your topic.* Read ahead of time on your topic so that you have some basic reference points and questions. Find out who in your organization (parish, university), circle of colleagues or acquaintances, or

agencies (government, nonprofit organization, NGO) has expertise in this area. Find some diverse opinions, too, so that you can do your own critical analysis in discerning action. You must also decide on the best use of specialists. Is it best to have the person meet with the entire group? Is an interview with a smaller group a good start? See how you might engage them most effectively, whether in person or by phone, social media, email, or letter. As you interact with the experts, think about whether they might be helpful later in the process as questions arise.

4. *Find research or articles that engage your topic from a value base close to your own and begin collecting those resources.* You will not always agree, but see how your faith tradition and value system consider the intersection between faith and the issue. Resources from particular groups within a faith tradition (for example, for Catholics, the Vatican, the US Conference of Catholic Bishops [USCCB], dioceses, theologians, faith-based organizations) or from a grouping of faith traditions (e.g., the World Council of Churches, faith-based UN groups such as the Temple of Understanding) are important and often helpful. Journals that clearly name their values are also helpful. Popular Catholic journals such as *America*, *Commonweal*, and *The Tablet* (London), while not necessarily writing from the same position, have a particular faith perspective.

5. *Find information from more than one perspective* (even or especially when you know your value system or leaning). Gaining a variety of perspectives, especially conflicting ones, is very helpful for discernment and for dialogue. Where are the discrepancies? If someone claims that capital punishment deters murder, does the data support this? If someone says that many immigrants are here to support their families in their countries of origin rather than to engage in drug trafficking or organized crime, what do we know about the amount of remittances going to particular countries? If someone says that hydraulic drilling is unsafe, what do data from both sides of the drilling indicate and what are the sources of the data?

6. *Where are the voices of those most impacted, and how does the data fit (or not fit) the experiences and narratives?* Are there any discrepancies?

7. *Ask more questions until you get to what you consider the central focus of your issue.* What questions underlie your questions (refer to the Five Whys in chapter 3)?

8. *Create visuals for the information you are gathering.* People can only absorb so much information. Present the information in more than one media. Some people better understand verbal explanations; some, written explanations; and still others, visual explanations. A combination is a helpful tool since we have such different learning styles. Visuals help us see what we are seeing, see what is missing, and imagine what might be possible. Visuals are used also in the third and fourth phases of the pastoral spiral.

9. *As information is gathered, consider yourself a conversation partner with the information.* No information ultimately substitutes for your own judgment. Thomas Clarke suggests that experts serve as helpful mentors but are not the ultimate judge:

> Social analysis is not the prerogative of an elite. If a participatory, democratic way of life is to be a possibility, it requires a basic confidence and skill on the part of ordinary people in making critical and informed judgments regarding the social contexts of their lives. To say this is not to deny the importance of specialized knowledge, or the difficulty which most of us have in being reasonably well informed on scores of major and complex issues, and in deciding just what sources of information and analytical helps to critical judgment deserve our trust.[6]

Your own wisdom and the group's wisdom emerge in this process. Test both your informed learning and your instincts with the group. One day I was waiting for baggage to arrive after a flight and entered into a conversation with a man who taught in a mining school and worked with oil extraction, an area I had been researching for some time. I realized quickly that we looked at the issue very differently, but I needed to hear his perspective and converse with him about the research I had done. In the end he gave me his card and offered to answer further questions. My instincts told me that I had much to learn from him, even though I heard us speaking of water safety assurances (or the lack thereof) quite differently. Just as students have the responsibility to question me in ethical areas (which I teach) and should not simply defer to my statements, so his actual mining experience didn't remove my responsibility to ask questions that still were unanswered and to question his accountability. We both spoke of caring for the Earth, though differently, so further dialogue would be essential.

10. *Discuss regularly what you are finding.* Remember that this is a community project, and communal discernment must be part of the information gathering. Regular gatherings and sharing of information and impressions will help you see what is emerging among you and what is happening at many levels on your topic. Communication is going to be key, especially since the information gathering is about transformation. Reflective consideration is part of decisionmaking, and doing so with others can build a transformative community.

THE STEPS OF SOCIAL ANALYSIS

We are now ready for the steps of social analysis.[7] The remainder of this chapter includes a detailed explanation and guide to the key areas of social analysis. Specifically we consider

- Sociological analysis
- Economic analysis
- Political analysis
- Cultural analysis
- Environmental analysis
- Religious analysis

Figure 2. The Pastoral Spiral

SOCIOLOGICAL ANALYSIS

As noted at the opening of this chapter, "The basic aim of good analysis is to discover the *why* of the *what*—the causes of the occurrences that we have described." In order to discover the *why*, we look at *who* is involved in *what* is happening. Sociological analysis takes its lead from the field of *sociology*, the study of human social behavior that analyzes the origins, development, organization, and institutions of human society. Sociology addresses how institutions or societies are organized within themselves and within a broader society.

Social analysis, as we know, examines the structures that cause or contribute directly or indirectly to issues of injustice, and so we begin by looking at the persons and groups connected to our topic. We first ask some questions revolving around the question "Who is involved?"

- Who are the actors in this situation, and what are the roles of each?
- What groups or organizations do they belong or are they connected to?
- What organizations are involved in this situation, directly or indirectly?[8]
- How are the persons and groups connected, associated, or interconnected? Or not?
- What, if any, parts of the Earth community are involved?[9]
- What is *your* involvement or role(s)? What groups are you part of? What roles do you play?
- What is the history of the situation, and what are the important relationships?

In the beginning, include every possible link in your brainstorming, for they all contribute to obtaining the widest and most detailed picture possible.

One example comes from participants in a social analysis workshop in San Antonio, Texas, who decided to look at the negative impact of plastic bags on the environment. Many had noticed the large number of plastic bags (and even double bagging) used in grocery stores and wondered about alternatives. Values they named included concern for creation, greater simplicity, and saving resources. A participant from Ireland pointed out that in Ireland, according to a government initiative, if you went to the grocery store and didn't have your own bags, you were charged for bags. Others found hope in the woman's narrative, wondering what they might do to change patterns and practices in their city. Interestingly, the first impulse of many was to see what could be changed via grassroots efforts rather than turning first to the government to mandate a solution. They were interested in changing minds and hearts first.

The group's initial research showed that some cities and countries already were selling sturdier bags that could be reused indefinitely. While this was not the case in their home city, they realized that some momentum and probably good published rationales were already present for their concern.

An informal survey of several grocery store managers and shoppers in the area found that not many people were thinking about this issue. People asked about its practicality: Will people remember to bring their bags to the store? Some reflected that just as people have a habit of having groceries packed into paper or plastic bags in stores, a new habit would need to be formed in which people bring their own bags to a grocery store. A shift in understanding was needed, and perhaps some incentive as well. The group's interest in the project of finding alternatives to plastic bag use and even paper bag use in grocery stores was piqued by this point, and so they began their analysis. They asked themselves what it would take to make a case for alternatives to plastic bags and thus started a list of who the "actors" in this issue would be.

Whom would they need to engage in order to change shoppers' habits? The list began with some of the most obvious individuals:

- Consumers
- Grocery bag packers
- Grocery store owners or managers
- Plastic bag manufacturers

Then they began a list of organizations or companies connected to the use of bags in some way:

- Grocery stores
- Families
- Grocery store franchises
- Companies that sell plastic bags
- Companies that produce plastic
- Plastic bag recycling companies
- Companies that created alternatives to plastic bags

Someone mentioned at one point that, within each parish community, parishioners buy groceries and thus are consumers as a group and as individuals. Now the list also included,

- Parishes
- Dioceses

This list seemed to offer potential for later use and advocacy. The group realized that, even as they were individual consumers, they were also part of a larger group. Moreover, as a community they could have an even wider impact if they found a way to connect this issue to their church community, as well as to a diocese and perhaps a city council district or city or state. Some saw possible collaboration across religious traditions as well as various civic groups. Members were beginning to think in terms of systems and to see how they might have more connections and more impact if they united with others around a common issue.

Categories Involving the Earth

The next focus was the way in which the Earth was impacted by plastic bags (and thus a player in the story), and the group listed landfill, recycled products, and litter on land and water. Now was the time to see if any actors were still missing and to list them as follows:

- Locally
- Regionally
- Nationally
- Internationally and globally

Now the themes and groups of actors were separated into groups themselves:

Local
- City sanitation workers
- Persons taking trash out using grocery plastic bags

- Persons using plastic bags for other things (carrying shoes, dog waste, small trash bags)
- Schools that educate on the environment, students, teachers
- Recycling bag bin makers
- Recycling companies
- City recycling policymakers

Regional
- Companies and employees of plastic bag manufacturers
- Local economies
- State environmental agencies
- Environmental groups
- States that have invested in alternatives and education on the use of plastic bags

National
- EPA guidelines
- Faith traditions with writing and efforts related to a responsible relationship with the environment
- Websites on plastic and recycling alternatives
- Countries with policies on plastic bags
- Legislators (local, state, or national)
- Companies that sell the chemicals that make plastic
- Companies that use plastics in different ways (helping us realize that plastic can be helpful, e.g., in medical equipment, and invites our imagination to consider options)
- Companies that make recycled bags for groceries and shopping/carrying
- National grocery chains

International and global
- Environmental groups researching plastic bag uses and misuses
- International groups or communities speaking out on plastic bags
- Earth impacted by plastics on ground, water, and in the air

Charting and Organizing

There are a variety of ways to organize the lists of actors for an issue. The following are a few samples. For linear thinkers the *listing* we just covered offers spaces for roles.

A more *visual* way of organizing is to create circles or webs of connection, as in the following figure. The center circle names the issue and then places the actors in self-contained circles somewhere around the topic circle. The most directly connected actors can be larger circles or be placed closest to the issue. Note the interconnections among the actors creating lines to link the players together. Note that this may get messy, so have a large sheet available for this exercise.

Figure 3. Three Circles

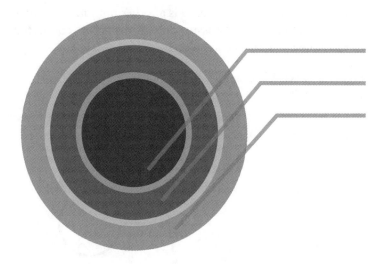

Another possibility is to create a chart much like a genealogy chart, listing the roles emerging from the issue, beginning with the directly connected actors followed by supporting connections.

Figure 4. Text Tree

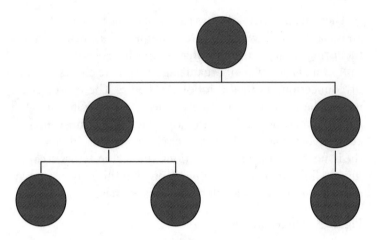

Creating a wheel with spokes is another option. The center of the wheel identifies the issue, and all the actors connected to the issue emanate out as spokes.

Figure 5. Text Wheel with Spokes

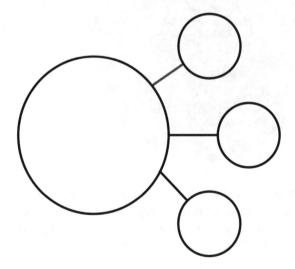

Different methods work for different types of focus and for different groups. Experimenting with different methods helps determine the best method for the particular issue. However, be sure to mark *your own connections with the various actors*, both as roles and as relationships. Note what groups you are part of, what roles you play, and how you are connected to the people or groups relating to this issue.

The group considering plastic grocery bags began with a listing and then from that listing created a circle chart showing with lines how the different actors were interconnected. The consumer was now connected to the grocery store owner, the city, the church, plastic distributors in the city, and so on.

No matter which organizing method you use, be sure at some point to note how the groups and actors may be related to one another, which is crucial for seeing what systems are at work and what connections are helpful and harmful. For example, if lobbyists for plastic corporations have a strong relationship with elected officials in a city and have a bias for continuing current uses of plastic grocery bags, groups looking at the topic need to question how others have their voices heard by elected officials. Seeing relationships and interconnections is essential for social analysis.

Keep two key mantras in mind as you work on lists, connections, and information gathering. First, *keep it manageable*. Even if complicated, your activity must be manageable. By separating the topic into various components, you can get a clearer idea of the areas in which you can best engage. You will also learn how the areas intersect, so that when action is needed, you have a better sense of which area taps into what other area.

The second mantra is: *Together we can*. Practically speaking, a group should divvy up the areas of analysis. However, a group dividing tasks needs to meet regularly to share learnings and research. Meeting regularly with an outline and information sharing from each member (in writing—either electronically or as a one-page handout) allows for accountability among members and offers a space for the connections to be made as one piece of information taps into another group's research.[10]

ECONOMIC ANALYSIS

After naming the various actors (and you may add to your list as analysis continues and deepens), see how economics relates to the issue. While all analysis has a bias—and ours is for the poor and marginalized—if we are to discern a proper response, we must try to understand the issue from all angles and see the various perspectives that inform the situation. Economic analysis looks at the organization of resources and seeks to understand and find the links between the organization of resources and the issue to be addressed. Economic analysis asks the following questions:

- What is the role of economics in this issue?
- What are the economic structures and dynamics involved in this issue?
- What economic systems are the various groups working with?
- What resources do the major actors have?
- Who benefits?
- Who is burdened?
- Who is responsible?
- How are resources being used to influence or affect this topic?
- What are the relationships or potential relationships in this area?
- Where are your relationships in this area?
- What role does economics play in this issue's history?

Whether you begin at the local or international level is often determined by where the issue first engages people. On April 24, 2013, the collapse of a building used by the garment industry in Dhaka, Bangladesh, killed over eleven hundred people and created a global and public outcry to investigate the cause of the tragedy. When investigations by the Bangladesh government's committee determined that "the defects and errors that led to the world's deadliest garment-industry accident extend from the swampy ground the doomed Rana Plaza was built on to 'extremely poor quality' construction materials, to the massive vibrating equipment operating when the eight-story building collapsed," public clothing companies with connections to the United States and Europe were deluged with demands for a change in practices that allowed such unsafe conditions.[11]

Calls for systemic change came because of ensuing analysis. One article noted, "The disaster highlighted the hazardous working conditions in Bangladesh's $20 billion garment in-dustry and the lack of safety for millions of workers who are paid as low as $38 a month," and that, "Since the disaster, many international clothing retailers have signed on to a five-year, legally binding contract that requires them to help pay for fire safety and building improvements in Bangladesh. Most American brands have not; the National Retail Federation is leading a coalition of North American retail and apparel groups to develop an alternative broader proposal that would go beyond Bangladesh."[12] Economic factors, from the wages of employees to companies that have garments made in these factories to the builders and government regulators whose job it is to ensure safety, are all part of changing the practices that contributed to the death of "at least 1,800 Bangladesh garment-industry workers killed in fires or building collapses since 2005."[13]

In considering the economic structures, look at venues such as corporations, banks, tax measures, trade patterns, and unions. Also look at the local dynamics to determine how eco-nomics motivates and moves each group. Topics such as food shortages can begin from the local and move more broadly or flow locally from the global. At other times the global impacts affect the local quite directly, such as the cost of oil at a local gas station. The point is to begin somewhere and expand so that you can see the large picture as well as the details.

Let's turn again to the case of the plastic grocery bags. Look at six major actors and begin some economic analysis to see how resources are organized. The actors are consumers, grocery store managers and owners, plastic bag manufacturing companies, environmental education groups, trash disposal and trash dump companies, and parishes. How are these actors connected to economic systems, and how are the various actors interconnected economically and thus able to impact one another?

Consumers go to grocery stores, purchase goods, and use plastic bags to pack and carry their goods home. The cost of the plastic bags is included in the grocery store costs. Consumers then own the bags and need to choose what to do with them. They have a responsibility for proper disposal or reuse. A benefit of plastic bags is that consumers do not need to carry anything to the store for carrying the groceries, but they pay for this service.

Additional questions for the consumer include how much money the person pays each year for groceries, and how many bags the consumer uses each year. This gives the consumer information and economic clout. (A family exercise could be counting the number of bags used in a given month.) A related question is the cost of trash collection.

Grocery store managers and owners are responsible for choosing and purchasing the types of bags they use. They contract with a particular company for the bags. The store has at least an informal contract of sorts with consumers, assuming that consumers want the bags and therefore will pay for them. Owners figure out the cost of bags within the overall costs of operating a grocery store and indirectly charge consumers. Owners have the economic and environmental burden or responsibility for the kinds of bags available to consumers. If they want to order bags that can be reused, they can advertise and educate about different kinds of bags. One year the Whole Foods store in San Antonio had a significant advertisement and education plan before Earth Day in order to encourage the use of reusable bags. Owners can also articulate their desires for particular kinds of bags with their vendors, including encouraging plastic bag makers to create reusable bags. Economics played a role in one grocery store in San Diego that offered a five-cent discount per bag that customers brought with them for packing groceries. A variety of motivations and incentives emerge, including and encompassing more than economics.

Additional questions for owners include the weight of various economic factors alongside other factors, such as environment and culture (some US cities have adopted a recycled grocery bag culture recently, but this was not always so). Also, are owners soliciting preferences from consumers about bags, and are vendors already developing alternative bags or alternative commodities to plastic bags if this consumer need significantly diminishes?

Plastic bag manufacturing companies make money producing and selling plastic bags. They buy the natural gas that is used for making plastic.[14] Natural gas distributors are thus another group to be considered. An entire system is at work in manufacturing, and knowing how the pieces interact is helpful. Plastic manufacturing companies are a direct economic partner with grocery stores, plastic bag distributors, and natural gas distributors, and all of these groups have employees and interact with the environment. In addition, since plastic is used for many things, the manufacturing companies may be making more than one item. Plastic bags are a livelihood for some companies, so not using plastic bags could mean lost jobs or a company closing.

Consider what other plastic products the company makes. Is the company open to alternative manufacturing products? Does the company recycle bags, use recycled materials, or perform research on biodegradable bags? What might they imagine that would help sustain their business *and* be better for the environment? Is the company local, regional, national, or international? The answers will indicate how relationships, educational efforts, and systems might be used.

Environmental education groups inform the public on issues such as recycling and bag use. They do research and have information that can serve as a fact check on what companies and grocers offer. They are the conduits between the consumer and the manufacturer and can speak for the Earth community. If the groups undertake their work with due diligence, they can offer further perspectives and questions on the wider issues, including: Is the information readily available to the public? Online? In journals or various other media?

Trash disposal sites and dumps involve a variety of economic issues and systems. First, the disposal sites are in a place that is owned or rented by one group that is paid by either public or private entities to take the group's trash and dispose of it. Disposal sites are on land or water and immensely impact the Earth community. Garbage such as paper and food items do disintegrate in a relatively short period of time, but plastic products have a very long life span. To the extent that garbage bags are thrown away, in a short or long span of use, the bags simply take up space in dumps. More dump sites are then needed, and already today some cities pay other cities to take their garbage. Space is a vital issue; disposal sites that take plastic bags must deal with the space and environmental issues that ensue. If garbage sites do not take garbage bags, the sheer amount of plastic bags requires someone to determine that dumpsters or garbage cans do not contain them.

Questions that emerge include the percentage of trash that consists of plastic bags. This gives information on space and cost. Does the site work with recycling programs, and if so, what is the impact? If not, why not? What is the environmental impact of plastic bags on the land? Environmental groups need to collaborate to find out the science of this question and also some suitable responses. A related question is the cost of trash collection and trash disposal. What benefits do the companies get for taking care of plastic bags, and what burdens do they have to contend with?

A *parish* is a group that holds economic and other systemic influence in a community. When the number of parishioners and families is multiplied by the amount of money spent on groceries, this economic impact is significant. Parishes also host events and thus use companies that offer food and other supplies. Even when parishioners bring goods, the ingredients that go into making the goods or the foods themselves are connected to grocery stores. Parishes also pay for trash collection services. Parishes are gospel centered, and so social and environmental justice questions emerge as the whole of a way of life for parishioners and for the parish as a whole. Parishes are connected to dioceses and also to national and international church communities. As a result, parishes have a burden of responsibility to engage as the church; as citizens of a city, state, and nation; and as global citizens.

Questions that emerge include: What level of awareness does the parish have about use of grocery bags as a church and as an issue of faith? How are reflection and action being fostered in the parish so that faith and citizenship are interconnected? Are there places in the parish where such issues and questions can come forth for discussion and discernment? Are the people who may have expertise and particular investments (employers, employees, environmental activists, and scripture and ethics students) invited to initiate conversations with the parish communities?

Clearly, many ways to do economic analysis are available. The method above is only one way. Another way might be to first brainstorm questions and then present them to one or more actors in the situation.[15] Some questions might include

- What benefit to the United States (or the country at issue) does this process offer?
- What money is being spent to care for and protect the Earth in this process?
- What is the economic base or situation of the state, region, or city?
- Are any companies giving money to political parties or political action committees (PACs)?

- If the water sources becomes toxic, who pays?
- What other groups are making money on an auxiliary level—restaurants, hotels, tool companies?

POLITICAL ANALYSIS

Political analysis looks at the organization of power and politics and asks questions such as

- What political structures are active in this situation?
- Who has power?
- What kind of power?
- What power does each major player have?
- What power dynamics are at play here?
- How are they related to each other?
- How are they related to you?
- What legislation, if any, concerns this issue?
- What lobbying groups are involved, and with whom and on behalf of whom?
- What is the role of social media on this topic in terms of political analysis?

Political analysis tells us where these various power structures are active or not active on a particular issue. It also yields insights into why a problem persists and what might be done to alleviate any injustice.

Knowing what political power is at play on any given issue is essential, for such information offers direction. For example, a group in the United States engaging the death penalty will quickly find out that, while this question is discussed nationally, politically it is a state issue. Each state decides its position, and different states have different laws about capital punishment. States also regulate the method of capital punishment. If you're addressing this issue, find out how the political system in a state has maintained, overturned, or reinstated the death penalty. Research will tell you whether political power to continue the death penalty is because of a number of high-profile criminal cases, a heinous murder of a child that galvanized a city and state, or some other reasons.

Note how media coverage affects public sentiment. Perhaps it investigates old cases and finds questionable evidence used. Movies such as *The Green Mile* show the horrors of the electrocution process, and *Dead Man Walking*, Sr. Helen Prejean's story about her ministry among death row inmates, invites a look at the complexities of the human situations of all involved. You may find that a state attorney general's office very publicly engages a particular point of view. In some states, faith-based groups advocate strongly to change public political perceptions about the death penalty, taking on their responsibilities as citizens with a faith tradition.

In one state, journalism students researched a death penalty case thoroughly enough to find that the judicial process was flawed, resulting in the prisoner's release and ultimately raising enough questions about the process that the governor first put a moratorium on the death penalty and then abolished it completely. Significantly, public opinion changed as well because of the students' research. In this case, journalism students and their professor were able to use the power of information to cause the system of capital punishment to be held in abeyance until further investigation was completed.

For some issues political power may reside on a national level, as is the case with immigration and calls for immigration reform. While states and even cities may decide how intensely they will seek out immigrants without documentation, immigration policies are national policies. At the same time, since Congress and the president of the United States are directly involved in legislation on this topic, many groups seek to assert political pressure and power during the debate. Some employers that rely on immigrants exert political pressure on lawmakers. Others may use public safety as political leverage and seek political methods for removing immigrants who do not enter by legal means. These groups may seek more funding for border patrols. Although both groups seek economic and political power, it is based on different agendas and values. And since the migration of peoples is present internationally, knowing the laws and processes of the country in which one resides is important, because there is much variation.

Here again, relationships among groups are important. For example, the agribusiness industry is quite aware of its political power. Because it meets important agricultural needs and is a multibillion-dollar industry, it has significant influence over jobs for migrants as well as for citizens; it has considerable access to decisionmakers in government and can provide substantial financial support. The agribusiness industry has relationships with management-labor, suppliers, governments (including lobbying—indeed it has one of the most powerful lobbying groups on state and national levels), consumer action groups, and the media. Their relationships also include those with other parts of the food sector, trade agreements (often transnational and international), and even social movements. The widespread desire in the United States for immigration reform has real implications for this industry; the industry thus seeks to influence agribusiness companies, lawmakers, and the public.

Sometimes political power originates with international groups. The UN Declaration on Human Rights names essential rights for every person that form a basis for international understanding. When violations occur, as in the case of genocide, torture, or unlawful imprisonment, anywhere in the world, not only the United Nations but also various groups such as Human Rights Watch and Amnesty International raise alarms and seek public political engagement with groups violating these basic human rights. Even in times of war there are still basic rights for the treatment of prisoners, as delineated in the Fourth Geneva Convention in 1949. International political analysis and pressure may come from any number of places when violations occur.

Political analysis reminds us that we need to look at various legislative processes and see what is in place, what is not present, where legislation has been amended, and where legislation is actively being resisted. Knowing the history of an issue is helpful. For example, while hydraulic drilling in its early form has been present for a few decades, the current method of fracking is relatively new, and procedures for regulatory guidelines and legislation are still being created in many states. Some guidelines are limited, and some are becoming more detailed as public concerns are increasingly voiced. Look beyond your own state and read about national and other states' conversations on this topic. Are any congressional hearings or investigations under way? How about hearings on the state and local levels? Do any international standards apply? Due to economic incentives to create a new energy resource in the United States, you need to understand if any legislation is directly or indirectly related to hydraulic drilling. If some groups have a financial stake, is there active lobbying? Do any stakeholders have political influence? Do any public officials have ties to this issue?

In recent years the Affordable Care Act addressing healthcare reform has been hotly debated, and many public and professional groups have spoken up. It is important to note, then, what the American Medical Association (AMA) advocates and why. What are corporations that manage long-term care facilities advocating and why? What values do the groups name? Consider what positions pharmaceutical companies, another of the most powerful lobbying groups, are promoting and why. While we speak more about this in the section on religious analysis, note the perspective of a faith-based group such as the Catholic Health Association (CHA). The same is true for the U.S. Conference of Catholic Bishops (USCCB) and other national religious bodies. If or when disagreements are voiced between groups with similar faith traditions, what are the differences, and how is political engagement being used and heard by the government groups and by members of their faith tradition? (For example, the Obama administration and the president personally spoke with leaders of the CHA and USCCB while the ACA was being crafted.)

CULTURAL ANALYSIS

We are all formed by a variety of cultures. Once we recognize this fact, we can begin to notice and identify the cultures that have shaped us, and we can make choices about whether to continue to form our impressions from that lens or not. Culture shapes how we look at issues, how we discuss issues, and which cultural lens we choose or prioritize in making decisions about issues. Overt as well as more subtle cultures form us.

Cultural analysis looks at various structures that determine how a society organizes meaning. Such structures can include traditions (such as Christmas, Labor Day, Fourth of July, and Thanksgiving), rituals (how we mark important events), language (how we describe immigrants, for example), art (perspectives on what we see or imagine), drama, song, initiation rites, communication media, myths (such as "Hard work always breeds success" or that radical individualism is possible today), and dreams (notably the American Dream).

As we undertake cultural analysis, we should ask,

- What are the cultural structures and dynamics at work?
- What cultural values and practices influence our thinking and acting?
- How does culture express meaning or value in this issue?
- How does culture frame the issues?
- Which cultures play a prominent role?

Cultures that have formed many of us include our family, school, faith community, nation, and social media/networking.

Family is the first culture that formed most of us. We have a way of looking at the world through the lens of our family. As we grow and mature, elements of our family culture[16] are kept, discarded, or more likely, blended into our own cultural framework. Special events like holidays—where "our family Christmas tradition is . . ."—are part of the lexicon of our lives, even if as adults and with our own families we make

other choices. Family life is replete with traditions and rituals (for example, choosing a meal of choice on a birthday, or
holding a yearly reunion for the extended family). Families
are also our first ways of looking at relationships and at the
world around us. Early on, children may be taught to take
care of younger siblings, as modeled by the adults caring for
the younger members.

Family culture offers a way of looking beyond the family as
well. When growing up, do you remember any conversations
in which politics was discussed? Did your family ever speak
of neighbors or others who were struggling financially? Was
there a sense of obligation to help those in need outside one's
own family? In your childhood, who were the guests at a family dinner table? What was the conversation about? Did you
discuss current events? Was disagreement allowed as part of a
discussion? Did family members share items, or did everyone
have their own phone, television, computer, car, toys, and so
on? The answers give a sense of your family culture.

We are also formed by our *school* cultures. Did the students
in your classes come from a background similar to yours? If
yes, how did you know? Was there racial and ethnic diversity?
Did your high school ethos have an expectation that you would
attend college? Was the environment competitive or collabora-
tive? What types of discussions were encouraged? Were you
taught to debate or to look at issues from various angles? Did
you go to school with people of diverse religious, political, and
economic backgrounds?

Geography forms us. Did you grow up in a city, suburb,
or rural environment? I grew up in cities and enjoy the hustle
and bustle of vehicles around me. A friend grew up in a rural
farming area and was much more attuned to weather patterns
and care of the Earth than I was. Except for visits to my aunt
Mimi, who gave us Bibb lettuce from her garden, we bought
lettuce and our other produce at the grocery store and knew
little about how our food grew.

We go into more detail with this when discussing religious

analysis, but suffice it to say for now that *faith communities* are also a forming culture. The faith community we are part of is a culture, yet even more so does the culture of our faith tradition tell us how to look at the world around us and give us tools to create meaning.

The *country in which we live* shapes us, as more than one culture is at work in most nations, and much of the culture we pick up depends on what we see, hear, and experience. In the United States, the Pledge of Allegiance gives a sense of a culture that includes "one nation under God, indivisible, with liberty and justice for all." The Declaration of Independence speaks of the right to life, liberty, and the pursuit of happiness, and our Constitution speaks to a culture that allows for freedom of speech and freedom of religion. The prevailing cultural assumption in the United States is still that there is abundant opportunity for all who are willing to work hard and that achieving the American Dream is still possible. While these same cultural assumptions often need to be checked out for verity, they represent the goals and dreams of many people in and outside the United States, which is one reason that immigrants still risk everything, including their lives, to enter the United States.

Another means by which culture is significantly shaped is the *media*. The media have their own biases as they seek to capture and shape their audiences' attention. The media also give us a lens into the US role in the global community by what stories they cover and by what they refuse to cover. During the 1994 genocide in Rwanda, much of the media was silent rather than absent. Reporting by CNN's Anderson Cooper during Hurricane Katrina and its aftermath challenged perceptions about our preparedness for emergencies, the quality of presidential and governmental responses to emergencies, and even racism. In Egypt during the uprisings of the Arab Spring, even when the television and radios were silenced by government forces, the Internet shaped the revolution that removed President Hosni Mubarak from power in a relatively peaceful manner. Media also shaped the understanding that many outside Egypt had of the nature of the revolution. Similarly YouTube videos that can go viral in a matter of minutes provoke global responses to human rights abuses. This instant information culture allows us to hear quickly about a tsunami in Asia as well as the marital infidelity of a local public official.

Television and *other entertainment media* have cultures that can be promoted or dismissed. For example, television series such as *CSI* or *Law and Order* presume a culture that says persons will lie about a crime until proven otherwise. This is a culture. Actual events, such as the scam of Bernard Madoff—whose investment scandal cost investors, including charitable organizations, losses in the billions—open up discussions of both a culture of greed ("Get as much as you can while you can and don't worry who suffers") and a culture of profit ("Don't ask me why I'm getting a larger return on my investments than most groups as long as I can benefit").

You should be aware of how US culture is described today and by whom, and be willing to ask whether we agree and how we do or do not participate in the actions that the culture designates. For example, the United States has been described by some as a "consumer culture," meaning that we consume more than save and often consume beyond what we need. We are also described as a "culture of affluence," implying the importance of wealth. Also, a culture of individualism still exists today, often connected to the rugged individualism of the earlier pioneer days. Individualism is also spoken about in opposition to the common good. At the same time, many in the United States would describe this as a "can do" culture, optimistically sensing that change and overcoming obstacles are part of the nation's ethos. Is any of this true in your experience? In your activity? In what you see around you? Can you offer examples of individualism as well as care for the common good? The United States is also often called a "fast-food" culture, with people choosing quick food options produced for us rather than making meals ourselves. This can be part of a "culture of convenience," where we give priority to something other than using time to prepare our food.

Pope Francis challenged global culture when he gave a talk in May 2013 to the Pontifical Council for Migrants: "In a world where there is so much talk about rights, it seems that the only thing that has rights is money. Dear brothers and sisters, we live in a world where money commands. We live in a world, in a culture, where money worship reigns."[17]

Cultural analysis asks us to identify and then assess the cultures that form us and frame particular discussions. An important step is to test the truthfulness and value of cultural assumptions, whether the culture is from family, media, or the nation. For example, is a sense that one is better than another because of one's salary, neighborhood, or race a cultural assumption that I am consciously or unconsciously holding? We need to understand the conscious and unconscious cultural understandings we have of events and circumstances, for they must be tested against intellectual reasoning and our deepest values (a topic for the next chapter).

We must also not slide into a pluralism that says that because so many possibilities are available, there is no way to understand and make choices among all the options. This can lead us to move nowhere and simply allow movements to lead us. Dean Brackley sagely wrote, "Pluralism slides into lazy relativism."[18]

Let us look briefly at some of the cultures that may be present in understanding the dilemma of plastic grocery bags. While every one of these assumptions must be checked out, the following are possible cultural lenses into the topic. For the *consumer* the issue may be about a culture of convenience. "If the bag is in the grocery store, that is one less thing for me to have to think about or remember." For the *grocer* and even the *manufacturer of plastic bags*, there may be some assumptions of "If it works, don't fix it," until some further education is done on plastic bags. *Environmental groups* may invest a lot of personnel and technology resources on the environmentally friendly culture and engage in steps to transform our culture into one that is more Earth-friendly and sustainability responsive. Environmental education groups may also note that an environmental culture is growing rapidly among schoolchildren, who can in turn impact their family cultures. Recently a grandfather noted that his granddaughter removed an empty milk carton he had thrown in the garbage. She said, "Grandpa, the Earth needs help with our garbage." She put the carton in the properly marked recycle bin.

ENVIRONMENTAL ANALYSIS

Because of the importance of environmental concerns involved in almost every issue today, we must consider the environmental impact in any political, economic, cultural, or religious analysis of issues.

Environmental analysis considers the structures that determine the organization of natural environments.[19] These may include, among many things, issues of sustainable agriculture and water use, issues of population and who or what populates a region, and more. Questions for environmental analysis include, but are not limited to, the following:

- How is the environment impacted (by the issue)?
- How is the issue impacted by the environment?
- How is the health of the Earth community (all living creatures) impacted?
- What is flourishing?
- What is languishing or dying? What is burdened?
- What is the state of elements related to air? water? land?
- What responsibility for the environment does each actor have? How is that responsibility being fulfilled?
- How is beauty being impacted by the issue?[20]

For our purposes, environmental analysis presumes five points. First, the analysis looks at both the immediate and long-term effects, including the use of resources and the impact on the environment. An important first look at issues is certainly the immediate impact. Although we may turn first to the immediate impact, the long-term impact is just as important. Our responsibility as stewards of God's creation is to look at all decisions through the lens of how they will impact the seventh generation to come.

Second, it is a false dichotomy to pit the environment against "the poor" or poor people. In the rhetoric around environmental issues one will eventually hear, "Look, I'm all for the environment, but if I have to choose between a tree and a human being, I will always choose the human being." This is a false choice. Of course, human beings are essential, but it is very short-sighted to say that we will give local people money to cut down virgin forest so that they can have enough food to sustain life. To the extent that rainforests are essential for our breathing and have immense medicinal potential, destroying a rainforest is eventually destroying all of us.

A powerful example is demonstrated by the story of Sr. Dorothy Stang, SNDdeN.[21] Dorothy left the United States to go to Brazil to work among the people. In being with them, she saw many issues that created hardships for them, and she advocated on their behalf. However, not until years later when she did some studies of the environment did she see the interconnection between the people made poor and the land on which they lived. With new eyes, she saw the efforts of the rancheros and loggers to remove the people from the land on which they did subsistence farming. Dorothy became aware of how the people knew how to use the land to produce medicine and food, and she saw how they were being intimidated by groups that were trying to take the land from the people and use it to sell timber and create grasslands for cows. She used her influence to educate the people about land use and their land rights, and she worked with the legal system in Brazil. Dorothy, however, angered the land grabbers and began to receive death threats, but she persisted. In the meantime she made known to her leadership in the United States and elsewhere the situation she was encountering. She communicated all the injustices among the people as well as the threats she was receiving. Her good work was lauded by the Brazilian law association, which honored her with their highest award. Not many months later, a group of armed men confronted Dorothy, and she was shot and killed as she read aloud the Beatitudes to them. Dorothy understood the connection between people made poor and the Earth, and others in Brazil continue her efforts even after her murder.

Third, environmental analysis must engage all other areas of analysis. In some ways environmental analysis poses an extra burden because it is not yet "naturally" part of every political, economic, cultural, or religious conversation. Environmental analysis must insert itself into other areas. Although awareness is growing, more work remains to be done.

Fourth, environmental analysis must play an equal role in discerning decisions. Clearly, some areas have more weight than others as many factors come into play. However, when a building is built, sustainable living options must be part of the blueprint conversations. Energy-efficient products must be part of the analysis, for example, when selecting a new appliance. When new landscaping is planned, the analysis should consider plants that use less of the earth's finite resources, such as water.

Fifth, geography matters. Where a chemical plant is built is important. Too many urban neighborhoods have been affected by factories that have not been responsible about their toxic chemical use or runoff, leaving the surrounding land toxic to people in the area.[22] When issues affect resources essential for life, such as water sources, air, and land use, human advocates must give voice to these resources and the Earth. If an oil spill in the Gulf of Mexico impacts not only life in the water but also the life of people, stringent regulations are essential to prevent more accidents such as the Gulf oil spill in 2010.

Clearly, environmental analysis asks crucial questions of every actor involved with an issue. Here, we again look at our major actors in the issue of plastic grocery bags, name an important environmental task, and pose a few related questions.

We begin with *environmental groups* because they have a major responsibility to make their area of expertise known and disseminate knowledge. They play a key role by sharing their expertise with consumers, grocery store owners, plastic bag manufacturers, and faith communities. They can make alliances to bring about positive change with trash disposal companies.

The *consumer* also must be accountable. What do you do with the bags after you empty your groceries? Do you throw them away? Where? Are they recycled? Where? Do you need plastic bags, or are you willing to find alternatives?

Grocery store owners are asked how their bags affect the environment. Would other bag options make less of a burden on the earth community and still be helpful to consumers?

Plastic bag manufacturing companies must be asked about the bags they produce. Are toxins present? Do the fumes from the chemicals used to make the bags get into the air? How much energy (and what kind) is used to make the bags? How are they transported? What amount of fuel is used for transport? Are the bags made for multiple use (reuse) or one use only? What alternative bag-making options would they consider?

Companies with landfills are asked to explain whether or how the land is burdened by the plastic bags. Are they biodegradable? How long will they take to biodegrade? Do they sort out the plastic bags from the rest of the trash? What changes need to be made so that less landfill space is used for plastic bags?

Parish and other community groups can do an environmental analysis of their parishes and among their members. Do people know what happens to the bags after their use? Do people recycle their bags? Do people know about alternatives to plastic bags? What would it take to get people to choose reusable bags? Parish and other community groups can also connect or partner with environmental groups that can supply resources and advocate for environmentally friendly positions.

RELIGIOUS ANALYSIS

In light of so much public debate on social issues and with the use of social, political, economic, and environmental analysis, people sometimes question if the category of religious analysis is still needed. Do religious beliefs, values, and institutions really play a role in the current issues and debates? One need only look at issues such as abortion, the Affordable Care Act, and current immigration reform initiatives in the United States to find that the answer is a solid yes. Whether people profess membership in a particular religious tradition or not, when people get serious about social issues, many talk about them as moral issues. And when we speak about moral issues, we need a base.

With so much religious partisanship, with every group declaring that "God is on *our* side," can we really know whose side God is on? I reply using the words of Abraham Lincoln, who once said, "My concern is not whether God is on our side; my greatest concern is to be on God's side."[23] Our call is to attune our minds, hearts, and our entire selves to where we sense that God's Spirit is leading us. There are markers for this understanding, and one is that we know the reality around us as it actually is, which is why we engage experience and social analysis.

As we read in chapter 2, we do know some things about God's love through our scripture, tradition, and experience. We have a sense of where God abides in areas of justice and dignity for all. However, even knowing this does not necessarily tell us which way(s) to best direct our actions. Discernment is important here—a desire to "act as God acts" (even as we are not God), which we have heard in the scriptures is to be the *imago Dei*. Religious analysis, in conjunction with the other areas of analysis we have discussed, offers us another tool for our information gathering by helping us look concretely at what our faith tradition says about an issue. Political leaders often evoke religious language to promote a position and even war. Faith-based groups also use religious language to influence people to vote and otherwise act. Some language has been properly used, and sometimes religious language has simply been co-opted. We need to listen to language and know how to assess it in light of a faith community's wisdom. Analysis also helps us locate the richness and depth of our traditions in service of God's mission.

Religion and religious traditions also participate in the social issues of the day, and we must responsibly assess religion's role, capacity, and responsibility on social justice issues. James Hug reminds us,

> If then, in answering the social-analysis question—What are the structures and dynamics at work creating the situation we are experiencing as it currently exists?—we discover that religious beliefs, values, institutions, and structures shape, motivate, legitimate and/or sustain the current situation, we must include them in the analysis. Only then will we be able to understand the situation accurately, evaluate it appropriately, and develop adequate plans for effective social change.[24]

Religious analysis thus looks at religious structures that organize our understandings of God, humanity, and creation and offer a faith- and value-based way of looking at the world. Religious analysis always asks what role religion plays in the issue and how religion engages the issue.

Questions you may want to consider include the following (these questions are particularly framed from the lens of the Roman Catholic tradition. The questions can be adapted or omitted as works within other traditions):

- What does the church say publicly about this social issue?
- Who is speaking?

- What do the official church offices say?
- Is this issue being engaged locally, nationally, globally? (Do we have speeches or documents from popes, bishops, Vatican offices, national church bodies?)
- What are theologians saying? (For example, much has recently been written about a theology of migration, so this would be a valuable resource.)
- How are dioceses engaged? Parishes? Bishops or bishops' groups? Lay groups?
- Who is speaking from the broader church communities? (Religious orders? Catholic nonprofit groups, advocacy groups such as Bread for the World?)
- What is the church's contribution to this topic?
- How is religious language used in this topic?
- What does scripture offer?
- What does Catholic social tradition offer directly or indirectly on this issue?
- In what way, if any, does our liturgical life connect to this social issue? (For example, bread and wine certainly have correlatives to poverty, community, table welcome, Jesus' example, and care of creation.)
- Are there any ecumenical, interfaith, or faithwide statements or efforts in this area?
- What are religious writers saying? (Consider publications such as *America*, *The Tablet* [London], *Commonweal*, *U.S. Catholic* [Catholic examples], and also *Sojourners* and *Christian Century* [two ecumenical publications]. What other faith-based groups are involved?
- What other concerned groups are we naturally connected to by values?

Sources and Resources

While many ways of approaching religious analysis are available, below are five significant resource areas with which to begin:

- Public statements from religious leaders
- Church documents and teachings
- Writings by scholars and persons with expertise in the topic and the tradition (or at least engaging both)
- Scripture and religious tradition
- Extended faith-community members and resources (denominational, ecumenical, faithwide contexts)

When considering a topic, begin by determining what your religious tradition is currently saying about it. What is to be found in newspapers or other media outlets? Is there anything on the topic on websites connected to the church leadership? For Catholics on a national level the website of the U.S. Conference of Catholic Bishops (www.usccb.org) includes a link to "Social Justice Issues" that covers a wide range of topics. The general website also offers a listing of statements by the bishops' conference. Another place to look for recent statements by church officials would be diocesan websites, beginning with your own.

Because the Roman Catholic Church is a worldwide community, finding out what the pope and various international church leaders are saying is important. From them we may see an issue more globally and find further connections around the world. Papal statements, talks from meetings of church leaders representing various offices, and the church's engagement with global groups such as the UN Human Rights Council, the World Health Organization, and others are places where particular social issues are discussed more directly.

In our technological age, this information is increasingly accessible via the Web or social media groups. The Vatican site, www.vatican.va, is a good resource and is in several languages. Websites such as www.zenit.org have daily listings of talks by the pope and other church leaders, both from Vatican offices and from around the world. Topics of current interest are often listed. Catholic News Service (CNS), a national documentary online news service, publishes texts from the Vatican, the pope, bishops, the US Congress and Supreme Court, and church leaders around the world. Current topics are often found, from human trafficking to immigration to war and much more. *Origins*, with both print and online options, is the documentary service of CNS. These are helpful first sources. You are also encouraged to see what other religious communities are writing, for this stimulates further thinking. Today we often find common cause across faith traditions, so finding resources across traditions is also important. Part of the research is seeking these out and seeing how the gospel message expands across religious borders.

Beyond recent statements, consider what has been written in the past. Many topics enter the public forum when a situation occurs that creates a need for public discourse and movement, so see what resources are already available. For example, the right of laborers was a concern written about in 1891 in *Rerum Novarum* (*Rights and Duties of Capital and Labor*) by Pope Leo XIII, and popes since then have continued that concern. By looking at various documents over the years you can also see how discussion of an issue has developed and become more nuanced over time, and how understandings of issues change.[25] It is also good to note that some church teaching has changed as insights deepened. Scholar and judge John T. Noonan offers the church's moral teaching about slavery and moneylending as two such examples as part of his excellent book, *A Church That Can and Cannot Change*.[26]

Church social teachings can serve to illuminate or underline social issues. On March 25, 1995, Pope John Paul II published *Evangelium Vitae* (*The Gospel of Life*). Among other issues, he wrote about capital punishment, indicating that virtually no circumstances in our time require recourse to capital punishment. This was widely quoted after Ursuline Sister Joanne Marie Mascha was raped and then murdered on the wooded grounds of her motherhouse in Pepper Pike, Ohio, on March 27, 1995. The state of Ohio has capital punishment, and the prosecutor's office clearly stated it would seek the death penalty for her murderer. The congregational leaders, in seeking a just conviction for the murder, also made clear that capital punishment was not what they wanted or what Sr. Joanne Marie would have wanted.[27] The church's teachings, including *The Gospel of Life*, providentially published only two days before Joanne Marie was murdered, were articulated, and many others were invited to urge the prosecutor's office to desist from seeking the death penalty. The case drew national and international attention, galvanizing the church's teachings and people's positions on the issue. The young man convicted of killing her is serving life in prison.[28]

Writers with expertise in both your issue and your faith tradition are good resources. Who is writing about torture? War? Immigration reform? Trafficking? As you read these perspectives, keep in mind your own values as well as the values you are reading in the texts. Note instances of resonance, where a new perspective or insight is being offered, and where there is dissonance. Try to note this with data. What is being written, and from what particular angle of faith? What sources are being used? What is new, and what is used regularly as part of a direction?

Another place to look for insight may be religiously based groups with a social issue agenda. The Catholic Campaign for Human Development, Catholic Charities, Catholic Relief Services, Pax Christi International, Caritas Internationalis, the Center of Concern, Maryknoll's Office of Global Concerns, Bread for the World, World Vision, Habitat for Humanity, and Lutheran World Relief are some groups that address national or international issues. Also see what local groups are involved in your topic. Again, look not only at your own faith community but see what other communities are writing to stimulate further thinking.

In all areas of analysis we must remember, as James Hug argues, "that we need to recognize the oftentimes implicit theology that informs our analysis."[29] For this reason we must comprehend what our scripture and tradition offer in framing and understanding our issues.

Scripture and tradition are absolute necessities for considering issues, whether the issues are implicitly or explicitly mentioned or not. Any life issue will somehow be connected, but it is essential to make connections cogently and with proper theological grounding. Too many people and groups knowingly or unknowingly can err by proof texting—that is, taking a scripture passage and making it fit an issue. This would be akin to picking a puzzle piece at random with no regard for its color or shape and trying to make it fit a particular spot. With scripture, in particular, we seek to understand the context (what comes before and after the selection) to identify how a scriptural message can respond to our issue, which requires scholarship and reflection. While scripture may not directly engage your topic, key scriptural and gospel values may be very helpful and useful for prayerful reflection.

This approach also applies to various areas of tradition. Know your own background and whether your group would benefit from the expertise of persons with more theological training. If you were looking at the care of the Earth and recycling, you might begin by considering what you know of how God looks at creation and how Jesus treated creation and spoke of it in scripture. You might have some passages in mind. Then you can get some background on the passage from the writings of scripture scholars. Although most of us doing social analysis are not biblical scholars, we can benefit greatly from their writings. Books and articles written on biblical themes can also be useful. Many scripture passages speak to the relationship that God invites us to with God and all of God's creation, including the Earth. You may choose to do some further research on what scholars are writing about the connection between liturgy, justice, and the care of creation.

Much in our scripture and tradition speaks to the poor and marginalized, so some areas are a bit easier to connect than others. Other areas—like the Trinity, for example—are parts of our tradition that we are learning to connect with on a more practical level, such as learning from the Trinity what community among distinct equals might look like. Scripture and tradition are both important resources in considering the role of our faith traditions on an issue.

DEALING WITH DIFFERENCES

What do we do in situations where people within the same faith community or in the same ecumenical communities look at the same issue and come up with completely different conclusions, citing their faith and tradition as a resource? How can this be? Is one person wrong and the other right? Can both positions be possible? If yes to the latter, then is religious analysis pretty relativistic?

Let us use the example of immigration reform and ask how two people who attend the same church and read the same documents and the same newspapers can maintain opposing viewpoints.

First, check that the people have accurate information. Someone might read the scripture passage, "The poor you will always have with you" (Matt. 26:11), and think Jesus is saying that we can do nothing about the poor and we should move on to something else. But if we have been reading scripture for a while, we might put that passage alongside many other passages where Jesus feeds the hungry, says he is here to offer release to prisoners, gives sight to those who are blind, and much more. Matthew 26:11 does not fit the general direction of the Gospel passages, so it is an invitation to look deeper. In such cases, reading commentaries can be helpful to put a passage into proper alignment with the rest of the Gospel texts.

Second, note which religious values hold what kind of weight in one's life and in one's issue analysis. There are some basic categories to consider that give a sense of where we might lean in particular areas and that may influence our standing.

Again, I want to caution that this is not the time for full discernment; this is when you do your research. The final weighing of issues in light of our faith tradition and deep values happens later. However, as you research, you will encounter other writers' deep values and convictions, and you need to be able to read diverse opinions with keen attention and a light hold.

Some questions that may help us see these divides include

- Are there differing theologies on this issue?
- If so, what are they?
- What are the key values in each position (overt and subtle)?
- What common values do the positions hold?
- Are there any inaccuracies in the positions? If yes, what are they?
- Where is concern for the individual, the community, and the Earth to be found?
- How is concern for the poor, vulnerable, and marginalized brought forth?

How we see God, ourselves, others, and basic morality all impact how we consider an issue at first; we need to be aware of this point as we consider the information we are gathering and as we read others' responses. One's views of God, humanity, community, society, good, evil, sin, and redemption permeate most choices and decisions we make, and all go into the transformative crucible of discernment described in the next chapter.

Notes

[1] This poem is an adaption by James Hug, SJ, of a meditation by Thich Nhat Hanh that may be found online at *Buddhadharma: The Practitioner's Quarterly Online,* http://www.thebuddhadharma.com.

[2] See, for example, the article by Jeanne Bonner, "Sustainable Wood Products," at http://www.mnn.com.

[3] Joe Holland and Peter Henriot, *Social Analysis: Linking Faith and Action,* rev. and enlarged ed. (Maryknoll, NY: Orbis Books, 1984), 14.

[4] James Hug, "Redeeming Social Analysis: Recovering the Hidden Re-

ligious Dimensions of Social Change," in *The Pastoral Circle Revisited: A Critical Quest for Truth and Transformation*, ed. Frans Wijsen, Peter Henriot, and Rodrigo Mejía (Maryknoll, NY: Orbis Books, 2005), 203.

[5]Wikipedia is one such example. It can be helpful and useful as a first look on a topic. However, these sources must be fact checked, both with the footnotes provided and with corroborating research data.

[6]Thomas E. Clarke, SJ, "Methodology," in *The Context of Our Ministries: Working Papers* (Washington, DC: Jesuit Conference, 1981), 7.

[7]The areas below are key starting points, and other areas of analysis may be added as your particular issue requires.

[8]List the organizations and institutions that first come to mind. Note which groups are directly and indirectly connected. For example, the US government is involved in the immigration process to the United States, but further organizations within the US government structures are very directly involved, such as USCIS (US Citizenship and Immigration Services), which facilitates immigration to citizenship processes. Another organization involved peripherally until a violation is to be investigated is Human Rights Watch, whose role is to make sure that individual human rights are followed in all cases. Next, note any significant groupings of people. You might consider groupings in terms of race or ethnicity, gender, class (low-income, blue-collar, white-collar, pink-collar, generations, regions represented), groupings by work (owners, construction, chemical, distributors, field workers, retail), and educational levels (high school, college, professional). The more you can begin seeing by raising various factors, the better you might note the systems at work and begin intuiting the places in the system into which you can tap and intersect.

[9]*Earth community* could be a passive or active actor, but here I do mean to continually remind us that the Earth is a vital part of social justice issues.

[10]I find this a very effective group tool. If each person has to give each person in the group a report with something in writing (electronically or as a handout), the accountability and effectiveness of the meetings remain high.

[11]Associated Press, "Building Materials Blamed for Bangladesh Factory Collapse," May 23, 2013.

[12]Ibid.

[13]Ibid.

[14]A misconception is that plastic bags are made from oil. Instead, natural gas resources are used, and arguments from some companies that it is a ready, available, and domestic resource must be considered alongside other values.

[15]This approach will be demonstrated in a case study of hydraulic drilling (fracking) in chapter 8.

[16]Here I do acknowledge that even in families a variety of cultures are at play. Each parent comes with a set of cultures, and as a family is formed, cultures are created yet again. The important point here is that we learn to recognize the cultures interacting around us and make choices according to our deepest values. To know how other cultures affect people is to have a lens that engages the culture and the social issue, among other analytical frameworks and values. We ultimately aim to discern out of our deepest values, and knowing how culture impacts us frees us to engage culture and values.

[17]Pope Francis, Address to Pontifical Council for Migrants, May 24, 2013.

[18]Dean Brackley, "Searching for Truth and the Right Thing to Do," in *The Pastoral Circle Revisited: A Critical Quest for Truth and Transformation*, ed. Frans Wijsen, Peter Henriot, Rodrigo Mejía (Maryknoll, NY: Orbis Books, 2005), 214.

[19]Appendix 1: Steps in the Pastoral Circle, *Pastoral Circle Revisited.*

[20]While some might consider this unnecessary, beauty is one of the gifs of creation and thus is to be maintained as a value. One could also make claims that because God has created beauty, beauty should be preserved.

[21]A good biography is Roseanne Murphy, *Martyr of the Amazon: The Life of Sister Dorothy Stang* (Maryknoll, NY: Orbis Books, 2007).

[22]See, for example, http://www.epa.gov/region5/littlevillagepilsen/.

[23]The original source appears to be Francis B. Carpenter, *Six Months in the White House with Abraham Lincoln* (1867), 282, that was published not long after Lincoln's death: "No nobler reply ever fell from the lips of a ruler, than that uttered by President Lincoln in response to the clergyman who ventured to say, in his presence, that he hoped 'the Lord was on our side.' 'I am not at all concerned about that,' replied Mr. Lincoln, 'for I know that the Lord is always on the side of the right. But it is my constant anxiety and prayer that I and this nation should be on the Lord's side' " (http://www.politifact.com).

[24]Hug, "Redeeming Social Analysis," 204.

[25]For example, today we would not speak of someone as "labor" but as persons who work. Language shapes thought.

[26]John T. Noonan, *A Church That Can and Cannot Change* (Notre Dame, IN: University of Notre Dame Press, 2005).

[27]Sr. Joanne Marie was a member of Pax Christi, an organization that "strives to create a world that reflects the Peace of Christ by exploring, articulating, and witnessing to the call of Christian nonviolence."

For more information on PaxChristiUSA, see http://paxchristiusa.org/about/our-mission/. For more information on PaxChristiInternational, see http://www.paxchristi.net/about-us/why-pax-christi.

[28]Note that the prosecutor's office still sought the death penalty, but the life sentence came from a confluence of events that included a misunderstanding by some jurors of various requirements for the death penalty. Those with religious convictions considered it a bit of help from the Spirit. For more in-depth analysis of the case from a faith and legal perspective, see Joanne Gross, OSU, "The Deliberations of Mortals and the Grace of God," *Texas Tech Law Review* 27 (1996): 1159–64.

[29]"Epilogue," in *Pastoral Circle Revisited*, 227.

5

Faith Reflection

Discernment for Decisionmaking

The disciples replied, "We have nothing here but five loaves and two fish." And he said, "Bring them here to me." Then he ordered the crowds to sit down on the grass. Taking the five loaves and the two fish, he looked up to heaven, and blessed and broke the loaves, and gave them to the disciples, and the disciples gave them to the crowds. And all ate and were filled; and they took up what was left over of the broken pieces, twelve baskets full. And those who ate were about five thousand men, besides women and children.

—Matthew 14:17–21

Action on behalf of justice and participation in the transformation of the world fully appear to us as a constitutive dimension of the preaching of the Gospel, or, in other words, of the Church's mission for the redemption of the human race and its liberation from every oppressive situation.

—*Justice in the World*

Faith reflection, the third movement in the pastoral spiral, is a decisive point in the process. This is the space in which our deepest religious values (gospel values, Catholic social teaching, tradition, and our religious imagination) are brought to the analysis and experience of the current situation to help determine the action to come. In faith reflection we engage issues with our religious imagination, creativity, and openness to possibility. This stage of the process is the point at which we discern the direction we sense that God is inviting us to respond.

Figure 6. Faith Reflection

As crucial as it is, faith reflection is often the step people want to skip or skim over in haste to respond actively to an issue. Once the experience is named and shared and the analysis is completed, a sense of urgency often moves us to say, "Let's act on this! Much is at stake, and time is of the essence!" The issue is important, and a desire to act is necessary and crucial. It is also true that immediate deadlines such as a congressional vote on immigration legislation or deadlines for proposals may require quick action. However, even in such cases, faith reflection must not be skipped. Even if a time-sensitive response may be necessary, faith reflection must continue. We risk a superficial, short-term, and inadequate response if we bypass the process of faith reflection. The time spent on social analysis is a clear reminder that the issues we engage are complex and value-laden, requiring discernment because of overlapping and competing values. However, faith reflection helps us sift and sort through these quagmires, leading to a fuller and deeper response.

Just as *experience* confirms a problem we are aware of, and *social analysis* reveals information about the structural elements involved in the problem, *faith reflection* opens spaces from which to respond to the issue through our deepest faith values. On one level, faith reflection goes on throughout this process, for we have a faith foundation and viewpoint from which we consider the world around us (see chapter 2), and we have spiritual practices that ground us. We bring all these together in faith reflection as we discern, envision what is possible, and make decisions.

James Hug reminds us,

> This is the pivotal point in the pastoral spiral process. Our analysis of the structural and historical dynamics creating our current reality is judged against the touchstone of our personal and communal faith experience. This is a discernment process by which we identify our own deepest values, determine the directions we must go to improve the situation as we have analyzed it so that it will accord more closely with those values, and then move to creating specific plans for bringing about a more just alternative social situation.[1]

At this point our deepest values and the best possible responses we can imagine converge and move. In this chapter we (1) examine the faith reflection process of discernment in greater depth, (2) consider particular challenges in this stage of discernment, and (3) note gifts that we can use.

While the order of these may vary, faith reflection includes the following:

- Openness
- Dependence on God
- Radical availability to God
- Deepest values
- Ownership
- Community discernment
- Gazing
- Religious imagination
- Insight
- Commitment to action

OPENNESS

Openness requires a freedom to envision what one cannot yet see. It is a stance that allows new insights to emerge rather than an expectation that the challenges we see are indelible marks of the terrain. The two previous stages—experience and social analysis—required openness, which is also true of faith reflection. Practices of prayer and reflection, a willingness to listen to the experiences of others, and an honest look at the results of the social analysis from many angles and diverse opinions are all practices of openness.

Freedom to see beyond what we can yet imagine at times also requires "de-linking" ourselves from our past experiences—those of success as well as challenge or failure. Openness doesn't mean that we forget the past, but instead that the past doesn't bind us or blind us from seeing new possibilities in the future. If we see only what we have already done or experienced, we cannot imagine something new.

This de-linking of memories in order to open ourselves to God's vision, God's future, is described by Carmelite Sr. Constance FitzGerald in her work on St. John of the Cross and the "purification of memory."[2] John of the Cross understood that human beings have an infinite capacity for God.[3] FitzGerald reminds us how important such openness is:

> Before memory is purified, we can thwart our encounter with the future, without even realizing it, by relying on the images which memory has saved for us—images of our past, joyful or sad, pleasant or unpleasant, fulfilling or detrimental. We project these images onto our vision of the future, we block the limitless possibilities of God by living according to an expectation shaped, not by hope, by our own desires, needs, and past experiences.[4]

Note, too, that even success stories can limit our capacity to hear God. Such limitation can happen if we think this (method of success in the past) is *how* something must happen rather than be attentive *that* something happened.

If, at this point, we encounter limits to our openness (noted in chapter 3 on experience), journaling or sharing this with the group may be helpful, not to forcibly change one's thinking (remember that the process is about transformation rather than coercion!), but to describe to God and to the group where we are stuck. Such an admission may help the whole group, because invariably others in the wider group may also find openness challenging.

Our experiences of success and experiences of pain can prevent us from listening and responding as fully and creatively as we might. For example, a successful business manager may think that her success comes solely from her hard work, which may lead the person to think that people who are unemployed are not working hard enough. What can happen, then, is that in considering the issue of unemployment in a city, the manager may be hindered from seeing all that is present in the issues surrounding employment (education, training, networking opportunities, and connections). Another person may have a family member who was injured in Iraq during a tour of duty in the US Army, and may feel much pain and anger toward

Iraqi people, which will influence the ability to consider ways of ending the war in Iraq and moving toward peace. Both individuals must attempt to open themselves, essentially a way of being and prayer, so that their memories of success or pain do not hold them back from imagining something new or from being transformed. A person need not forget the prior experience; instead, the experience simply no longer holds the person captive or dictates a response. The person is thus freed to a future that God is inviting.

How do we find that freedom? The more we pray for and practice openness, the more we sense the places of our freedom and lack of freedom. As we live into this, we ask God to free us from anything but what God is trying to offer. Peace abides, even as we don't immediately have a solution to the issue at hand; however, we do know we are on the right track.

In the processes of de-linking or letting go, we seek to offer a space where God can come in ever more fully and, through daily activity as well as silence, move and transform us to greater love. Such openness to God reminds us that we can do this only if we depend on God.

DEPENDENCE ON GOD

In the United States many may cringe at a word like *dependence*, for society offers the illusion that we can be self-sufficient. However, as we have mentioned throughout, personal transformation and societal transformation are dependent on more than just information. If we are to transform the values that create situations of oppression and injustice, we must dig deep to the root of issues. Uprooting injustice requires that our roots in God are strong. Sometimes well-meaning persons involved in social issues become hardened, cynical, or even violent. Just as de-linking requires openness to God's movement in us, regular "resting in" or depending on God is also required in responding to the wounded heart of Earth and humanity.

Practices we have mentioned, such as prayer, scripture

study, faith sharing, and liturgical worship, sustain us for this journey. Major movers and shakers in movements of justice very clearly named their dependence on God for the work they did. Martin Luther King Jr., Mahatma Gandhi, Oscar Romero, Mother Teresa of Calcutta, and many more were clear about the time needed for prayer. Actually, the more demanding the task is, the greater our dependence must be on God, with time given to God. This is the humility of knowing that we need God's help. Such dependence on God is, again, quite freeing. Spiritual wisdom has often declared that the more we have to do, the more we have to pray.

A story told of a friendship between Pope John XXIII and UN Secretary-General Dag Hammarskjöld illustrates this point. The two men met whenever Hammarskjöld was in Rome, and during a conversation about prayer, Hammarskjöld asked John XXIII about prayer. The pope told him to find ten minutes every day for prayer and that it would make a difference to his work. Hammarskjöld followed the pope's advice for a long time. At some point, as his life was increasingly busy, he stopped this practice. On his next visit with his friend, he told him that he just couldn't find time anymore. The pope's response: Give ten minutes to prayer anyway.

This stage of the process may cause some discouragement or frustration as we see all that needs to change, the amount of effort that change will take, and even how impossible structural change seems. We must not let these factors dissuade us from reliance on God, for this is exactly where we need to be. Notice when such feelings arise. Such self-doubt is not of God, and we must not succumb to this temptation. As we stay the course, a daily reminder of our dependence on God moves us to radical availability to God.

RADICAL AVAILABILITY

Radical availability is born of and cultivated by prayer and a desire to be open. As we recall from chapter 2, "radical" in this sense refers to the root, core, or essence. "Availability" here is more akin to the word *disponibilidad* in Spanish or *disponibilité* in French. *Disponibilidad* does not translate into an availability as in "I'm available for a meeting." Instead, *disponibilidad* is a complete offering of self. Radical availability is about a core offering of self, a complete willingness to go where needed, to do what is needed. It is the disciple's way of life.

Again, we grow into this way of life—the graced disposition we seek and a way of life we practice. It is a virtue—and grace, because God deeply desires to offer this gift to each of us. Our radical availability flows from our spirituality, the way we seek to live out our deepest values. We are again reminded of Richard Gula's definition of Christian spirituality as "a way of discipleship involving a personal relationship with Jesus under the power of the Holy Spirit working in and through the community of believers to bring about a world marked by justice and peace."[5] Radical availability is the stance in which we make ourselves utterly available for what might be asked of us, with Jesus as our model and guide, and God's reign as the vision we, too, seek to manifest.

Openness, dependence on God, and radical availability—all assist us as we listen to our deepest values emerging within the issue at hand.

DEEPEST VALUES

Our deep values help us sort through both the experiences and analysis of an issue. While seeking as much content as possible through social analysis, our values serve as a foundation and shape the direction of the analysis—for example, seeing what immigration policies or trafficking is doing to the poorest and most marginal people. Social analysis and stories also help us see the complexities of issues, and in this our deep values—principles, what we hold most dear and nonnegotiable—stand at the center of our approach to any injustice.

Naming these values, out loud and perhaps in writing, is

helpful. Notice which scripture passages, themes of Catholic social thought, virtues, or aspects of one's religious tradition emerge. Spend some time reflecting on the following questions:

- What faith values are emerging in light of this issue and with what you now know?
- Are new questions or insights emerging as you reflect on this issue?

Be attentive to your responses here, and the responses of your group members.

Be open to a possible reordering of values. For example, in immigration reform, a person's value could be that everyone has the same opportunity to emigrate to a country and the current immigration process is a just means. People who come via means other than the official immigration process are cheating, taking an unfair advantage as they "sneak" to work. However, various narratives and analysis may offer new perspectives. Now a group member may see those entering without documents as persons trying to feed their families. Common experiences are men without the money needed for the immigration process, and women who love their family so much that they sacrifice seeing their family—although vulnerable daily to arrest, deportation, unjust wages, unsafe working conditions, and physical abuse—in order to send money home so that their family will survive. Experience, analysis, and faith reflection may now reorder some values and indicate insights and values that need further discussion, given the current realities of immigration. A filtering process is beginning. This is part of discernment.

James Hug offers a chart to show how our values and theologies can come into play when we pray with an issue. Notice how different perspectives on immigration can come from different religious images of God, sin, love, freedom, goodness, and so on. Note that the descriptions are probably more extreme as a whole than those of most people. Although many find themselves in the middle on a particular issue, at some point there tends to be a greater leaning in one direction than another.

Figure 7. Spiritualities in Conflict

Spiritualities in Conflict
The Challenge in a Divided Nation

Anti-immigration reform:

God: Moral authority, lawgiver, teacher, judge

Sin: Disobedience, irresponsibility

Love: Tough love, not unconditional Love

Freedom: Responsible choice, discipline, self-reliance

Society: Competition

Goodness: Developing moral, strength, responsibility

Judgment: Reward/punishment

Concern for poor/margins: God helps those who help themselves

Pro-immigration reform:

God: Love, forgiveness, teacher

Sin: Unloving, nonnurturing, action, attitude

Love: Unconditional love as foundation for tough love

Freedom: Love, compassion, nuture

Society: Nurturing community

Goodness: Developing nurturing care, community

Judgment: Love relationship model rather than reward

Concern for poor/margins: Let all who are thirsty come to the water

---

Looking at this chart, how might these areas of our tradition translate into our understanding of immigration policy? Following the descriptors on the left, the person might look at someone without documents and at immigration reform in the following way: "I am against undocumented immigrants being accepted into the United States. If you came here without documents, you are breaking the law and you do not belong in the U.S. Most people came here legally, and you need to as well. This is a competitive society and you have to prove yourself. You broke the law and so do not deserve to be here but instead should be removed and returned to your country of origin. God loves those who help themselves, but you need to do so honestly and legally."

Using the descriptors on the right, the person might look at someone without documents in the following manner: "God loves you, however you came. Our community is to be a welcoming one, and you are welcome here. I believe you when you say you came here in order to feed your family. We know you and we will support you. We will find ways to work with the structures to help you find a way here, too."

Certainly these representations are potential stereotypes of theological views and positions, but the point is important. How we see God, ourselves, humanity, community, society, good, evil, sin, and redemption all impact how we consider an issue. Again we are reminded of the need to recognize the (often) implicit theology that informs our analysis.

While our deepest values do not yet inform us of our actions, they do inform our reflection on the level of our head, heart, and gut. Refrain from demonizing others or points of view and have a clearer view of the reality of what is, rather than simply what you would like to see. Values are also named and heard here, and all can listen deeply to what the group's members are offering. A helpful image is of a person standing with feet planted solidly yet able to move with ease and flexibility, with hands open to offer the values and issue to the group.

ROLE OWNERSHIP

As we begin to see an issue more fully and deeply, we begin to take ownership of our personal and communal roles in the problem. Seeking to respond as God would, with an open heart, we can see where we have and have not responded well. I may, for example, realize how often I have not bothered to bring recycled bags to the grocery store even as I see the need for the city to do more recycling. I may also realize that my desire in Chicago for inexpensive fruit and vegetables at any time of the year contributes to companies using extra fuel to bring food from more than one thousand miles away. I may realize that my silence when confronted with racist, homophobic, anti-Islam, or anti-immigrant comments either encourages or doesn't dissuade bullying. The point is not to take full responsibility for a city's recycling deficiency, increasing fuel use, or an increase in bullying. That would be unhelpful hubris. Instead, the point is to see how and where my own actions and that of my community (city, state, country, church, family, etc.) contribute to the problem. Since persons organize and run systems and structures, we each and all contribute to just and unjust structures.

When we take responsibility for our actions, acknowledge sin ("a failure to bother to love"[6]), and trust God's mercy,[7] we are free to make new choices. In order to truly transform a system and ourselves, we need to name and own the places where systems have become hardened ("it has always been that way") and perhaps even where our hearts have been hardened. If we can see how we have failed, even when our intentions were good, we can be willing to create more space for change to galvanize.

More positively, ownership of our own participation in a position or issue also taps into our sense of wonder, hope, and possibility. When we can see the larger picture and our role in it, when we ask to see God's movements, we seek "conversion of heart that attunes a person to the will of God for the world."[8] We ask to be shown another way and to allow that way to be a way of love. This does not remove our political, cultural, religious, and other biases, but it means that they inform rather than dictate the response. Given that our evaluation and judgment do take into account all prior experience and information, we now seek the way to shape the world according to a gospel vision of love.

COMMUNAL DISCERNMENT

Discernment by a community generally offers three particular contributions: support, an enlarged vision, and a deepened vision to provide a model for action. Chapter 4 on social analysis has already demonstrated the breadth of knowledge and information that can come from the work of analysis. Yet a community can encourage, offer energy for the longer haul of vision and action, and even bring accountability to the entire process. When challenges arise, as they inevitably do, the community offers the support of a common vision and encouragement to stay the course.

While more is not necessarily better, a community consisting of members who have experienced individual discernment has incredible potential. If each contribution is valued as part of the unity in diversity—part of the effort to see the larger goal and God's movements in response to the situation—so much is possible! As insights are offered, as people listen together and sit in silence, a powerful forging of insight and effort often results, bonding a community with a common vision.

Communal discernment models how a group of people can seek to live the gospel and promote God's reign to move toward a world marked by justice and peace. This approach is in direct opposition to efforts that create rancor or some form of oppression or demonize people or their beliefs. This communal process can model dialogue, collaboration, and communion if the group is committed to seeking the truth and working together to the same goal, seeing all the possibilities, and seeking to respond through the deepest faith values of the group.

GAZING

Gazing may be an apt descriptor for this next step, for here we hold all we have learned and understood in a relaxed yet attentive manner. Gazing is a way of contemplating, looking at what is, yet holding lightly enough so that we open ourselves to seeing something further and farther. It is a sacred space, asking for time in silence—in solitude or in a group—so that we can take in what is possible.

At the same time, this space also offers the freedom to sift and sort the pieces of what we have been pondering, ideas we

have engaged, scripture we have let abide in us. It may be helpful to bring some key passages from scripture to this step. Key
insights from one's tradition, a mission statement, inspirational
music, or a visual can serve as reminders that we are seeking
God's horizon and seeking to serve God's people and earth.[9]

RELIGIOUS (MORAL) IMAGINATION

Openness, dependence on God, radical availability to God,
our deepest values, and ownership for our roles free us personally and communally to see beyond the problem in front of us
toward responses and possibilities that we may not have yet
seen (for example, a hole in an argument or an opening for
legislation) or that may not have seemed possible earlier. This
space is one of the most creative and dynamic in the process
because it takes the problem at hand and the information
gained, alongside our deep faith values, and helps us see differently to imagine beyond where we are, transforming one way
of seeing to another. It is deeply rooted in reality and in one's
faith. The extent to which we give space to this process suggests
the depth to which we may engage the issue before us. This is
also one of the most critical junctures in the pastoral spiral,
for what we know and where we will go next hinges on this
step. This space is one of deep-rootedness in God, trusting God,
asking to see a way through an impasse. However, this is not
a "magic" step, hoping that if we say the right things we will
get what we want. We must deal with reality and not fantasy.

Religious imagination is connected to hope and our paschal
imagination, powerful conduits of grace. The life, death, and
resurrection of Jesus represent a message of hope that does not
evade or deny the suffering and dying that occur in life. Yet the
crucial and incarnated hope is that the end of the story is not
death but new life that may take a variety of forms. Imaginative hope does not evade reality but sees it and transforms it.[10]
At this step we bring all that we have done to the fore and sit

with it, allow it to steep, and be attentive to what emerges.

Some examples help us understand what this process might look like. At a speech accepting her Peacemaker Award in 2013 from the Catholic Theological Union in Chicago, former president of Ireland Mary McAleese said that when she became president she said to her husband, "We shall see how much we really believe in 'love your neighbor.' "[11] She made "Building Bridges" the theme of her presidency and reached out to the unionist community in Northern Ireland and to the Republic of Ireland, at times surprising people who thought this was not possible. Her religious imagination opened new relationships. President McAleese did what many could not imagine when she invited Queen Elizabeth II to make a state visit to the Republic of Ireland. On May 17, 2011, the Queen arrived in Ireland wearing a green dress, an intentionally symbolic gesture.

During the visit, several important moments opened spaces to imagine "more" between two countries that have had bitter conflicts in the past and have unhealed wounds that go back generations. At one point during the visit she planted an oak tree by the Peace Bell in the garden of Phoenix Park. Another moment that caught the attention of all was when Queen Elizabeth II and President McAleese each laid a wreath at the Garden of Remembrance, and the Queen bowed to honor those who had died for Irish freedom. People in Ireland were riveted to their televisions, and some even moved to tears. It was a very positive experience for people who were now invited to imagine new possibilities between the two countries. There was no way to anticipate or dictate the responses of the people of Ireland or England ahead of time, but McAleese took the risk to imagine a better relationship between the two countries by building bridges between the two leaders. Each step led to the next step, and much happened.

In a local example, an eighth-grader who recently offered a graduation reflection on behalf of his class spoke about how his education and faith taught him that there really was enough for everyone in the world today. He further reflected that he himself had enough, more than enough, and that his life was to be about making sure that more people had enough. His vision was wide, and it came from seeing the world as it is, with people who had much and with people who were not able to provide for their day-to-day needs. He said he knew he had enough food and enough clothes, and he didn't want more but instead wanted to help others. He was graduating from a school of well-educated students with financial resources and wealthy families. Afterward, a member of the school community commented he was teaching his family and school community by his example. This fourteen-year-old had a vision of what could be. He didn't need to see all the steps in front of him. He saw the next step and he responded.

INSIGHT

If we are faithful to the space needed for religious imagination, at some point insight emerges. Something flows through the impasse, be it a revelation, a way through that wasn't noticed earlier, or a combination that gives new vision. A direction emerges with greater clarity. The energy of a group is calm, yet the flow happens and a way emerges for what is possible. It's not always based on new information: at times it is an intuitive process, and at other times it is a very logical and practical process that leads to insights. We need to trust this kind of process as we do faith reflection. This is the point at which persons and groups know it is time to act and sense a direction for their activity. President McAleese and the eighth-grader both experienced a moment of insight that led them in a particular direction.

Another example is that of an ER physician enrolled in an ethics course I taught who was deeply concerned that the female patients he saw were at adverse risk for HIV and domestic violence. He tried to bring up such topics with some patients, but he felt stonewalled by their silence. As months went on, some of these women returned to the ER and tested positive for HIV. The doctor was frustrated and didn't know what to do. The entire class then began an exercise of contemplative walking. For thirty to forty-five minutes, doctors, chaplains, professionals, and students all left their phones, laptops, and other devices with me and exited the classroom to walk outside. They were allowed only a pen and a piece of paper in their pocket. They walked in silence, similar to the way one might at a monastery garden—walking without a physical arrival point but walking in order to reflect. They walked with a question: "I wonder what it would look like to. . . ." Prior to this exercise, the students had spent weeks reading and discussing various issues of ethics. Each person had questions and concerns regarding ethical problems, and each walked and wondered. Now they used time and space to imagine the "more" that flowed from their deepest faith values.

When they returned to the classroom, their energy was noticeably different. They returned with a quiet focus (rather than the unabated frustration they had left the room with forty-five minutes before). They returned from this walk with insights, and they began to articulate them. The ER doctor said that he began wondering what it would be like if he asked the nurses and physician assistants to talk with the women about their situations after he left the examining room and they had a few minutes to think about the questions. He wondered if extra time for nurses to talk with the women could help open up some spaces.

He left that night and discussed his ideas during a staff meeting the following week. When our class next met, he pointed out that the entire staff decided on a plan and that it came after the staff, also taking time to "wonder," contributed further insight and direction. They also invited some female patients to join them in considering possibilities to better assist women coming to the ER. The staff, as concerned as the doctor, found more effective responses to the needs around them.

COMMITMENT TO ACTION

Once an insight emerges, committing to action is important, no matter how small the initial act may be. Insight has its own natural flow and energy, and it seeks a lived response. As we see in the next step, action, there is much to be done. However, at this point a commitment to act is crucial.

A commitment calls for accountability, prayer, and some initial small steps. Telling someone, even one another in the group, about a direction emerging fuels energy and accountability. Something internally and externally begins to move in the group as energies are released. Prayer at this time can be directed to perseverance and right judgment, as both are needed to bring about systemic change. Similarly, listing the next possible few steps gives momentum to a longer-range vision. While this topic is more for the next chapter, keep it in mind as you begin to undertake even a small act in the direction you seek.

Some years ago when a group of students spent a month in Zambia, they found amazing responses to HIV as well as appalling circumstances related to HIV. They visited a clinic that distributed infant formula to people caring for infants whose mothers had HIV and were too sick to care for their children. One grandmother caught the group's heart when she came to the clinic with infant twin girls. The twins were healthy, without HIV, but they were not gaining weight. The clinic's funds for infant formula were not increasing even as needs were. In essence, the grandmother had to divide the infant formula between the two since she was not able to get a double portion.

One of the students in the class, a married woman with two teenage children, spoke with the clinic directors. When she returned from Zambia she gathered other mothers from her local church, and they created a fund to take care of infant formula for the twins for eighteen months. This was not a solution to the wider issues of HIV, treatment for mothers, children of parents living with HIV, elder generations caring for children, or even the others at this clinic. However, it was a necessary first step. It significantly impacted one family, connecting the mothers in this parish to the realities in a town in Zambia, and it brought further questions and possibilities to the table. The mothers in the United States, seeing what was possible on a small scale, began learning more because they "wondered," *How might we make a larger impact?* Taking even a small step is also important so that people do not feel overwhelmed by the enormity of the issue. As one step is taken, other steps emerge. These stories inculcate hope, and hope is a necessary virtue in dealing with most social issues.

The process of discernment is transformative, inviting significant change in us and our society, and it brings challenges and gifts.

Challenges

The spiritual wisdom of our Christian tradition tells us that good is challenged by evil and by forces that seek to hinder efforts for the good of all. To not get waylaid by these challenges, we need to identify and prepare for them. We should notice challenges or bumps in the road so that we are not unexpectedly tripped up by them or by temptations. Internal or external voices may say,

- We don't know enough.
- We can't take this on. It's too big, too much.
- We can't write or speak well enough for this. There are larger groups in power in this issue that want no change. Can we really counter this?
- We are risking our resources [wealth, time, talent], reputation, and power . . . and for what? Is this really worth it?
- This will take more time than we have to give.
- There are others far more capable to take this on.
- Who do we think we are?

Feelings that show up and can overwhelm include fear, confusion, and discouragement. We can be tempted to focus on what we lack rather than what we have to offer. We may even seek out God to convince God, "Surely you don't mean me? Surely you know there are others far better, far more skilled, far smarter, sophisticated, strategic, skilled, and connected, than I? You know my weaknesses. How do you see me doing this?" This is why it is important to continue steeping ourselves in prayer and in our sense of call. Communal support helps us to stay grounded.

Another way to deal with such challenges is to connect to beauty. Openness to woundedness require regular drinks at the well of refreshment, particularly the well of beauty. John O'Donohue wisely reminds us,

> Constant struggle leaves us tired and empty. Our struggle for reform needs to be tempered and balanced with a capacity for celebration. When we lose sight of beauty our struggle becomes tired and functional. When we expect and engage the Beautiful, a new fluency is set free within us and between us. The heart becomes rekindled, and our lives brighten with unexpected courage. It is courage that restores hope to the heart. In our day-to-day lives, we often show courage without realizing it. However, it is only when we are afraid that courage becomes a question. Courage is amazing because it can tap into the heart of fear, taking that frightened energy and turning it towards initiative, creativity, action, and hope. When courage comes alive, imprisoning walls become frontiers of new possibility, difficulty becomes invitation and the heart comes into a new rhythm of trust and sureness. There are secret sources of courage inside every human heart, yet courage needs to be awakened in us. The encounter with the Beautiful can bring such awakening. Courage is a spark that can become the flame of hope, lighting

new and exciting pathways in what seemed to be dead, dark landscapes.[12]

Gifts

Whatever challenges we might encounter, there are also abundant gifts. Some of the gifts that grow and deepen in this process include the following:

- Interiority deepens and our potential activates.
- Waiting becomes an active prayer of seeing God's movements.
- We see differently, looking at the world around us with a wider horizon and a sense of God's immediacy.
- Community moves us beyond ideologies to a communal vision that seeks God's vision.
- Radical dependence on God grows.
- Steadfastness and strength (spirituality) for the long haul grow.
- Celebration and gratitude for insights grow.
- Our religious imagination and creativity are cultivated and seep into more areas.
- We experience the joy and feelings of satisfaction that can come from working with like-minded people in community.

CONCLUSION

Faith reflection, while ongoing, is a contemplative process of engaging as we gaze; it requires an attentive receptivity and a desire to listen to the Spirit's invitation to respond to the cries of our world today. People who seek to live in this way offer a form of leadership that is deeply needed in the church and world. This is possible only with openness, radical dependence on and availability to God, community, religious imagination, and insight that commits to act. Then the space opens up. When it does, we move to action, to which we now turn.

Notes

[1]James Hug, "Redeeming Social Analysis: Recovering the Hidden Religious Dimensions of Social Change," *The Pastoral Circle Revisited: A Critical Quest for Truth and Transformation*, ed. Frans Wijsen, Peter Henriot, and Rodrigo Mejía (Maryknoll, NY: Orbis Books, 2005), 204.

[2]Constance FitzGerald, OCD, "From Impasse to Prophetic Hope: Crisis of Memory," *CTSA Proceedings* 64 (2009): 21–42, http://www.ctsa-online.org.

[3]Ibid., 24.

[4]Ibid., 32.

[5]Richard M. Gula, *The Call to Holiness: Embracing a Fully Christian Life* (New York: Paulist Press, 2003), 21. Gula's definition also describes the moral life.

[6]This definition is attributed to James F. Keenan, SJ.

[7]This message is replete in Pope Francis's *Joy of the Gospel*.

[8]Joan Chittister, *The Monastery of the Heart: An Invitation to a Meaningful Life* (Katonah, NY: BlueBridge Press, 2012), 203.

[9]Poetry or other inspirational reading or music can be equally helpful.

[10]I take this from my book, *When God's People Have HIV/AIDS: An Approach to Ethics* (Maryknoll, NY: Orbis Books, 2005), 46.

[11]Part of her acceptance remarks at the Peacemakers Dinner, Chicago, IL, April 17, 2013.

[12]John O'Donohue, *Beauty: The Invisible Embrace*, repr. ed. (New York: HarperCollins, 2005), 6.

6

Action

Service in Solidarity

See, I am doing something new! Now it springs forth,
do you not perceive it? In the wilderness I make a way,
in the wasteland, rivers.

—Isaiah 43:19

In this context we can understand Jesus' command
to his disciples: "You yourselves give them something
to eat!" (Mark 6:37): it means working to eliminate
the structural causes of poverty and to promote the
integral development of the poor, as well as small daily
acts of solidarity in meeting the real needs which we
encounter. The word "solidarity" is a little worn and
at times poorly understood, but it refers to something
more than a few sporadic acts of generosity. It presumes the creation of a new mindset which thinks in
terms of community and the priority of the life of all
over the appropriation of goods by a few.

—Pope Francis, *The Joy of the Gospel*

This chapter asks, "In light of our experience, analysis,
and faith reflection, how do we respond to this issue?" and it
moves us through several steps to a concrete response. Once
a decision is made to act, we begin the steps of planning, acting, and evaluating in order to bring about the change we
desire, considering both the short- and long-term strategies

and steps toward the desired end. The action must include the participation and vision of the group affected by the chosen issue. It is also essential to have a tool for evaluation, which is why the pastoral spiral is indeed a spiral, helping us evaluate and continually focus, adapt, and fine-tune our thinking. A spiral reminds us of the continual movement through layers of response in order to achieve a desired end.

Figure 8. Action

The first part of the chapter offers some insights to guide the planning and action that follow. The second part explains the various steps of the action process and offers sample questions in each area (economic, political, environmental, cultural, and religious) that can be used to measure progress. The third section names some of the resistances, responses, and gifts that often accompany the action phase.

THREE GUIDING INSIGHTS

In beginning to decide on a plan of action, three points are important:

1. Trust the vision that led you here.
2. See and respond to the group's energy.
3. Manage the structure of the process and maintain flexibility.

Trust the Vision

Trusting the vision that has brought a group to this point is essential in both the short-term and the long-term work. A discernment process led to the decision to act, and just as moving to action is an act of trust in God, following the lead of the "befriending Spirit" (*Gaudium et Spes*, 3) continues to require trust. Find a way to keep the vision clearly in front of you and in front of your group, perhaps by displaying an image or saying together a specific prayer. Also keep in mind that the process of bringing about structural change is a spiral rather than a circle; there is the continuous movement of evaluating and modifying to effectively bring about change.

Pope Francis offers a helpful reminder about the type of action needed and the process required:

> What we need, then, is to give priority to actions which generate new processes in society and engage other persons and groups who can develop them to the point where they bear fruit in significant historical events. Without anxiety, but with clear convictions and tenacity . . .
>
> Sometimes I wonder if there are people in today's world who are really concerned about generating processes of people-building, as opposed to obtaining immediate results which yield easy, quick short-term political gains, but do not enhance human fullness. (*Joy of the Gospel*, 223, 224)

Keep moving and remember that if your chosen path is not the way of the Spirit, you will become aware of it. Continue moving forward in the set direction as you have sought out information, prayed about it, consulted with persons with expertise, determined a course of action, and made a decision to act.

See and Respond to the Energy

Once a group opens itself to move in a particular direction, a natural flow begins. Scottish explorer W. H. Murray affirmed this movement:

> Until one is committed, there is hesitancy, the chance to draw back, always ineffectiveness. Concerning all acts of initiative (and creation), there is one elementary truth, the ignorance of which kills countless ideas and splendid plans: that the moment one definitely commits oneself, then providence moves too.
>
> A whole stream of events issues from the decision, raising in one's favor all manner of unforeseen incidents, meetings and material assistance, which no man [or woman] could have dreamt would have come his way.[1]

Listen, especially early on, to the sources of the energy and direction. The creativity and process of problem-solving to bring about systemic change emanate from the inspiring vision that had brought us to this point. Using religious language, we might say it is listening to the guidance of the "befriending Spirit."[2] The specific direction will be tested later, but here it is important to listen to this initial energy because it does offer direction. Listening is especially key since it is coming from the time and space of faith reflection, consistent attentiveness to the world around you, your sense of needs in the world, and your hope that change can come about.

Begin where you can create movement. The elements for action are structurally the same as for social analysis: sociological, economic, political, environmental, cultural, and religious. From which of these does the energy come? Initially, the players or actors are the same ones you named when doing social analysis. Do any particular persons or groups share your first instincts to respond to this issue? Consider these questions:

- In what direction is your energy generally moving?
- Are any insights emerging for you as you begin leaning into what you might do?
- If the areas of need give no indication of a possible response, how will you proceed? What could you do?

While some people find this kind of intuitive questioning and thinking contrary to conventional wisdom, significant figures in organizational behavior, such as Otto Scharmer, note, "The biggest mistake when dealing with innovation is to first focus on the rational mind."[3] Instead, listen to the energy and direction of the group. Listen to who is speaking and leading on a given area. Who might take the lead? I say more about this point in the second part of this chapter on envisioning, but be keenly attentive to the group's flow of energy.

Noting and heeding the creative guiding instinct among you are important steps throughout this process. Allow insights to evolve as you individually and communally "lean into" the issues. Sometimes insights emerge on a walk or a run, and sometimes they emerge as we struggle to put images or words into an insight that is still emerging. Keep the creative spaces open. Sometimes when I need to invite insights or energy to flow, I walk contemplatively, gazing at beauty outside or inside, or I play with juggling balls in my hands. None of these distracts me in the way that checking email or going online or making a phone call does. Invite the group to do one of these exercises whenever you come to some kind of impasse. This is part of noticing where the energy flow is going and opening spaces up for this energy. Attentiveness and understanding the use of energy are key practices of leadership (more on leadership in chapter 7).

Leaning into the new and emerging possibilities takes more than one set of insights; similarly we cannot simply add up pieces and come up with the whole. The process is more like looking at a field or horizon to see what emerges. Sometimes this happens as a whole and sometimes in bits and pieces. The process of choosing an action requires structure and flexibility.

Structure and Flexibility

Finding a way to offer a structure to the compelling insights emerging in a group is important, but so is flexibility. Structure is necessary to give people some assurance of direction and a plan for action. Structure helps you see what you are doing and, subsequently, note what is missing or what you are choosing not to do. Structure also gives people places to direct their gifts and energies, helps us set priorities, and reminds us of the large vision and the immediate needs. These factors assist us when establishing timelines and assessments.

Flexibility is also needed in planning action, as action and implementation require a continual willingness to adapt to changing situations and the signs of the times. Issues involving social change often have a dynamic and fluid nature. For example, questions about immigration reform continue to shift even during a presidential administration as situations and legislation arise, so knowing how to enter the current point of a discussion is important. Be attentive to social and political developments; for example, a serious incident at a border or the treatment of a local undocumented family may influence a group's plans. Remember that remaining grounded in your deepest (gospel) values allows you to manage the shifting sands and tides.

Flexibility is important because trying something new nearly always involves some risk taking. A group's chosen path of action may require some experimenting with planning, modeling, and implementation. Experimenting means you are making adjustments as needed and inviting others to collaborate and assist. Because this is a learning process, some directions inevitably will not work. Flexibility then becomes important, for all actions that suggest possibilities won't come about. However, flexibility of spirit allows us to learn from our mistakes and thus see the problem more accurately. Finally, flexibility is necessary in order to regularly test the Spirit's direction as you seek to move toward action. We must be free to ask questions like the following and respond in light of what we hear:

- Does this action express the guiding instinct we had?
- How does this action respond to the issue, both systemically and locally?

In planning for action, try to determine who in the group naturally tends toward structure and who welcomes flexibility, for people with gifts in each area will help immensely. With these caveats assisting our general direction, we move now to the process for taking action.

TAKING ACTION

Action is built around seven key movements:

1. Envision.
2. Set priorities; utilize social analysis categories for short- and long-term organizing and planning.
3. Create models.
4. Experiment.
5. Get to work.
6. Assess and revise.
7. Repeat as needed.

Envision

In order to envision what can be done, it is necessary to

- Maintain a large vision to see the big picture.
- Articulate what we see.
- Invite others to see, and then see together.

- Seek out others as needed.
- Imagine long-term and short-term possibilities.

The group's process of faith reflection will understandably move the group in a direction that coincides and responds in light of what we hear in the group's deepest values. For example, a group may determine that the best way to end capital punishment is to change the legal system, because that speaks to one root of what justice is and is not in society today. The timing of action also connects to the restlessness in the state about what good comes from the process and costs of capital punishment. That provides a general direction, and then envisioning suggests what might come next.

Envisioning imagines future possibilities, visualizing what is not yet, and is deeper than seeing what is around you and taking in information. Envisioning is the sense that something else can be and gives language, albeit incomplete, to it.

Because action may involve a number of areas, keep in the forefront what is most important to the group. The big picture is the lens from which particular actions flow and to which any action must connect. As mentioned earlier, many social issues have multifaceted roots and sources, so they do not lend themselves to obvious or easy solutions. If the big picture is clearly visible, the smaller steps will be parts of the whole but will not be substituted for the whole.

Invite group members to name what they envision flowing from the direction that was set during their faith reflection. Each person may have ideas to share. Articulating in written and spoken word assists the person and the group to more concretely imagine the possible from the issues before us. This move is key, for this step involves risk taking. Being attentive to the large vision and articulating our vision concretely helps us not succumb to fear.

By sharing what we envision, we begin to see possibilities together. Disagreements may flow from the deep call heard in the group for change. At the same time, sharing invites others to join in on a particular possibility or may suggest other jumping-off points. A number of initiatives can enter the process as collaboration begins.

At this moment you may realize that the vision requires that more people join you at the table. We must ask once more who is missing from the table in order to help plan any action. This can be done concretely or even imaginatively. Finally, envision both short- and long-term goals. The next step will be to set priorities, but first create an initial listing of all that might be possible.

Setting Priorities

Now is the time to return to the categories of social analysis that we used to gather information. With the information we have and a named vision, the group needs to list what actions need to be done, when, and in what order. The following categories of questions can help develop and shape action. You are encouraged to adapt these or create your own. Also, remember that the ordering here of economic, political, and other actions does not mean your action needs to begin in such an order. Choose that which flows from your reading of the signs and times, analysis, and faith reflection.

As a group, notice which areas (economic, political, environmental, cultural, and religious) generate energy and whether particular needs call for priority.

- Which area(s) are most immediately needed to move toward your goal?
- How do these areas move you closer to your long-term goals?
- Which areas have short-term goals that lead to the long-term goal?
- Where does the energy of the group members lean?
- Are there time-sensitive events you need to incorporate into your choices—for example: Is legislation possible or pending? Is an important parish meeting coming up? Is action within an academic year important?

First, depending on the group's size, choose one or two short-term goals to prioritize and then designate subgroups for each. You may wish to chart the different areas and see how each connects to the larger goal. Meet regularly to see how your efforts are contributing to the larger goal. Second, once you have a goal and a sense of timing in mind, draft a timeline so that all can see a visual of what is needed next (see Figure 9).

Figure 9. Timeline

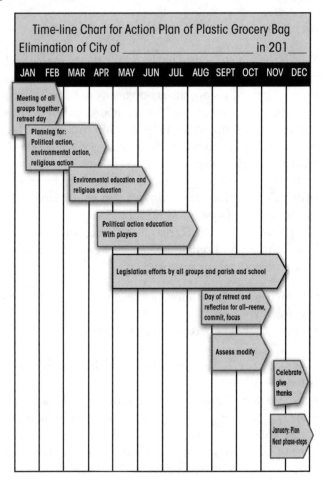

In thinking about possible action, some categories of questions often prove helpful: *guiding questions, creating questions,* and *organizing questions.* Possible questions in each area of social analysis include the following:

Economic Factors

Guiding questions
- How is economics connected to the systemic change you seek to bring about?
- What role does economics play in your short-term plan? In your long-term plan?
- What faith values need to impact the economic factors in this issue (for example, immigration reform must also consider human dignity, justice, solidarity, rights, and responsibilities)?
- Is there a particular form of action that flows from your particular group (for example, a Franciscan- or Jesuit-run parish, an educational ministry, a healing ministry, and so on)?

Creating questions
- If there were a blank slate for economic factors, what kind of system would you create?
- How would you change the economic structures in place to the vision required that more closely reflects your faith values?

Organizing questions
- Who is needed for this action here?
- What skills are needed?
- Who has expertise?
- What persons are still needed? (This may be in the specific area, or you may invite a few persons who imagine beyond economics or across disciplines with a good deal of imagination to stimulate your thinking.)

Political Action

Guiding questions
- How is politics connected to the systemic change you seek to create?
- What role does political action play in your short-term plan? In your long-term plan?
- What faith values need to impact politics and law in this issue?
- Is there a particular form of action that flows from your particular group—for example, a Franciscan- or Jesuit-run parish, an educational ministry, a healing ministry, and so on?

Creating questions
- If there were a blank slate for political factors, what kind of system would you create that would be different?
- How would you change the political structures in place to achieve a vision that more closely reflects your faith values?

Organizing questions
- Who is needed for action here?
- What skills are needed?
- Who has expertise?
- What persons are still needed?

Cultural Action

Guiding questions
- How is culture connected to the systemic change you seek to bring about?
- What role does culture play in your short-term plan? In your long-term plan?
- What faith values need to impact culture?
- Is there a particular form of action that flows from your particular group (for example, a Franciscan- or Jesuit-

run parish, an educational ministry, a healing ministry, and so on)?

Creating questions

- If there were a blank slate for culture, what kind of system would you create?
- How would you change the cultural structures in place to achieve a vision that more closely reflects your faith values?

Organizing questions

- Who is needed for action here?
- What skills are needed?
- Who has expertise?
- What persons are still needed?

Environmental Action

Guiding questions

- How is the environment connected to the systemic change you seek to bring about?
- What role does the environment play in your short-term plan? In your long-term plan?
- What faith values need to impact environmental efforts in this area?
- Is there a particular form of action that flows from your particular group?

Creating questions

- If there were a blank slate for the environment, what would you do to create a workable system?
- How would you change the environmental structures in place to achieve a vision that more closely reflects your faith values?

Organizing questions

- Who is needed for action here?
- What skills are needed?

- Who has expertise?
- What persons are still needed?

Religious Action

Guiding questions
- How is religion connected to the systemic change you seek to bring about?
- What role does religion play in your short-term plan? In your long-term plan?
- What faith values need to impact religious structures?
- Is there a particular form of action that flows from your particular group (for example, a Franciscan- or Jesuit-run parish, an educational ministry, a healing ministry, and so on)?

Creating questions
- If there were a blank slate for religious factors, what kind of system would you create?
- How would you change the religious structures now in place to achieve a vision that more closely reflects your faith values?

Organizing questions
- Who is needed for action here?
- What skills are needed?
- Who has expertise?
- What persons are still needed?

Create Models

Now let's try out in miniature scale some of the ideas and plans generated. To do so, we

- Group people according to vision and energy.
- Maintain time limits.
- Design what we envision.
- Fill in details for the vision.

- Communicate often with whole group.
- Adjust models as needed for the vision.
- Create models that may be parts of the process or the whole.

Get a sense of where the energy is moving and begin with the priorities you have set. Create groupings around the possibilities that garner the most energy.

Give the groups a limited time for creating models or steps for what the group envisions. Time limits are important because the earlier that options can be identified, the sooner the group will provide feedback and further direction on where to fine-tune the model. The first version may not be the best one. In fact, the learning will probably increase because you have only a limited time; the goal of brainstorming is to quickly get a range of ideas on the table. Sharing thoughts early on a model will help develop any subsequent models. This is part of the early layers of co-creating where you may already have a small group putting together a model and a slightly larger or equal-sized group offering feedback.

At this time you should consider if your group has a particular lens from which you naturally work and you use to create models. Some powerful examples are described in a book by Timothy A. Byrnes called *Reverse Mission: Transnational Religious Communities and the Making of U.S. Foreign Policy*.[4] Byrnes documents how the Society of Jesus (Jesuits), the Maryknoll Sisters, and the Benedictine Monks of Weston Priory, Vermont, responded to injustices using the distinctive characteristics and charisms (spiritual gifts) of their communities. The US Jesuits engaged various legislative power structures when their brother Jesuits were murdered in 1989 at the University of Central America (UCA) in El Salvador. Concerned with atrocities in Nicaragua, the Maryknoll sisters went to the parishes and spoke out about the funding the US government was sending to the Nicaraguan government, which was harming innocent people during the civil war. The Benedictine monks saw the great poverty in Mexico through the eyes of Benedictine sisters in Mexico and co-created a center of education and prayer called Guadalupe Center in Cuernavaca, in which US citizens can learn, pray, reflect, and find ways to respond to poverty and other injustices. Each group used its spiritual strengths in creative ways to effectively affect systems, whether their engagement was short-term or long-term. Each responded to the cries of the poor.

Also invite some out-of-the-box thinking so that creativity can be further unleashed. For example, one way to create a model is to imagine what would be best for a situation if all the pieces currently in place, problematic or not, were absent. What would be best for functioning at the optimal level no matter the issue—childhood obesity, immigration laws, hydraulic drilling, homelessness in a city, and so on. Consider everything that is currently happening, including factors of politics (laws on this issue), economics (costs related to the problem/solution), the environment (types of materials), culture (what vision is needed?), and religion (what is needed to be said and modeled?) You have already practiced this type of thinking in the preceding section as you answered the question, "If there were a blank slate for _____, what kind of system would you create that would be different?"

This approach helps with creative envisioning and plans that engage the present. Note that once the model is properly created, it does not turn to the past but moves creatively from the present into a future way of living that responds to the cries of the world. Energy does need to be galvanized, for there may be negative energy telling you not to step beyond "How we've always done it" and instead to "Just tweak the process a little bit." These tests and doubts must be acknowledged and then put aside.

Adjust the models—and there will be more than one—as small groups regularly receive feedback from the larger group. Communication with the whole group is important because it reminds everyone of the vision and how the parts connect to it. As you create models you will need to try them out, which is done by experimentation.

Experimentation

Now is the time to try out your model on a small scale. Four points to remember include the following:

1. This is a learning space where you can reach, risk, and play.
2. Failure can be your friend and teacher.
3. Protect the space and time for experimentation.
4. Keep an eye on the rest of the system.

You are encouraged to reach as far as you can toward what you sense needs to be created. If, for example, you are trying to move twenty steps toward your vision, you may achieve only ten steps. However, if you try moving only ten steps, then five steps may be as far as you go. Of course, as the model develops so will your keenness of perception and your ability to see where strategic moves be made.

Be willing to take risks as you experiment. See what is possible in light of your highest aspirations. See what is possible even if your efforts will be incomplete in these early stages. As much as possible, experiment in a manner that prevents you from holding too tightly onto either the process or the product. Held lightly, the important pieces will remain in place and you will more easily be open to what is still possible though not yet identified.

Failure is your friend and teacher. We are taught early on in life that failure is bad, that it reflects poorly on us as persons and on our ability. No one seeks to be a failure. However, the wise person is one who takes sufficient risks and tries new ideas even if some or many do not succeed in full or in part. The wise person has a longer vision and sees that each effort is a piece of the movement that gets you closer to your goal. *The failure is to not try beyond what you can see, and therefore only get more of what already is.* A meeting facilitator once noted that when her father, who helped invent a particular type of X-ray machine, was asked how many failures he had before his invention worked, he said that over 99 percent of his efforts failed before he succeeded.

Protect the time and the space for trying out new ideas so that there is sufficient room for the ideas to grow and be adapted. It is too easy to subject early ideas to outside review only to be rejected before being properly considered. (I did earlier suggest getting feedback early and often from the larger group. This is good. Feedback does not mean the rejection of ideas but rather the opportunity to have others interact and make suggestions.) Sometimes critiques may come too soon to be able to be integrated. Some critiques may simply stem from the newness of an idea that does not fit the established patterns. Ideas and projects need some time to germinate and to grow. This is a somewhat fragile stage when a nourishing environment may be more helpful than an intensive testing environment. This is not yet the time for public scrutiny, though certainly people with expertise can offer assistance; however, the group must carefully choose those with the willingness and capacity to help create something new.

As the group tests its models, have at least one person keep an eye on the larger picture, attentive to how a proposed model may be shifting or affecting the goal (the situation you ultimately seek to change). From time to time the group should ask how a particular model is impacting the system we seek to change (prison reform, immigration policy, childhood poverty, human trafficking, environmental pollution, and so on).

Assessment and Revision

Once you have created, experimented with, and followed certain steps of action, you need to see what is working and what requires modification or improvement. Assessment is essential for initial and ongoing efforts. In the early stages of experimentation, assessment makes use of feedback from group members as well as other players and experts. Collaboration greatly assists in co-creating and bringing others with you into the project. Group members know the vision and goal of the project and can assess results in light of that vision. Players can contribute role-specific insights and details that wider visioning may have missed. Experts can clarify questions and direct adjustments in the model in their area of expertise. Assessment affords opportunities for more people to participate in creating what will emerge. Ultimately, as more people take ownership (no matter their extent of involvement), the more venues there will be for realizing the vision.

Assessment is aided by questions. Questions are meant to help continually assess and revise sections of the action and to ask some relevant personal and global questions, as follows:

- How is your particular area (economic, political, political, environmental, cultural, religious) being put to action?
- Are there gaps between what you are trying to do and the results? If so, what is necessary to close the gap?
- What next step is needed in your area?
- What major players are involved? Are there others you have not yet considered?
- How are you impacting the system you are seeking to change?
- What is happening to the persons (or Earth community) most adversely impacted by the system of injustice that you area addressing?
- How is your action connected to creating a world marked by justice and peace?
- Where are you finding God in this?
- Is your deepest envisioning present? If not, why? What next step could improve this?
- Who are you becoming in the midst of this?
- Who is your group-community becoming in the midst of this?
- What is the possible impact on civic and international life?

The spiral of experience, social analysis, faith reflection, and action is repeated and continued as long as necessary, based on energy, needs, and priorities.

CHALLENGES, RESPONSES, AND GIFTS— SPIRITUALITY FOR THE LONG HAUL

Let us take a moment now to name some of the challenges that can arise during this process as well as some of the gifts. "Success" in systemic change often happens over the long haul as well as in bits and pieces along the way. Because it is a "long haul," having spiritual practices and community support is absolutely essential. Challenges will be posed throughout the process. In fact, the extent to which you are taking on and proposing significant change to the status quo will in some ways be measured by the response. If you are not asking for much beyond what already is, there will probably be little response or opposition. Those whose way of being in society and the world is ensured by the way the present system is working will be keen to notice any changes, and if you propose no real changes (or simply rearrange the chairs on the deck of a ship), there will be little resistance.

However, if you propose (as this book presumes) a change on behalf of the poor, vulnerable, marginalized—the wounded heart of humanity and creation—and if the change is based on deep gospel values, you will most certainly encounter some resistance. While the next chapter deals quite directly with resistance to change and how to manage it, I simply point out a few challenges to increase awareness.

1. As noted above, if you are taking on the roots and effects of an injustice, those in power will naturally seek to maintain their power. If you are dealing with roots of injustice and the roots run very deep, uprooting them takes effort. This is part of the process; do not let adversity overwhelm or paralyze you. Change nearly always generates some form of challenge.

2. Anticipate challenges to your ideas at a number of stages,

but do not self-sabotage. Challenges are generally both good and normal—good because someone is paying attention to your efforts or is getting an inkling of what you are doing that is different. Sincere questioning is a compliment and indicates that someone is paying attention. When a student in my classroom asks a sincere question, I consider it a compliment because the person cares enough to think, to try to clarify, and even to differ. If you can anticipate questions, you may also generate questions of greater depth.

3. Be aware of the fear factor in the challenges as action becomes more public. Is resistance happening as more people are realizing the implications of the change? Is the response generated by fear? This gives you an understanding of what is happening.

4. Know that sometimes the voices of challenge are internal. Sociologist Otto Scharmer helpfully offers three forces of resistance within us that show up where the weakness is greatest:

- Voice of Judgment (VOJ): Old and limiting patterns of judgment and thought. Without the capacity to shut down or suspend the VOJ, we will make no progress toward accessing creativity.
- Voice of Cynicism (VOC): Emotions of disconnection, such as cynicism, arrogance, and callousness (that prevent us from diving into the fields around us).
- Voice of Fear (VOF): Fear of letting go of the familiar self and world; fear of going forth; fear of surrendering into the space of nothingness. [5]

Many of us have had one or more of these voices visit, and to each of these the Christian faith offers a response:

- The gift of *faith in God* counters the voice of judgment. Our identity and sense of belonging give voice to a truth greater than ourselves.
- The gift of *hope* counters the voice of cynicism. Hope is deeply connected to the reality around us and sees a vi-

sion that God intends for the world. Such hope replaces cynicism with creativity and imagination.

- The gift of *love* counters the voice of fear, for love leads us beyond ourselves. Love replaces fear and moves us to live the justice found in a spirituality of communion and a globalizing solidarity.

The challenges we encounter all have responses in communities of faith that reach out in love to the wounded heart of humanity and the earth. This we believe, and with faith, hope, and love, together we act.

Notes

[1]W. H. Murray, *The Scottish Himalayan Expedition* (England: Dent, 1951), cited at http://www.goethesociety.org.

[2]This reference to the Holy Spirit is found in #3 of *The Pastoral Constitution on the Church in the Modern World*, http://www.vatican.va.

[3]C. Otto Scharmer, "Addressing the Blind Spot of Our Time: An Executive Summary of the New Book by Otto Scharmer, *Theory U: Leading from the Future as It Emerges*," 11, https://www.presencing.com.

[4]Timothy A. Byrnes, *Reverse Mission: Transnational Religious Communities and the Making of U.S. Foreign Policy* (Washington, DC: Georgetown University Press, 2011).

[5]C. Otto Scharmer, *Theory U: Leading from the Future as It Emerges* (San Francisco: Berrett-Koehler, 2009), 245.

7

Leadership for Change
How to Help Change Efforts Succeed

Every economic, political, social, or religious project
involves the inclusion or exclusion of the wounded lying on the side of the road. Each day, each of us faces
the choice of being a good Samaritan or an indifferent
bystander.
> —Cardinal Jorge Bergoglio, "Homily on the
> Good Samaritan," May 2003

Real leadership is a choice. . . . It is a willingness to be
responsible for what goes on in the world and take the
necessary stands and make the necessary interventions.
It requires thoughtful, creative, strategic, and courageous action to mobilize enough people to confront
reality, tackle their problems, and generate solutions
that produce morally based progress.
> —Dean Williams, *Real Leadership*

In the preceding chapters we have considered the world
around us through the lens of faith and our faith tradition. We
saw both the gifts and challenges present in our world today
and used the pastoral spiral process to bring forth experience
and engage in social analysis, faith reflection, and action to
respond to the cries of the world and to create a more just and
loving world. In essence, this is participating in living out the
reign of God today.

The pastoral spiral method is a tool to bring about a greater good, yet this process is not always easy or straightforward. We have all seen good persons as well as good organizations and countries founded on great values arrive at impasses. In 2011 the US Congress's impasse on budgets and taxes showed the level of vitriol and rancor that can emerge when leaders who pledge allegiance to the same flag choose not to or are unable to dialogue. The resistance can be so great that not even a "supercommittee" can resolve key issues. History and lived experience remind us that while change efforts don't always work, some change efforts are successful.

This brings us to two major questions. First, why don't great ideas that have come out of solid processes work? Second, could a problem be solved given better leadership? There are, in fact, many different ways we ask these questions. For example, if a "great idea" doesn't work, could it be because the proposed idea or solution is not so great after all? Or is it because of a lack of good leadership? Should competent leaders be able to solve all the issues we have today?

The process of the pastoral spiral can and does help many groups engage in positive change. At the same time, certain dynamics need to be considered if we are to be effective leaders for change. What is now happening in society and our churches indicates the complexities of our time. There must always be an ever attentive eye to the environment around us and to the gospel values we espouse. Good ideas require clear, well-thought-out strategies.

Second, we must look at the kind of leadership needed for change to transpire. Leadership for change and personal transformation is the focus of this chapter. While change usually deals with external differences that can occur a deeper shift essential for effective leadership is personal transformation, a gift of God's Spirit. When we open ourselves to a deep change of heart (*metanoia*), we are moved to more deeply respond together to God's invitation to create a kinder world. Transformation by its very nature forms us anew as we work *with* God to change and re-create structures.

The first section of the chapter identifies factors that contribute to the challenges we face. The second section considers the type of leadership needed to overcome these various challenges. A third section names some of the dynamics of change and explains why any change, even if positive, can run into resistance. How can leaders effectively manage such resistance? Finally, the last section examines some qualities of innovative leadership.

WHY IS THIS TIME SO CHALLENGING?

Three particular challenges represent potential directions for responses: (1) scale and complexity, (2) interdependence, and (3) the presence of new realities that require new skills.

The *scale and complexity of issues* continue to grow. The more carefully we look at a tree, the more we see the different elements, from the roots to the tips of new leaves. The more carefully we look at a topic such as global climate change, the more we see that it is impacting every region of the globe. A nuclear plant damaged in Japan by a tsunami leaks radiation all the way across the Pacific Ocean to San Diego and Seattle in the United States. While a global economy may raise the income of more people in developing countries, jobs being outsourced from the United States negatively impact unemployment figures in the United States.[1] What appears to be a solution to one part of the world may introduce a new challenge in another.

A related challenge is *interdependence*. For example, challenges to U.S. immigration reform are not simply legal challenges. Immigration questions connect issues of politics, economics, culture, religion, and many more. The European debt crisis impacts not only the Eurozone countries but Asian and North American markets as well. While the United Nations creates a global community committed to protecting human rights, it takes only one veto in the UN Security Council to prevent any action generally sought by the members.

A third challenge is that we are dealing with both *new realities* and *familiar realities that require new skills*, and we are at a loss at times on where to begin. Some of the problems we are facing today are beyond our known means of addressing them. The Arab Spring of 2011, which was unanticipated by most and greatly assisted by social media, continues to struggle to find its "summer of stability" in new governments in some countries, while others continue in turmoil. Economic policies that for a period of time created wealth have resulted in increasing austerity measures, antigovernment demonstrations, and new issues (for example, debt relief and bailouts in Greece, Spain, and Italy; the crisis of the euro; and the steadily increasing gap between the wealthy and the poor). Israel and Palestine continue to dance around elements of a permanent peace without finding a path to which both can commit, and at the time of this writing, Russia's push toward its former territories in Eastern Europe continues to result in global tensions. While we know that change is a constant, both in the world and in our lives, the world around us presents challenges that do not seem to respond to our current skill set. In some instances we are aware that certain practices need to change or adapt but we either resist or do not know how to approach the needed change. The paucity of civil, meaningful, and productive discourse and dialogue toward the common good is a clarion call in our time of vitriol and rancor. This seems to hold true from the US Congress to Venezuela, from Myanmar to Ukraine.

Nevertheless, deteriorating situations in the areas of economics, education, religious bodies, politics, and environment insist that we need a new way of leading and living. What we have done in the past is working for fewer people and is not sustaining our life on the planet. It is no longer enough just to stop injustice; instead we must try to create a new way forward. It is not enough to problem-solve; instead, we must try to create a new way that more closely resembles the vision of Jesus' reign. However, when we hear leaders suggest that we may have to change our use of goods, our ways of living, we often resist. The word "sacrifice" does not hold well with many.[2] Giving up for the common good something of what we want or think we need doesn't generally sit well with us. Suggestions that *we* sacrifice stir visions of wasted effort rather than an image of the One who loved us even unto death.

We seem to be in a quandary. We're often furious with leaders, even as we know that somehow we ourselves are as much part of the problem as they are. Both of these areas create resistance and fear as well as possibility and hope. This is part of what makes these times so challenging. And yet we want to go beyond problem-solving to creating something new. As we shall see later, this move creates its own frustrations that we must address.

All these challenges in themselves offer clues and possible directions for our response. Three essential skills that offer a response to these challenges include (1) seeing the big picture, (2) being willing to collaborate, and (3) being creatively innovative.

TYPES OF LEADERSHIP REQUIRED

Harvard University's Leadership Education Project offers a helpful lens for looking at the challenges of this time, identifying two key distinctions that leaders must make as they consider problems today: technical problems and adaptive problems.[3] *Technical problems* are those routine problems for which there are technical or certain answers that experts in particular areas can fix. For example, if your sink is leaking and you are not able to easily fix it, usually a plumber can. If your engine does not start, you need a mechanic rather than the Ford Motors CEO to fix your car. If your heart valve is leaking, you need a cardiologist rather than a general practitioner to help you.

Some problems need immediate attention and others need ongoing attention. When building a house in areas prone to earthquakes, architectural and engineering expertise is needed for the placement and dimensions of a building that can best withstand them. Ongoing expertise is needed across disciplines to adapt knowledge about earthquakes and construction into best practices and building codes and laws. Technical problems may be straightforward or complex, but experts know how to fix them.

Adaptive problems, on the other hand, require learning and innovation, and experts, even as they will have a role, cannot simply solve them as they would a technical problem. Adaptive problems generally require people to make choices based on greatest values. For example, an accountant can meet with the mayor of a city and say that the current spending will result in bankruptcy in five years and that the only way to keep the city solvent is to cut spending by 25 percent. A "technical" solution of cutting 25 percent of the education budget or of city pension payments would only create an uprising. Instead, controlling spending requires adaptive measures that seriously consider the greatest values of the community in creating a reasonable budget.

What do we do in light of our greatest values? For example, changing the death penalty law in a certain state will require adaptive measures rather than technical measures because the community's values about justice, punishment, and restitution need to be engaged. If not, even as changing the law is crucial, the law may change but the value supporting capital punishment will remain and perhaps become more entrenched than ever. Further, if experienced and otherwise successful teachers who are trained in new methods that promote higher literacy do not shift and use them in the classroom, even if it may take some trial and error in light of their particular students, the new methods will be of no use. In general, adaptive problems are initially more difficult because they require that we go beyond a technical solution, which requires a change in our thinking as well as acting.

Theresa M. Monroe, an expert in leadership, describes this kind of adaptive leadership:[4]

[In] a crisis we tend to look for the wrong kind of leadership. We call for someone with answers, decisiveness, strength, and a map of the future, someone who knows where we ought to be going; in short, someone who can make hard problems simple. But many of our problems are not simple. Instead of looking for saviors, we should be calling for leadership that will challenge us to face those situations for which there are no simple, painless solutions—the problems that require us to change our ways.[5]

In other words, instead of looking in vain for technical leadership to solve the problems, we must instead offer leadership that develops our adaptive capacities.[6] This is transformative leadership that creates a team or community of leaders for change.

Monroe further describes the defining characteristic of leadership to be "not simply the activity of gaining authority and influence, although these are important tools, but the mobilization of people to clarify aspirations and do the adaptive work of defining and solving the problems created by the gap between those aspirations and current conditions. In short, leadership is the activity of getting people to tackle tough problems."[7]

While we may say we want these difficult problems and situations resolved, we usually mean that we want to have the problems solved without any significant changes on *our* part or on *our* way of life. For example, while I may want healthcare reform to include all people in need of health care, I may want this reform only as long as it does not affect *my* level of care or the amount of money *I* pay. Or I may say that I want to be less dependent on foreign oil and also care for the environment in any further exploration of energy, but am I willing to look also at my own consumption of energy and start driving less? Am I willing to pay more for clothes so that garment workers can earn a living wage? Am I willing to eat mainly seasonal foods (that is, limit my food selections) if I want to support more locally grown products? To say yes requires personal adaptation as well as dialogue among groups with different visions and interests. As we shall see later, it means naming and facing our fears and working beyond that to common hopes and visions.[8]

Dean Williams, who works with adaptive leadership methods, offers this marker for measuring success:

> Leadership that targets authentic progress must gauge success by the degrees to which people are engaging the *real* problem versus symptoms, decoy concerns, or false tasks. That is, are the people facing or avoiding reality? Answers to tough problems are rarely obvious, and real solutions are elusive precisely because they require due regard for the ingrained values and habits of the groups, which members of the group protect with daily striving and sacrifice.
>
> Therefore, real leadership demands that the people make adjustments in their values, thinking, and priorities to deal with threats, accommodate new realities, and take advantage of emerging opportunities. At its essence, real leadership orchestrates social learning in regard to complex problems and demanding challenges.[9]

Such systemic change, Williams reminds us, is possible only through adaptive leadership, calling forth work across different values and priorities. He observes, "[Tough] problems often require an evolution of values, the development of new practices, and the revision of priorities."[10]

ELEMENTS OF ADAPTIVE AND CREATIVE LEADERSHIP

Leadership in these times requires a different skill set than simply "managing what is" more effectively. "What is" is no longer serving us well, and thus change is needed. Even the phrase, "It is what it is," no longer serves as a response.

Some of the biggest problems we are facing today require us to learn more adaptive skills, which in turn open us to create something beyond what we may initially imagine (see also chapter 5). Researchers in leadership name seven components that lead to adaptive and creative leadership.[11] Leaders must

- Name the issues clearly.
- Identify and clearly name the highest values from which we wish to act.
- Encourage and find ways to support different people and groups to find ways toward the goals that underline our great values.
- Stay focused and on course when we veer away from the vision.
- Engage our creativity.
- Take responsibility for what belongs to each person and each group as well as take particular responsibility for leading the group toward the goal.
- Build skill in communal discernment and decision-making.

What follows provides a broad mapping that groups can, in turn, adapt to meet their particular needs.

1. *Name the adaptive issues* clearly. Identifying the challenges means that we must acknowledge that the issue/problem is not a technical one, and so we must submit to a deeper process. This step invites both a big vision and a reflective lens.

2. *Identify and clearly name the highest values* from which we wish to act. Each member of the group needs to clearly state the key values early on so that the values are at the forefront later on when decisions are to be made. For example, Christian faith-based groups will articulate the deep values within the gospel tradition.

3. *Encourage and support different people and groups* to find ways toward the goals that underlie our greatest values. Leaders must know the people with whom they are working

and listen carefully to what is happening. This will include naming as many times as necessary core values and inviting people to live those values. Listening and pointing in a broad direction are important.

4. *Stay focused and on course* when there are efforts to veer away from the vision. Leaders need to keep "directing disciplined attention to the issues (counteracting human tendencies toward generating distractions, which we call work avoidance mechanisms)"[12] with both gentleness and firm, disciplined focus so that the movement toward change is not derailed. If derailing happens, the leader must emphasize the greater values to the group as encouragement and reminder.

An understanding of relationships, your colleagues, and the wider community is important. You must be attentive to the visible and invisible cues. If a group is working on a project, breaks, laughter, decent food, encouragement, and a voicing of progress will all be needed. Flexibility is also needed; sometimes a break will be postponed because the group is very close to a breakthrough. An effective leader doesn't push too much or too little but seeks a delicate and essential balance. A leader must regulate the level of social equilibrium to keep it within a productive zone of stress.

5. *Engage the creativity* in the group. The call to creativity is important at each step in the process of bringing about change. In *Evangelii Gaudium* (*The Joy of the Gospel*), as Pope Francis writes about the common good and society, and social issues in general, he addresses the need for creativity: "What we need, then, is to give priority to actions which generate new processes in society and engage other persons and groups who can develop them to the point where they bear fruit in significant historical events. (Without anxiety, but with clear convictions and tenacity.)"[13]

6. An effective leader must *take responsibility for what belongs to each person and each group* as well as take particular responsibility for leading the group toward the goal. Adaptive learning's premise is that the solution or movement

forward on an issue is the end result of each person in a group, and therefore each person needs to know how essential she or he is. Each person and each group have influence and thus participate in leadership. Each person has a role in opening up the complexity of the task to its manageable parts. This is part of learning how to solve adaptive problems. There is a point at which every person offers observations, including taking responsibility for where each helped or hindered the wider vision. Stay at the table and continue to ponder, probe, and walk with the problem. Leaders need to be present for coaching and encouragement, but they should not try to solve the problem by themselves apart from the group.

One effective adaptive leadership building tool is the format of the PeerSpirit Circle process, developed by Christina Baldwin and Ann Linnea, authors of *The Circle Way: A Leader in Every Chair*.[14] In circles that are convened, people take turns serving as host (organizers of the meeting), guardian (keeping people focused on important movements and calling for focusing silence as needed), and harvester (gathering the important points in the discussion and giving them to the group). This is one way to build skill and community.

7. *Build skill in communal discernment and decisionmaking.* The need for communal discussion throughout any process leading toward transformation is essential, which is stressed throughout each step of the pastoral spiral. Each member of the group must own any outcome for the process to be successful and long-lasting.

DYNAMICS OF CHANGE AND STRATEGIES FOR MANAGING RESISTANCE TO CHANGE

Knowledge of the dynamics of change is essential for adaptive and creative leaders, and ignorance of these dynamics has torpedoed and destroyed many good possibilities for change. Such knowledge also requires identifying and managing any resistance to change. This section examines ten dynamics of change and then five areas of resistance. Understanding these dynamics is essential for our time.

Ten Dynamics of Change

1. *A majority of change efforts fail.* A vast body of professional literature suggests that over 70 percent (and even higher) of change efforts end in failure.[15] This information is sobering yet helpful, as it invites us to look at what we can do to learn from "failure" in order, ultimately, to bring about positive change. To do so, we must attend to what helps change come about *and* what creates resistance or what thwarts change. Change efforts that begin with the externals but do not enter into deeper levels of experience will not be long-lasting, which is why so many efforts to change are not completed.

2. *The reason for change must be compelling.* Change, even positive change, usually results in anxiety. Change means that it may be a while before we know where we are going. This point is not easily accepted for most persons or organizations, even though as a people we are constantly changing. The needed change must be connected to our identity in some way. We must be able to clearly articulate the values we hold most deeply in order to create an inspiring vision for our journey. For example, changing our system of primary education requires much time, effort, and relearning. Most people have to be strongly motivated to accept this amount of work. Either something must not be working well (often the cause for change) or someone is likely dissatisfied enough to ask a question that cuts to the core of what we believe. Such questions might include: Are our children kinder and better able to lead in a world as diverse and global as ours as a result of our education? Will the way we educate give skills for living and learning in the world that is currently evolving? Otherwise, change remains on the surface and never penetrates the level needed for transformation.

3. *Tensions need to be managed.* For change to occur, there needs to be enough tension to initiate movement but not so

much tension or stress that people become paralyzed or revolt, thus stifling creativity. In other words, we need enough stress to shift but not enough to push people to fight back and undermine change efforts. In addition, the amount of time that change takes will itself be a tension. Some will say, "Change takes time, so let us give this more time." While change does take time, our gospel values often tell us that we must begin.

4. *Deep respect for the other is essential.* Some of the factors we deal with may be intangible, at least initially. Cultural, social, and many other factors are at least a bit shaken in adaptive change. This kind of change impacts not only a particular way of doing but a particular way of being. When a parish decides to focus more energy on the care of creation, for example, its liturgy, community life, and its other ministries, as good as they are, will be affected. Change needs to be approached with great respect for what has come before and with respect and care for the people who have brought the parish vision to the present. Respect for one another is a sacred trust that asks that we allow ourselves to change and are gentle with ourselves and one another as the changes occur. Even though there is likely some continuity, the shift in word, deed, and attitude may be significant and may also represent loss. (We discuss loss in the section on transition.) Gerald Arbuckle, a social anthropologist, hones in particularly on the need to respect and attend to cultural dynamics, "or culture will eat strategy for lunch every day."[16]

5. *Skill and capacity building are important.* Because change often means going in new directions, people may feel lost and unsure how to proceed—a sure way to hinder change efforts. Some areas of change, even adaptive ones, require new skills. When a significant change is introduced, the competence of a group and persons may decrease for a time. It will undoubtedly increase again, but the in-between time can generate a lot of anxiety. The new style, both technical and adaptive, will probably result in people feeling less competent and also that they are losing valuable time while they are trying to learn

and implement this new way of being together and working. Someone invariably asks if the implementation could be delayed until a better time—for example, when no projects and deadlines are pending, or when the election season is over. In truth, there is rarely a "better time." This is when the leaders must remind one another of the vision. (Here a reading of the Genesis account of the Israelites fleeing from Egypt and spending forty years in the wilderness may be helpful.)

Not only skills but capacities must be built, which requires persistence and patience. In his book *In Over Our Heads* Robert Kegan writes that adult development stages have to do with capacity and that even as adults we are continually growing in capacities to understand.[17] This would suggest the need for an awareness that people will be in different places, not because of intelligence, but perhaps because of differing cultures of learning.

6. *This is a time of great creativity*. As we approach the process of bringing about change we don't know exactly where we are going; as a result, many things that we took for granted ("this is how we've been doing it") can be opened up and examined. "Possibilitizing" is possible again. Leaders must offer continual encouragement because people in changing times may feel more anxiety about their jobs and organization. Hearing regular encouragement to be creative is important.

7. *Complexities increase during times of change*. In *Engaging Emergence: Turning Upheaval into Opportunity*, Peggy Holman writes, "Complexity increases as more diversity, connectivity, interdependence, or interactions become part of a system. The disruptive shifts occurring in our current systems are signs that these characteristics are on the rise."[18] There is good news in this statement. "Today's unprecedented conditions could lead to chaos and collapse, but they also contain the seeds of renewal. We can choose to coalesce into a vibrant, inclusive society through creative interactions among diverse people facing seemingly intractable challenges. In many ways, this path is counterintuitive. It breaks with traditional thinking

about change, including the ideas that it occurs top-down and that it follows an orderly plan, one step at a time."[19] If we try to be attentive to what we see and listen communally to what others are seeing, instead of being like the proverbial people who touched different parts of the elephant in the dark and could only "see" their part of the elephant, we together name what we are seeing, which then not only includes the elephant but also finds the way to walk, step by step, on the path we are called. Complexity requires persons and communities. We see and create better when we are doing so together.

8. *Clear and inclusive communication is essential.* Because change involves so much movement, it may be easy to neglect people, which can lead to misunderstandings, rumors, and obstruction. Establish clear lines of communication and keep them open to all, perhaps through a letter that is regularly updated or by means of lunches or other gatherings with leaders so that the various groups can be aware of what is happening and clearly communicate developments to everyone else. (Before a new building and residence hall were built a few years ago at a university, for example, many meetings, including public ones, were held to ask faculty, students, IT staff, and others about what would be essential. Then, once the building project began, emails were sent almost weekly to inform people about what had been done.) In addition, because most forms of change elicit so much anxiety, people's insecurities are often affected. Leaders must continue to find ways to build relationships with one another so that each person feels worth and belonging in the project.

9. *Change is not always good for everyone.* Even if change is inevitably good for the long haul, change may be a burden for some more than others, even in the short term. While it must not stop change, it must make us aware of the need for sensitivity. For example, I have a friend who works for the US Postal Service. At this time the organization is in financial difficulty and changes are needed if it is to survive. I commented to my friend, sympathetically I thought, that our house gets

lots of unsolicited and unwanted catalogs, unnecessary weight that he has to carry. His immediate response was, "But that's what's keeping my job at the moment!"

For me, the amount of paper used for unwanted catalogs is a justice issue based on my environmental concerns. I don't want to have catalogs mailed simply so that postal workers can have jobs. This seems an incredible lack of imagination! Other jobs are needed in our country. However, I did understand how changes that are to come will not be easy for some, especially those immediately affected. Do I believe a new way of communicating would cost the Postal Service far less? Yes. Do I also believe that people could be trained in other jobs that are more contemporary with our needs? Yes. However, this will not satisfy my friend, who would rather have his job than change jobs. Yet, imagine what life would be without change. Because change may not benefit all, the possibility of loss must be considered.

10. *Hope is found in the midst of change*, though sometimes you have to look very hard for it! The vision we seek should be our goal, but we must also celebrate markers along the way; even if they are incremental and small, they are still signs of hope.

Leaving Time for Transition

André Gide, a twentieth-century novelist, wrote, "One doesn't discover new lands without consenting to lose sight of the shore for a very long time."[20] Gide describes clearly the need to leave something behind in order to move on. At this stage we realize that what we have been doing is not working or needs to be changed, and this point is often when we begin to consider implementing change. This is really an in-between stage, a liminal stage, that must be attended to, or the changes implemented may find further resistance or not be fully implemented. William Bridges, in *Managing Transitions: Making the Most of Change*, calls this space the "neutral zone."[21] Difficult to pin down, many of us can probably describe it better than name it. An image might be someone on the trapeze who has just let go of one set of bars but hasn't yet gotten to the other set of bars or to the arms of the catcher. Major transitions of any kind contain some liminal or in-between spaces.

Effective leaders must be good at leading in a time of enormous changes. As we go through change, we must attend to transitions if we are to manage the change well. Bridges encouragingly writes that "chaos is not simply 'a mess.' Rather, it is the primal state of pure energy to which the person (or an organization, society, or anything else in transition) must return for every true new beginning."[22] With this in mind, we move to managing resistance.

Managing Resistance to Change

Now that we have named some of the dynamics of change to which leaders must attend, we turn to how we might deal with another natural part of dealing with change—resisting it. Resistance gives us information. It tells us that some change is being felt, and the level and kind of resistance tell us how we might proceed. While this phase is difficult, knowing that resistance is a part of the process may also save leaders from premature failure. What might the fear or anxiety about change or the resistance to change look like, and how might we deal with it? Let us look at five modes of resistance and some ways to manage them.

1. One form of resistance to change comes in the form of *criticism*.[23] If individuals or members of a group experience their own incompetence to a high degree, a leader will likely be attacked. Given a certain level of tension, the attacks can be very personal, including comments about appearances. An unfortunate example in 2010–2011 was the continuing attack on President Obama's citizenship. This was a personal attack that stemmed from political, economic, social, and cultural tensions. While there is no real excuse for this sort of personal attack, the challenges of change can create an environment that results in this kind of public questioning.

However, leaders must not be surprised by such criticism. The reality is that the criticism is not about the person, but rather about the person's role or authority. On that level the criticism is not personal but is a manifestation of tensions. However, such criticism still often feels hurtful. The task here is to not be surprised by such a response. People hit walls and resort to criticism because many do not have the capacity for change in these times. The task is to invite and raise people's capacity for change, and this task has stages as well. It may take some time, however, and purists or idealists who want it all at the same time will not survive as leaders even though their goals are admirable. All people need to maintain respect for the other, carefully pacing the rate at which people experience stress and frustration.

2. *Denial and avoidance are part of the process.* Dean Williams, in *Real Leadership: Helping People and Organizations Face Their Toughest Challenges*, writes,

> Humans will go to great lengths to avoid facing their real problems. As individuals and in groups, people tend to shy away from addressing tough, complex, painful problems that are caused, perpetuated, or protected by their own values, habits, and priorities. Rather than look at the reality of the predicament they are in, they often distort what they see, put the problem outside themselves, scapegoat others, and create distractions—all as a way of distancing themselves from responsibility for the real issue.[24]

We often deny or avoid something when we know that naming a problem means we will have to address it. Sometimes employees do not want to name a problem because an investigation will reveal more than they wish. Sometimes workers do not want to name a problem with a product because it will mean a large recall or loss of profit. Sometimes avoidance and denial happen because a group does not know how to deal with an issue. An interesting example comes from the newspaper industry.

In 2009, fifteen thousand newspaper employees lost jobs, and over one hundred papers closed. "The decline was predictable, yet virtually every newspaper is choosing extinction over experimentation."[25] In addition, "Even when we know we must change, 90% of us won't alter our behavior to fit the new situation. We choose death over adaption." So writes change and leadership expert Alan Deutschman, author of *Change or Die: The Three Keys to Change at Work or in Life*.[26] For 10 percent of newspaper owners, however, that invitation turned upheaval into opportunity. What could have been done? Instead of avoiding the situation, the newspaper industry could have worked cooperatively. If the true value was providing newsworthy information to the public, a reading of the signs of the times could have reframed the disaster as an opening to design a format that would keep news flowing. This approach requires looking more deeply and pausing to see how best to serve the community where the need still exists for news.

A less drastic example is my experience a few years ago in learning to teach online courses. Some years ago, a graduate school where I was teaching hired an expert to work with the faculty to develop online education courses. Generally, the faculty was not eager to do so, but a few adventurous members started learning and teaching (after some coaxing). I resisted. I knew at some point I would need to learn how to teach using this new model, but I avoided taking on this responsibility in part because I had other priorities and didn't want to give the extra time that would be needed to learn this new set of skills. In addition, I was not convinced pedagogically that online education was of equal merit to person-to-person live education. At the same time I knew that there were people who weren't able to take advantage of graduate theological education because of where they lived. I had traveled to such areas, where online education is the only possible way to get an education. This could meet an unmet need, something I support.

What chipped away and eventually removed my resistance, however, was a year when I was required to commute often between two cities. At that point, learning online education was part of keeping my job (i.e., change or die!). To my surprise, with coaching from a wonderfully skilled IT educator, I was soon able to experiment with the media, using not only voice but also video, PowerPoint, music, sidebar commentaries, YouTube sites, and more. I actually did find what was effective and what wasn't, learning from my failures as well as my successes. But my earlier resistance that resulted in avoidance went by the wayside once there was a very compelling reason to learn: my employment was at stake.

3. *Decreased productivity happens*. When major changes are afoot, an initial decrease in productivity occurs. Theresa Monroe calls this an "implementation dip."[27] (This decrease is not intentional the way a worker's strike is. It is simply that the changes take more time to learn and implement and is part of the learning process. Here, leaders can either push to have more done or they could use this time to engage different dimensions of the work that would introduce colleagues to a new perspective or a new interest base. Encouragement in various forms is necessary.

4. *Quick solutions are not necessarily the best solutions*. In a challenging situation, looking for the first or easiest way to lower the stress is only natural. While this may not solve an adaptive problem, it may offer a temporary *technical* solution. The leader's task is to encourage further pondering and experimentation. The strategy to postpone problem-solving until change comes is a long-lasting *adaptive* change that is accepted by the people involved.

5. *Identify the roots of resistance*.[28] Perhaps the best way to deal with resistance to change is to identify the actual root of the resistance and slowly chip away at it. Deep resistance may not go away with argument or reasoning but only by the slower process of building up people's skills and awareness. If, for example, there is resistance in a parish to working on immigration reform because of great division among members on the topic, the leader may need to begin by developing skills

for dialogue. If financial concerns are significant in a rural community and money is a major determinant for openness to fracking (hydraulic drilling), then consideration must be given to all the financial implications as well as issues of safety and property use. Knowing that finances are a key concern provides a leader with important information. It indicates what further information is needed and what options might be available if financial concerns govern decisionmaking.

QUALITIES OF INNOVATIVE LEADERSHIP

What qualities or virtues are necessary for leadership in this time of great change? As indicated in earlier chapters, virtues, like our human nature, are also dynamic. Therefore, as we continue to learn, grow, and mature, our level of understanding and our ability to deeply live the virtues evolve.

This section highlights eight core virtues for innovative leaders:

- Vision
- Reflection
- Courage
- Collaboration
- Commitment to sustainability
- Compassionate solidarity
- Curiosity
- Joy

The qualities or virtues of leadership can be both personal and collective. While each virtue is developed by an individual, social or societal virtues can be increasingly embodied by a group. In addition, while no leader may fully embody all of these virtues, working as a group allows each member to bring his or her gifts to be used by and for the whole. Further, some of these virtues are naturally interconnected and will reinforce each other. Certainly other virtues can be named, especially to fit a particular context. Finally, the virtue of love grounds all the rest.

I describe each of these virtues or qualities briefly, using the lenses of theology and contemporary insights into effective leadership. Each description of a virtue is then followed by a reflection question and a related practice. You are also invited to engage your own creativity by posing further questions and creating a brief exercise of your own.

Vision. Two different, though not unrelated, types of vision are necessary. The first is a vision that can see interconnections in the big picture, in the larger system. Leaders try to see how the whole works in order to understand the parts and their interconnections. First and foremost, the leader needs to see the whole as part of an ever larger whole. The second type of vision is the vision to create. Effective leaders can see where they desire to go, even if the details are not at all clear in the beginning. Thus, the leader is prophetic, not only seeing where the current vision fails but also where the vision (of the reign of God) invites us to go.

- Reflection: Who would have either type of vision described above?
- Practice: (1) Look at one current issue and write what you see as the big picture of the issue. (2) Offer a vision of what you see as the direction that is needed for this issue to be transformed.

Reflection. Reflection is a virtue that frames our highest values by connecting us with God and with one another. A life that includes regular time for silence and reflection—thoughtful openness to hearing and seeing what is being invited—moves us toward wisdom; it bridges our various experiences of life, sets aside time with God, and provides insights. While there is no guarantee, wisdom generally does flow out of this open space in one's life for the connection with God and the spiritual life. Reflection serves as a sifting and sorting space. Reflective space can open up our blind spots and also give us the insight for the next steps. Self-knowledge (of self and of group) grows here, as does knowledge about one's resistances and one's deepest values and hopes. The need for reflection and reflective space is considerable.

Interestingly, Dean Williams writes that wisdom in leadership is difficult to find:

> Real leadership is not easy. It requires considerable wisdom to be a leader on multiple adaptive challenges and succeed. The work of real leadership is often to defend or promote particular values and practices, while discouraging or phasing out other values and practices that impede progress, even though some people hold dearly to the impeding values and practices. Therefore, whoever exercises real leadership must *discern* (italics mine) which values to promote and protect, and which values need to be challenged or changed. It takes a degree of wisdom, not simply experience or intelligence, to know what to promote and how to promote it so a group can do the adaptive work.[29]

A faith dimension with a tradition of wisdom and practices of prayer, contemplation, and reflection that flows into action can well serve the wider community. Discernment, conscience formation, prayer, and communal reflection all promote and serve wisdom, and can make more possible the transformation of self, group, and the world. Dean Williams also notes that wisdom is part of the path to success and is "an ongoing process of continuous learning and discovery—for the one leading and also the people."[30]

One of the byproducts of such reflection is the ability to reflect without immediately rushing into premature action. This can create an intermediate space that enables one to continue to think in difficult situations. Researchers further point out that "alongside such positive capabilities there is a need to consider the contribution of negative capability, that is, the capacity to sustain reflective inaction. This is described as 'negative' because it involves the ability not to do something, to resist the tendency to disperse into actions that are defensive rather than relevant for the task."[31] It "requires a capability, which manifests in behaviors such as waiting, observing, and listening, that are not negative per se but are, as it were, at the opposite pole to action as intervention."[32]

- Reflection: When have you found "negative capability" assisting people in deepening their reflection?
- Practice: Take twenty minutes each day to sit in silence. If this is not your regular practice, begin with a timer and have five minutes of silence. Each week add a minute of silence until you reach twenty minutes.
- Group practice: Before a meeting begins, sit in silence together for five minutes.

Courage is the virtue that leaders need to enact what they most believe, even if the responses or results may not be satisfactory. Courage is a virtue, the ability to make a choice and act on it even in difficulty. A person must have the capacity to face the fears, resistance, and even unknowns that may occur when making a difficult decision. The kind of courage required is evidenced by the Latin root, *cor*, meaning heart. Courage is the capacity to act out of our deepest values, from our heart; at its best, courage flows out of contemplation and encourages creativity.

A powerful and sometimes forgotten image of courage comes from Mary, who said yes to mystery when she was asked to be the mother of God. The poem "Annunciation" by Denise Levertov, which we mentioned in chapter 2, offers a glimpse of courage that required consent on many levels. In speaking of Mary, Levertov states simply, "But we are told of meek obedience. No one mentions courage." I would suggest that in Mary's yes we find four moments of courage. First, courage implies choice. The person must be free to choose. Second, while God gives the gift of courage, God also waits for the person to choose. Waiting happens. Third, courage means a choice is made with neither a poor sense of self nor anger at being forced to do something. Fourth, courage requires conscious consent, a yes, and genuine openness. This strong image of Mary reminds us that courage requires deep freedom for consent, which is very different than saying yes while resisting the entire way. Only a reflective, contemplative spirit can have this type of courage.

Courage also helps leaders honestly see what is happening in a situation. Courage allows one to name truths and to make the necessary changes to change a situation for the better. Courageous leaders continually face the challenging realities, helping others deal with them.

Courage requires dealing with voices of judgment, cynicism, and fear so that they do not unhinge the process of change that will flow out of risk-taking and experimenting.[33] Leaders must be particularly attuned to this. *Responsibility* is thus one of the markers of courage for individuals as well as for groups; to take action is to be able to respond to problems.

When we can live out of a contemplative lens and a willingness to see the world through the eyes of God and a heart of love, we can let go of what is not essential and move toward what will bring more life. Although our actions may bear a considerable cost at times, such sacrifice is a natural outpouring of love.

Finally, a wonderful connection exists between beauty, imagination, creativity, and courage. To spend time in beauty, with nature, and in the arts stimulates the contemplative and creative, ultimately linking us to solidarity and justice. John O'Donohue expresses this beautifully when he writes,

> When we lose sight of beauty our struggle becomes tired and functional. When we expect and engage the Beautiful, a new fluency is set free within us and between us. The heart becomes rekindled and our lives brighten with unexpected courage. It is courage that restores hope to the heart. In our day-to-day lives, we often show courage without realizing it. However, it is only when we are afraid that courage becomes a question. Courage is

amazing because it can tap in to the heart of fear, taking that frightened energy and turning it toward initiative, creativity, action, and hope. When courage comes alive, imprisoning walls become frontiers of new possibility, difficulty becomes invitation, and the heart comes into a new rhythm of trust and sureness. There are secret sources of courage inside every human heart; yet courage needs to be awakened in us. The encounter with the Beautiful can bring such awakening. Courage is a spark that can become the flame of hope, lighting new and exciting pathways in what seemed to be dead, dark landscapes.[34]

- Reflection: When have you acted with courage? What helped you do so?
- Practice: List a practice that will help you maintain courage (i.e., chanting a mantra, having accountability to someone, etc.).
- Do something. Take one very small step that acts on your deepest values.

Collaboration. Leaders build teams, form circles, and invite a community of conversation, reflection, and action to build relationships and create new systems and structures. Collaboration replaces competition, but not the energy to learn, succeed, or do one's very best. The community of conversation includes not only the specific group looking at a reality or situation but continually invites others beyond the circle to join an ever-widening circle. Leadership is a collective phenomenon that requires persons to work together. Leaders create the spaces for collaboration to happen, realizing that all are needed in the reign of God, and demonstrate their trust in persons and the group by their participation.

A marker of collaboration as a virtue is the practice and disposition of welcoming the other in a way that sees and promotes the possibilities and gifts in others. Leaders must also create, hold, and encourage spaces for community to be built. This may be allowing time for breaks, play, and conversations that matter. Dialogue is essential because, in the course of living, hurts happen and forgiveness and reconciliation are needed. The virtue of community attends to all these pieces.

Finally, communal discernment, flowing from contemplation and solidarity, is an essential element of community. So often discernment is limited to the individual; however, communal discernment today has much to offer the group and the world.

- Reflection: When have you experienced collaboration? What were the elements of collaboration that made collaboration successful?
- Practice: Decide on a weekly practice to build community in your neighborhood, family, or work. Do it.

Commitment to sustainability. Effective leaders must be attentive that every practice and action consider the sustainability of Earth. New actions must underscore care for Earth. In addition, leaders must ensure that sustainability education is part of any action, and that the process can withstand scrutiny.

- Reflection: What practice do you have that is intentional about Earth sustainability (e.g., using recycled bags for grocery shopping; eating locally grown foods; travel and carbon footprints)?
- Practice: Find one quote or image that speaks to you of Earth sustainability and place it on your computer or some other place where you will regularly see it when you work on projects.

Compassionate solidarity. Solidarity is necessary for leaders and communities to be prophetic and capable of transformation, and solidarity will need to be grounded in compassion. The Greek word *splanchnon* is about the gut's wrenching in response to the suffering of another, moving a person to seek another way beyond the suffering. Compassion calls forth solidarity.

Solidarity connects me to my neighbor so that my neighbor's

joys, hopes, struggles, and sorrows are mine. My humanity is linked with the humanity of the other, and any inhumanity toward my neighbor demeans my humanity as well. Solidarity calls me to look at life alongside my neighbor, particularly asking my neighbor who has been excluded or in any way marginalized from the human community how we might together change that reality. I act in conjunction with my neighbor. Solidarity makes neighbors interdependent. Matthew 25:31–46 is an apt description of the neighbor who calls us to solidarity.

Pope Francis writes about solidarity in *Evangelii Gaudium* (*The Joy of the Gospel*). He reminds us of the need for structural changes and mindset changes as he interprets Jesus' command to his disciples:

> "You yourselves give them something to eat!" (Mark 6:37): it means working to eliminate the structural causes of poverty and to promote the integral development of the poor, as well as small daily acts of solidarity in meeting the real needs which we encounter. The word "solidarity" is a little worn and at times poorly understood, but it refers to something more than a few sporadic acts of generosity. It presumes the creation of a new mindset which thinks in terms of community and the priority of the life of all over the appropriation of goods by a few.[35]

The transformation and conversion required for solidarity are clear: "These convictions and habits of solidarity, when they are put into practice, open the way to other structural transformations and make them possible. Changing structures without generating new convictions and attitudes will only ensure that those same structures will become, sooner or later, corrupt, oppressive, and ineffectual."[36]

Markers of solidarity include pragmatism, accompaniment, radical availability, and a global focus.

- Reflection: Where have you seen solidarity (rather than simple charity) in practice?

- Practice: Choose one, just one area of need that you are aware of in the world. Learn about it. Tell someone else about it. Choose one small act in response.

Curiosity. Curiosity is an essential attribute for our time. Curiosity is an interest in the other—in the other's interests and perspectives. Curiosity requires respect for the other, acknowledging that what another thinks or desires deserves consideration. Curiosity rooted in respect will be sensitive to what the other holds as a value and seeks to understand. Thus, curiosity is also rooted in humility. Humility, which means truth, uses curiosity in order to find the truth that the other offers. Statements such as, "Please tell me more about this priority," or "Help me see how you understand this issue so I can see it more fully," move us to deeper understandings of the other and of the structure of the topic we are considering. Curiosity also allows us to delve more deeply into conversation with others, some of whom have a vision and view different from ours.

Curiosity leads us to creativity (which we have noted above, particularly in chapter 5). We know that creativity, too, is a virtue that can be learned. Robert E. Franken, in *Human Motivation*, writes, "Creativity is defined as the tendency to generate or recognize ideas, alternatives, or possibilities that may be useful in solving problems, communicating with others, and entertaining ourselves and others."[37] In addition,

> In order to be creative, you need to be able to view things in new ways or from a different perspective. Among other things, you need to be able to generate new possibilities or new alternatives. Tests of creativity measure not only the number of alternatives that people can generate but the uniqueness of those alternatives. The ability to generate alternatives or to see things uniquely does not occur by chance; it is linked to other, more fundamental qualities of thinking, such as flexibility, tolerance of ambiguity or unpredictability, and the enjoyment of things heretofore unknown.[38]

Curiosity and creativity often involve experimentation, and the response to a question of "I don't know" is an invitation to explore, as possibilities abound. Such experimentation or exploration can make available to us that which we have not yet noticed. It can be a very productive time. Freedom is yet another marker, and leaders must both encourage and protect the spaces for creativity—for others and for oneself. A learning curve naturally develops when we engage our curiosity and creativity as our adaptive capacities and capabilities grow and mature.

- Reflection: What were you curious about at a younger age that led you to learn and explore more?
- Practice: Choose one person, issue, or decision you don't understand or which you differ about yet do not completely understand. Create some curiosity questions (ones that come out of a sincere desire to understand rather than trap the other) and find someone who can offer some insights. (If no person is available, as a second option, look for an answer and insight on a website that is supportive of the person, issue, or decision.)

Joy. A final quality of leadership is joy. Joy comes from a source much deeper than optimism or even hearing good news, though joy is not unaware of these. Joy, like hope, comes from a belief that beyond suffering or what seems intractable are more possibilities for change and transformation. Joy emanates from the risen Christ, from the resurrection experience we celebrate on Easter Sunday. Joy comes from a deep conviction; it is a gift of faith that tells us that God can redeem and transform all things to God's desire for creation. Choice is not left out, but joy emanates from a belief that God is in the midst of all we do. Joy comes from *disponibilidad*, radical availability, which is an act of surrender to God. It is not the surrender that comes from defeat but a surrender that is a letting go into God. Hence we hear of "risking joy," which means a letting go ultimately into God's plans for humanity and all of creation, knowing that in God all is possible.

- Reflection: What does joy look like for you? Where have you seen it? When have you found it in yourself? What was the most recent cause of your joy?
- Practice: Find someone you consider joyful and see what the fruits of this joy are. Find out more about the person.
- Practice: Reread selections from Pope Francis's *Gospel of Joy*. Choose one practice that invites joy (allowing Jesus to encounter you; being with the people ["smell like the sheep"], etc.).

Notes

[1] Eduardo Porter, "A Global Boom, but Only for Some," *New York Times,* March 18, 2014, http://www.nytimes.com.

[2] I am not here speaking of sacrifices that demean the dignity or rights of another, female or male.

[3] The ideas on technical and adaptive leadership are indebted to the work of Martin Linsky and Ronald A. Heifetz, *Leadership on the Line: Staying Alive through the Dangers of Leading* (Boston: Harvard Business Review Press, 2002).

[4] I am greatly indebted to the work of Theresa M. Monroe, RSCJ, on leadership. Her work on leadership is an underlying resource for this section and the third section.

[5] Theresa M. Monroe, "Leadership in Tough Times," *Touchstone*, Winter 1996, 14–15. Monroe also writes, "What kind of leader do we need in these times? While we tend to say we'd like to have someone who could solve all our problems (savior or magician)," the call is really for "leadership that will challenge us to face those situations for which there are no simple, painless solutions—the problems that require us to change our ways. . . . We need a different idea of leadership that develops our adaptive capacities, rather than inappropriate expectations of authority."

[6] Ibid., 14.

[7] Ibid., 14–15.

[8] Ibid., 15. Monroe reminds us, "[Yet,] although many people claim that they yearn for leadership, they often seek protection instead. They may want to reduce the budget deficit, for example, but then they instruct their political representatives, 'Don't close my factory, my army

base, or raise my taxes!' When the situation involves complex problems for which technical remedies and easy answers do not exist, making progress often requires engaging the community of interested parties. Resolving issues demands getting various factions with competing interests and problem definitions to incorporate to some degree one another's perspective and evidence. Thus, leadership frequently means getting people to face the internal contradictions in their own lives and communities" (15).

[9]Williams, *Real Leadership*, 5. Williams also writes, "People must learn why they are in a particular condition in order to invent pathways forward that produce genuine progress, as opposed to hollow and temporary gains. If the people refuse to face hard truths, are weak at learning, or learn the wrong things, then their problem-solving capacity will suffer, and their group or enterprise may eventually wither and die" (5).

[10]Ibid., 7.

[11]Monroe offers four points. I use the basics of the four points (see below) and then develop some; I also add three more essential tasks for leadership today. I bring them together because the seven together are essential tasks for leadership and adaptive and creative change for this time. Monroe places these elements into four basic parts of the leadership task: (1) identifying the adaptive challenges (which requires both the clarification of orienting values and the diagnosis of the problem situation); (2) directing disciplined attention to the issues (counteracting human tendencies toward generating distractions, which we call work avoidance mechanisms); (3) developing responsibility-taking for solving complex problems among members of the community or organization, without abandoning them (giving the work back to people while holding them through the adaptive change process); and (4) regulating the level of social disequilibrium (chaos, confusion, conflict) to keep it within a productive zone of stress. In these ways, those who lead direct a process whereby the organization or community learns its way toward a solution, ("Leadership in Tough Times," 15).

[12]Ibid., 15.

[13]Pope Francis, *The Joy of the Gospel* (Washington, DC: United States Conference of Catholic Bishops, 2013), 223.

[14]Christina Baldwin and Ann Linnea, *The Circle Way: A Leader in Every Chair* (San Francisco: Berrett-Koehler, 2010).

[15]See, for example, William J. Rothwell and Roland Sullivan, eds., *Practicing Organization Development: A Guide for Consultants* (San Francisco: Pfeiffer, 2005), 15; Norman Wolfe, "Change Efforts Fail Over 70% of the Time—Why?" December 10, 2010, http://www.fastcompany.com; Linsky and Heifetz, *Leadership on the Line*.

[16]Gerald A. Arbuckle, "Change and Culture," lecture at Catholic Theological Union, Chicago, October 7, 2013.

[17]Robert Kegan, *In Over Our Heads: The Mental Demands of Modern Life*, 4th ed. (Boston: Harvard University Press, 1998).

[18]Peggy Holman, *Engaging Emergence: Turning Upheaval into Opportunity* (San Francisco: Berret Kohler, 2010), 9.

[19]Ibid.

[20]André Gide, *The Counterfeiters* (New York: Vintage, 1973).

[21]William Bridges, *Managing Transitions: Making the Most of Change*, 3rd rev. ed. (Boston: Nicholas Brealey, 2010).

[22]William Bridges, *Transitions: Making Sense of Life's Changes*, Revised 25th Anniversary Edition. (Cambridge, MA: Da Capo Press, 2004).

[23]Many insights on this point come from a lecture by Theresa Monroe, "Challenge of Leadership," University of San Diego, Fall 2010.

[24]Williams, *Real Leadership*, 11.

[25]Holman, *Engaging Emergence*, 7.

[26]Alan Deutschman, *Change or Die: The Three Keys to Change at Work or in Life* (New York: HarperCollins, 2007).

[27]Monroe, lecture at San Diego, 2010.

[28]Ibid.

[29]Williams, *Real Leadership*, 7–8 (emphasis added).

[30]Ibid., 10.

[31]Peter Simpson, Robert French, and Charles E. Harvey, "Leadership and Negative Capability," *Human Relations* 55, no. 10 (2002): 1210.

[32]Ibid., 1211.

[33]See Otto Scharmer, *Theory U: Leading from the Future as It Emerges* (Cambridge, MA: SOL, 2007); for further explanations of these three voices, see 42–43, 245–46.

[34]John O'Donohue, *Beauty: The Invisible Embrace* (New York: HarperCollins, 2005), 6.

[35]Pope Francis, *Joy of the Gospel*, 188.

[36]Ibid., 189.

[37]Robert E. Franken, *Human Motivation*, 3rd ed. (Independence, KY: Cengage Learning, 1993), 396.

[38]Ibid., 394.

8

Doing Social Analysis Using the Pastoral Spiral

A Sampling of Cases

By this time some readers must be asking themselves, "Does this really work? Can I do this, or can we do this in our context?" This chapter offers two specific and very different case studies of situations in which the pastoral spiral was used to bring about positive change. The final section of the chapter offers brief examples of how this method has been used in international contexts.

We have come a long way, having begun in the first two chapters by considering the world around us and the world with God in our midst. The next four chapters kept these frameworks of world and God and looked at the process of the pastoral spiral through four stages: experience, social analysis, faith reflection, and action. Chapter 7 explored the role of leadership in bringing about change and transformation. This chapter reports on two groups that used the process of the pastoral spiral to deal with a specific issue.[1] It is interesting to note how the pastoral spiral was put into practice by each group because each group adapted it to its context and need. These narratives tell about ordinary people who were concerned enough about an issue to choose to walk together through a process in order to make change happen. The hope is that readers understand how they, too, can bring about needed transformation.

Each narrative describes what concerned or motivated the group in the first place, some of the experience they already had and what they needed to add, what they found in their analysis, and why and how they chose certain directions for action.

CASE STUDY 1: FROM DOMESTIC VIOLENCE TO DOMESTIC PEACE

This first case emerged from a capstone project for students graduating from a school of theology in which they had to take on a project of social analysis. Groups of three formed with a desire to take on an "unmet need" but without a particular project in mind. Two groups involved with a city parish decided to see if an unmet need existed that the parish would like them to consider; this is the account of one group's project.

Choosing a Topic

The three students made individual appointments with the pastor and the pastoral team, including pastoral staff members such as the parish receptionist. What slowly began to emerge, first in hints and then in stated concerns, was the issue of domestic violence. Newspaper accounts that year gave alarming statistics about domestic violence in the city and even the state. Interviews with parish staff elicited stories of suspected domestic violence within families, although they provided no direct evidence of abuse. Staff learned that when this issue surfaced in families, and particularly in younger families, those families often disappeared from the parish roster and events. The staff was unsure of what to do, concerned that speaking up without proof would offend or alienate the family, removing any further opportunity to assist.

When the group met together after these preliminary conversations, the three members discovered that the concern came up in more than one venue, which motivated them to pursue the issue. However, none of the three had much experience in this area, so they recognized the need to do basic research. As they went online, they realized that their city was getting quite a bit of attention because of the increasing numbers of instances of domestic violence.

Gathering Information for Social Analysis

The group of three then made an appointment with the director of the city's Center for Domestic Violence. Their conversation with Gloria, the center's director, confirmed what they were seeing online. They also learned that generally there are far more incidents of domestic violence than are reported, so the statistics likely indicated that the issue was already far more serious than appeared in the news.

The group now realized that it had a topic that was limited enough to begin further work. The group also decided to connect its effort somehow to that specific parish. At this point, the students began to undertake *social analysis*.

As they began dividing up areas of responsibility, Gloria offered to ask some of her clients if they would be willing to share their stories. Because no group member personally knew anyone who was a survivor of domestic violence, Gloria felt that the group might easily come up with some stereotypes of who might experience such violence, so one evening two women whom Gloria invited shared their stories in a way that galvanized the students. Their eyes were opened, their hearts were moved, and their energy was focused. In later reflections each of the group members shared how the reality of domestic violence became personal for the first time.

As the group approached the actual task of social analysis, they began to examine all the factors connected to domestic violence, and they listed all the individuals, groups, and institutions that they thought in any way intersected with domestic violence. Each student used a different charting system in an effort to visualize the largest number of possibilities. As their research continued, they added names and groups. This stage was the beginning of seeing the connections, understanding how some relationships could interrupt and stop domestic abuse, and observing where new systems could be created to prevent further abuse.

Their *economic analysis* revealed the impact that poverty or a fear of poverty had on whether someone experiencing abuse actually left a spouse or partner. Mothers often decided to stay with their abusive partner "for the sake of the children." Later, Gloria also connected the group with a young man whose mother had stayed in an abusive marriage for the sake of the children. His nightmare ended only after his father died in a car accident while under the influence of alcohol. He told of how difficult it was for his mom to take care of the kids financially. This conversation was typical of how individual stories were transforming all members of the group. They realized that all this information needed to be shared with the parish staff, but initially they were not sure how to go about doing so. Eventually, they did share some of the stories they heard with the parish team, including directors of programs such as the Rite of Christian Initiation of Adults (RCIA), those working with youth and young adults, religious education coordinators, and sacramental coordinators.

As the group began to analyze *political* factors, they discovered very uneven laws for intervening with and prosecuting offenders. States had different definitions of domestic violence and different processes for dealing with it. State support for victims and survivors was weak or lacking altogether, and most victims regarded shelters as a last resort. *Cultural analysis* showed them how diversely people think of what constitutes abuse or violence. They began by developing a very clear and basic definition of domestic violence, and quickly realized that various cultures and cultural traditions regarded domestic disputes and domestic violence quite differently. They encountered the shame that came with admitting to abuse, whether male or female. They learned that the culture of silence in families, ethnic groups, countries, and churches was deafening.

When they started looking at *religious* perspectives, they wondered what they would find. Did churches actually address the issue? Beginning with their own Roman Catholic tradition, much to their surprise, they found that in 1992 the Catholic bishops of the United States had prepared a statement, *When I Call for Help: A Pastoral Response to Domestic Violence against Women*, and then updated it in 2002. They were heartened to see this resource, for it includes some definitions, data, understandings of the people's realities, and resources for pastoral staffs. This led to further research about churches and domestic violence, and they found that over the past ten years there has been a slow increase in the amount of literature available. While the social sciences were clearly addressing the issue of domestic violence, theologians and churches were only beginning to take on this topic.

At one point the group decided it had completed sufficient analysis to see the different "leveraging" points influential in stopping domestic violence. Culture, economics, politics, and religion all played a part and could be used to respond in some way to what seemed to be a growing crisis. Yet what was this small group of three students to do? Although they had no clear plan in mind, they knew something had to be done. At this point, it became apparent that undertaking this project as a graduation requirement was now in the background; by this time it had become a matter of personal interest for the students. But where should they begin?

Faith Reflection

They then turned to the next step in the process of the pastoral spiral—directed faith reflection. Faith reflection had been part of their experience from the time they chose the topic of domestic violence. Each person had committed to personally praying daily for victims, survivors, and abusers. They also prayed each day for the various players and actors who either do or can offer assistance to stop abuse and to stop the systems that allow for abuse. The personal realities of domestic violence were already part of their prayer, and as they shared their research with friends and classmates they invited them to pray as well. The parish staff and program directors were now also more attuned to the reality, and domestic violence became part of their prayer as they prayed for this small group, for their parishioners, and for all people affected.

As the group met and reflected on what they were reading, hearing, and seeing, one thing became clear. They did not want to create yet another program focused on domestic violence. Once violence did happen and was noticed or reported, as terrible as it was, other groups could be engaged, including the city's Center for Domestic Violence. As they realized that something more was needed, they spent time together and apart, in silence and in sharing, struggling with this question for a few weeks.

Planning for Action

The idea of domestic peace emerged. When one student first said it out loud, the other two immediately affirmed the idea. Even the wording was attractive, leaning toward what they wanted to create. Yes, domestic violence needed to be stopped; that is one way of changing a system. Another way is to create something new that would eliminate the abuse. Domestic peace was their chosen lens. The students knew it was where they were being called to go, and the group's energy was strengthened as it immediately latched on to the idea of domestic peace. Quickly ideas began to emerge. While the group could not take on everything related to domestic violence, it could take on domestic peace, which would be both prevention and creation.

Since their project was parish-oriented, they studied the information at hand. This parish had a lot of young families. The very basic baptism program consisted of a one-hour meeting with either the pastor or a parish staff member or a large group meeting after the last Mass on the first Sunday of each month. This is where religious imagination came into play, and they started speculating: *I wonder what it would be like if we could find a way to connect families together early on? I wonder how we might bring more families together to share their lives and time together, bonding so that if problems emerged, all would have people with whom to share their concerns, conflicts, and challenges before violence actually surfaced? Could we create a program for young families, connecting people who are bringing their children to be baptized?* They realized that they would not reach everyone on the first round, but they had to start somewhere.

They engaged in conversation with the sacramental program leaders to share ideas. A few were reticent (naturally there are always some who are reluctant about change), but many found that this idea had possibilities, especially since the baptismal program was so basic, emphasizing doctrine and some of the formal procedures for a baptism in the parish. The pastor offered encouragement and support and told them to begin. There would be time later for fine-tuning, he said, but he wanted them to come up with a plan. In addition, he said he wanted the program to develop faith and build community. He wanted a plan for pastoral ministry, not a plan for counseling or social work. Grounding a pastoral plan theologically was already part of the school project, which reinforced the understanding for future ministers that theology does indeed have a ministerial outreach.

During the next few weeks the group created a detailed plan. They looked at how they would invite young families to the groups and how they would make sure that communication, conflict resolution, and other resources for young families were available. In terms of faith formation, in addition to baptism, they focused on the four themes of community, Trinity, gospel relationships, and forgiveness and reconciliation, offering some instruction but also creating processes that would allow families to get to know one another. They also dealt with practical issues, such as providing time for age-appropriate discussions for older children while babies and parents were together. The group also wanted such family clustering to be done within the larger parish family. From that came the idea to invite a few "experienced couples" to join clusters of perhaps four "new family" couples. It was also proposed to hold a Family Festival on a weekend to kick off this initiative. After consulting some parish staff and parishioners, it was decided that another group would take responsibility for the festival and be attentive to how the new families could be welcomed to the parish. (Action plans, though they can be expansive, need to be manageable as well. Although planning the festival was too much for this small group to take on, another group in the parish willingly took on that leadership.)

Presenting the Plan

The class requires that the final projects of graduating students be presented publicly. Faculty and students attend the presentations, and group members have the option of inviting outsiders as well. The students must be accountable and thus are encouraged to invite all of their conversation partners— those who have shared stories and provided information and other support. This particular group invited the pastor, parish staff, the program directors, Gloria, and any of her staff and clients and their families who wished to come. Interestingly, the pastor also invited some of his fellow pastors in neighboring parishes. He clearly was very interested in this project.

The group agreed in advance to give a copy of the project to the parish as both a reference and a thank-you. Three members of the pastoral team who had read a copy before the presentation offered helpful suggestions about specific facets of the action plan, contributions that could be made only by current staff with their insights into the parish based on experience. Also, the group asked Gloria, the director of the domestic violence center, to vet the project before the presentation. Their analysis needed to be well done and accurate if they were to present the information publicly. Again, this is a reminder of the importance of working together: a community can generally produce a more viable project than an individual or a small group. Group members simply need to offer what they can and seek out others to supply the needed missing information and expertise.

The very well attended public presentation was a huge success. In just under an hour the group presented significant narratives and statistics that illuminated the importance of stopping and preventing domestic violence, including a Power-Point presentation and a few video clips. The group recognized that people could be overwhelmed by too much information, so the group carefully selected images, statistics, and various steps in the plan. They wanted people to have basic information through stories and data analysis, but they also wanted people to make a faith connection—to understand that the issue is important because these are our brothers and sisters, and faith must be turned into action. The group described the role of faith reflection throughout and invited attendees to participate briefly.

At the end of the presentation, the plan for action was laid out. The goal was to help people see that a plan for domestic peace was a means of preventing domestic violence by creating a way for families to grow together peacefully. A handout of the pastoral plan was distributed so that attendees could clearly see the details and study it later. The handout also demonstrated how the pastoral spiral could be used as an effective tool for addressing other social needs. Finally, the group offered suggestions for how to evaluate the pastoral plan for domestic peace after implementation. (These were tentative, as actual evaluation would be the parish's responsibility.)

As a conclusion, the three members of the group briefly described how this experience of doing social analysis using the pastoral spiral personally transformed them. They included their feelings of encountering the wounded and vulnerable people of God in need and also connecting with each other and with God. Their accounts were a powerful witness to the reign of God.

In the discussion that followed the presentation, a number

of people admitted that they knew so little about domestic violence. Most had no idea that the Catholic Church offered resources and said they were planning on turning to them. The diocesan staff who attended the gathering acknowledged that this was likely the first program in this area, creating a resource that needed to be more widely known. Then, after adequate time for comments, questions, and answers, the pastor and staff announced that they had decided to implement the project. This small group of three graduate students had found a way using their theology and the tools of social analysis to meet a real need in their community. Two of the students were going to do ministry in two different regions in the United States, and the third was going to minister in another country. All three future ministers now had resources to bring to, adapt to, engage with, and offer to their new communities. The parish also had a detailed plan for a program it would now be able to use, adapt, and offer to families to create a more peaceful and loving parish and community.

CASE STUDY 2: TO FRACK OR NOT TO FRACK

A few years ago a group of women religious in the United States began to hear some of their rural neighbors talk about people coming to their homes and offering to pay them generously (many thousands of dollars per acre) for the right to drill on their land and extract any chemicals that might be found there. When the landowners asked what chemicals the company was looking for, they were told that the area had great potential for natural gas. These company representatives emphasized that this method of drilling, hydraulic fracturing, known popularly as "fracking," was a much used, tested, and safe process and that it was important to explore any alternate forms of energy that could decrease the current US dependence on oil from the Middle East and elsewhere. These potential sources of natural gas could be tapped only if people were willing to let the experts have access to their land, and the people would be paid well for such access. Finally, the visitors mentioned that a number of the neighbors in the area were in the process of accepting. They intimated that it would be wise to get on the bandwagon and earn some cash, particularly during such difficult economic times in that region.

Many local politicians who were trying to figure out how to get more money, income, and jobs into the area also joined the bandwagon. No laws for fracking existed in that state, and the governor was pressuring people to accept the offers, reminding them that this would be good for a state hit hard by the recession.

Some property owners saw this as an unexpected economic boon that could help them provide for their retirement—and this was in the midst of the economic recession—and signed up right away. Others felt that if they didn't sign up, their neighbors would get all the profit and they would end up with nothing. They felt their neighbors were sensible, careful people, so if they were signing up, surely there was something to this. There was also a sense of patriotism in signing up. While they were not serving in Afghanistan or Iraq, people could help their country this way while providing for their own economic future. The visitors were very friendly and informed and answered questions about how intrusive this would be to their property. They explained that the drilling would not be intrusive but would hover at the edges of property as much as possible away from the view from the house. Finally, the drilling process would be a great boon to the entire region, bringing in much-needed jobs. The few who signed up rather quickly felt good about their decision on many levels.

Some property owners were skeptical from the very beginning. The visitors arrived unexpectedly, without first calling. They were not from the region, and the company they represented was not known in the state. Too many people had read about insurance scam artists who signed people up, took hard-earned money from good working-class people, and were never heard from again, even after legal efforts. This group of landowners was quite resistant. Yes, they could use the extra money, especially to pay for the college education of their children, which was a worry. However, the process was not clear, and rarely was anything so easy and simple.

They asked many questions, and while answers were readily given, they felt they needed to do further research and get other opinions about this method of drilling. They said they would consider the option, but that while the price was good, they needed some time to find out more before they could sign up. They were not influenced by comments that a number of their neighbors had already signed up. They wanted to discuss this more with some of their neighbors and understand why their neighbors had decided to sign up. The landowners didn't want to succumb to the peer pressure that the company reps exerted. If the offer was good, having other neighbors sign on before them was fine. They could miss out on this opportunity, but for the moment they felt they could take more time to get more information. So, while open and willing to take the forms (which the visitors left with a little hesitation), they decided to wait.

A third group of property owners, and definitely a numerical minority in the area, had internal alarm bells ringing within the first five minutes of the visitors' proposal. These owners had often come to the land more recently, having chosen to live in a rural area instead of a city, having decided to raise their children to be more aware of land and nature and their value. Some still worked in the city, but they had had a conversion of sorts that moved them from the pace and pollution of city life to what they saw as a healthier and more holistic way of life that connected more with nature. Their great value was nature, uninterrupted and unpolluted. This process of drilling sounded somewhat familiar, but the owners had a number of questions. What impact would this have on their property? Where else was this done? Where there any reports about safety? Had there been any accidents? What would this do to the quiet of the area, and for how long would the equipment be there? Were there any laws about how this was to be done? These property owners took the materials and contact information and said that they were very hesitant about any drilling in this area, and that they would do some further research and would get back to the representatives. They added that they did *not* want their names included in any conversations about "interested neighbors."

Choosing a Topic

As they listened to these stories, the sisters started asking themselves what they should do. While they were not approached by the people seeking drilling and chemical rights, this was their region and the landowners were their neighbors. In addition, they didn't really understand what the companies were trying to do. They started hearing phrases like "hydraulic drilling" and "fracking" to describe the process, but many didn't know what this meant or what would be involved. As a group of religious sisters who sought to put their faith in action through a variety of ministries, including education, they realized that they needed to understand exactly what was happening. They were also becoming ever more aware of the connections between various justice issues and the environment, and they sensed this issue could be an invitation to deepen their living out this call. The sisters began talking with one another, wondering whether they could contribute to understanding what was happening in the region by using the lens of social analysis and then offering the knowledge gained to their neighbors.

The sisters became more attuned to what their neighbors were saying, to short articles that began appearing in the regional newspaper, and to some early reports on national television. They then realized that the topic was being more widely discussed, not only in their region but in other parts of the country. A few people on their justice, peace, and integrity of creation (JPIC) committee began doing basic research to determine whether to recommend this topic to the community as a topic for an ongoing educational session that summer involving the congregation and its associates and collaborators. They quickly identified issues that needed to be addressed and learned that legislation was being done state by state, with their state joining the debates on both sides of the issue. They ordered a copy of the documentary *Gasland* and watched it together. The committee determined that this would be an appropriate topic for the summer gathering. While they had no idea of the outcome, they could begin by learning more about this type of drilling. The JPIC committee decided to use the pastoral spiral as its model for doing social analysis.

Gathering Information for Social Analysis

The summer assembly began with an opening prayer that in word, image, and music spoke of the community's charism and spirituality and the calls to and commitments of the congregation. The prayer was planned to help people enter into more stillness and openness and gain focus. As people were coming from all over the country to the assembly, it was important to allow time for everyone to enter into the process with a reflective, mindful, focused lens. The prayer also included images of beauty, beginning with photos of the region around them and extending all over the country and into the universe.

Members of the JPIC committee then explained why they had chosen this topic and asked attendees, with a raising of hands, to indicate how much they knew about the topic. Over half had heard of the topic but knew little more than what was in brief newspaper articles. A third were unfamiliar with the topic. Others (about a quarter) were familiar with the topic and eager to learn more to see what their community might do in the midst of this pressing issue.

The process began by explaining terms so that everyone would be working from a common set of definitions. Some of the basics included were as follows:

Hydraulic fracturing, or fracking, is a technique designed to recover gas and oil from shale rock. . . . Fracking is the process of drilling down into the earth before a high-pressure water mixture is directed at the rock to release the gas inside. Water, sand, and chemicals are injected into the rock at high pressure, which allows the gas to flow out to the head of the well. The process is carried out vertically or, more commonly, by drilling horizontally to the rock layer. The process can create new pathways to release gas or can be used to extend existing channels. It is shorthand for hydraulic fracturing and refers to how the rock is fractured apart by the high pressure mixture.[2]

Drawings and images were also included so that people could see and understand what the actual process of fracking entailed. After a few questions, with answers supplied by a science teacher on the JPIC committee, committee members recounted some of the narratives from neighboring property owners.

The committee made clear from the outset that these two days would not provide an answer to "How should we stand or act in the midst of hydraulic fracking in our region and world?" It would, however, give some direction to the needed next steps and help people understand the process and the decisions to be made in light of their deep gospel values and spirituality. An added hope was that this time together would capture the interest of people who wanted to do more on fracking, and that they could join with the committee already working on the project. For example, an attorney at the meeting offered to explore the legislative issues. One member, a high school science teacher, offered to take up this question with her students and also ask the social ethics teacher at the school to do the same. By the time the analysis was completed, the number of people engaged had tripled.

When listing the actors and players involved in fracking, the group quickly became aware of the systems involved. They made use of the charting options (see chapter 4 and Appendix), placing large copies of the charts on walls so that they could be added to as needed. People quickly saw how they could offer something to this process. A few people likened it to piecing a puzzle together, and others saw it as a "search for the clues" in a treasure hunt, with the treasure being the best way to proceed.

The next step was to look at the various areas of analysis: *economic*, *political*, *cultural*, *religious*, and *environmental*. After a short break, people were invited to form small groups, and each small group was assigned two of the areas of analysis (e.g., economic and cultural; political and religious; environmental and political). Looking at two different areas of analysis often illuminated more insights. For example, economics questions were deepened when people also looked at the culture that would say yes or no to fracking. How does a high jobless rate in the state affect a culture that otherwise would be more cautious about a drilling process that could potentially impact the water supply? How does the Catholic Church's greater involvement in Earth issues engage political systems on justice issues that impact both the vulnerability of living things and of the Earth?

The small groups met for a considerable amount of time, generating further questions. Before the groups parted for the day, three things happened. First, a brief selection from the religious community's mission statement was read, followed by five minutes of silence. This grounded the group, quietly reminding all of their deep core values. Second, the results of the groups were offered to the whole visually (large sheets of paper on each table) and placed on the wall under categories. Each group then had a maximum of two minutes to offer highlights—questions they had raised, insights gained, and intersecting connections made. Then all were invited to five more minutes of silence. Finally, before the day ended, each person was asked to write down any further questions or insights.

The second day began with prayer that intentionally brought

together justice, peace, and integrity of creation as issues that intersect with hydraulic fracking. People were then free to study the wall charts or sit silently listening to music for about five to seven minutes. Then relevant quotations from the community's rich heritage were read and given to each, followed by an invitation to go outside in nature or to the chapel. The only request was that people remain silent in solitude for about forty-five minutes and wonder about possibilities in light of the questions raised about hydraulic drilling and the work of the congregation. This initial "wondering" is an important step and a reminder that faith reflection is to happen throughout the process. It would be repeated later on during the stage of faith reflection and also during the move to further action.

Upon returning, the group was quiet, yet the room was filled with energy. The time with nature, with prayer, and wondering led to some profound insights that were presented to the large group. Many participants spoke about being moved by feeling their closeness to the Earth, by the challenges their neighbors faced, and by the resources—human and in all creation—that God has offered us all with love. They felt a call to respond to God's call by caring for God's entire creation, human and beyond.

The group made a commitment to take this issue on formally as a community and to probe more deeply into the issue, beginning with a town hall meeting in the fall. However, they wanted to do their work before that meeting, so they found ways for the various groups to bring together answers to the questions in the different categories. Different people offered, as needed, to contact people with expertise in specific areas. It was agreed that their action plan would be a process of education. As a whole they would engage more deeply with the pastoral spiral to discern what they should do next. Each person was invited to make some commitment, from active participation in an area to prayer for all involved. People wrote down their commitments, shared them in their small groups, and placed them in a basket during the offering of gifts at the evening liturgy.

Information and ideas evolved over the next few months. People slowly began to gather more information for the areas of social analysis. Their prayer also now included the Earth and discernment about hydraulic fracking. Their conversations were ever more informed as they invited all kinds of people to assist them, including parishes and schools. Indeed, the entire region would be affected by decisions taken. Over the next months the information was disseminated to those who lived nearby and via the Internet for those at a distance. Keenly aware now of how much was happening in the public sphere, with international standards on fracking, legislative debates across more than thirty states, and other nations also getting into this debate, the community realized that it could offer an informed space for sharing information, organizing public responses, and engaging in dialogue on an issue that was now increasingly polarizing. The group as a whole committed to this, asking their collaborators to continue to join them. Different people organized in different areas, including, for example, political outreach (to the governor, mayor, and EPA head in the region), environmental outreach (to environmental groups with this as a key issue, groups looking for alternative energy sources, and groups looking at sustainability and our use of resources), religious outreach (to Roman Catholic, other Christian, and interfaith groups), cultural outreach, and economic outreach (learning more about the region's economic issues).

The religious community offered its large meeting space for a public gathering of neighbors to discuss this issue. When the town hall meeting was held, many members of the workshop came to it with an informed perspective, interest in learning more, and the ability to speak from their deep values. As of this writing, the issue of hydraulic fracking is still evolving, and this group continues to gather information, reflect, and educate in the region, providing resources for interested groups around the country. In this case, the process of social analysis is ongoing.

INTERNATIONAL APPLICATIONS

While these two cases, quite different from each other, come from the United States, such cases can certainly be found elsewhere in the world as the process of using the pastoral spiral has been applied internationally as well. Many of its learnings and insights are applicable beyond country borders even as particularities are found across cultures, political systems, economic systems, religious traditions, and environmental lenses. A few brief examples illustrate some ways the process has been useful globally.

In Africa

One student from the Democratic Republic of Congo used the pastoral spiral to work with the challenge of dealing with efforts within her government to change the national constitution to remove term limits for national office holders. Some powerful insights emerged, and one of the most significant insights was cultural. While sharing her political and economic analysis with a large group, she found to her own surprise that many people in her country immediately associated a president with a tribal chief. A chief never stops being chief; this is a lifetime role, and a replacement is named after death. She had to begin by explaining that a president is not a chief and then demonstrate the value of term limits. This major insight gave her possible directions for further action.

She also explained that as long as an individual holds an office, that person is exempt from any legal charges, whether stemming from corruption or the misuse of power. However, once someone leaves a position, charges can be filed. Even while presuming the best in officials, she explained that this is often why those in power are reluctant to give it up.

In another location in Africa, people were invited during the component of faith reflection to consider, "What could this [engagement in action or simply taking on the issue publicly] cost?" After several minutes of silence, one participant said, "This could cost me my life," and it was literally true. That was a truly profound moment.

In a Developing Country

Another profound moment came in a small group of people from several countries when a man told of a challenge in his region. There had been an increase in the number of young teenagers becoming pregnant and allowing others (who never met the teens) to adopt the infants. The girls were then paid a sum of money that was used to pay for their education. This was not publicly spoken about, even among the teenagers' families. Instead, the teens, once they started outwardly showing signs of their pregnancy, went elsewhere to "work" and live until they gave birth. Then health care workers took the infants, the girls received their money, and not long after they returned home. The teens had a source of income, but something was deeply wrong about this situation on many levels.

It was extremely difficult to clearly piece together the situation because influential persons and groups were trying to keep it hidden. Finally, one person in the group raised a hand and said, "Wait." He stood up and said, "What we are talking about here is human trafficking. This is the trafficking of children." The import was stunning. This issue affected many developing countries, and the group had now named it, giving it further global significance.

In South America

Sometimes social analysis is undertaken according to a plan, and other times use of the pastoral spiral can be helpful in situations that simply arise. This happened in Brazil. A group was running a workshop that was both an interlanguage and international immersion experience. As part of the workshop, a Brazilian sociologist spoke about Brazil's plan to host the

World Cup in 2014 and the Summer Olympics in 2016. He spoke about the economic costs to the country for creating a new highway infrastructure and the buildings and hotels that the events would require in addition to the cost of needed security. He cited recent cities and countries that hosted such events, demonstrating that the great economic costs were not balanced by revenue. In the wake of the Games, some countries had to resort to austerity measures. He forecasted a probable economic outcome for Brazil, concluding that it was possible and quite probable that the country (i.e., national/regional governments) would pay for about 95 percent of the costs with perhaps only 5 percent coming from private sources. He added that nonetheless it was private money that was behind the effort to bring the games to Rio and Brazil.

The sociologist presented a very helpful context for what participants in the workshop were seeing and hearing. Before and during their time in Brazil, news reports described and showed people protesting in the streets, demanding that money be spent on the basic human needs of the people—education, food, water, medical care, sanitation, and housing. These issues had been covered by the international press in many countries prior to the group's arrival. This was a clear invitation to do social analysis to determine what, if anything, they could do. The reality had multiple entry points for them, both in Brazil and in their home countries. And so they began.

In Higher Education

The Hesburgh Sabbatical Program at Catholic Theological Union in Chicago makes regular use of the pastoral spiral. One semester a participant from Bangladesh who worked with the spiral returned to Bangladesh knowing that he had a tool to address ethical issues in his home country. He focused on gathering people together to stop the use of toxic chemicals to preserve fruits and vegetables. While the produce was lasting longer, it was poisoning the people.

CONCLUSION

These cases demonstrate how, with careful preparation and analysis, problems can be identified and transformed positively. This can be done locally on small issues as well as larger ones; it can also be applied regionally, nationally, and even internationally. The process takes time and requires the presence of thoughtful, committed people, but bringing about change is possible, and it can begin with a small group of people rather than millions of dollars and a dozen lobbyists.

A common point in each of these stories is that people are learning from and with their sisters and brothers about what is of great concern, not only to them, but because we are mutually responsible, to one another and to our Earth community. In each of these stories people became more alive to not just the issues but to the people who experienced their negative effects and suffered from them. What the pastoral spiral offers is a way to say, "How can I be a peacemaker in this situation? How can I give a cup of water" (see Matt. 25)? Participants have realized that they are not just "out there" as observers but that they can play a role in making a difference, however small or large, for the people and the Earth. This is why we do analysis in the first place. Such study can take place in classrooms, in parishes, and among families and people of faith and passion. We need not hide from or be overwhelmed by the situations of need around us. There is a process to be used—a process that can reframe realities for us, transform all involved, and be a concrete response to the gospel call to participate with God in bringing about the reign of God.

Notes

[1] Due to the nature of some of the cases, some details were modified.

[2] This is an updated definition and explanation of the process from the BBC News UK. See "What Is Fracking and Why Is It Controversial?" http://www.bbc.com.

Epilogue

Ultimately, this book is about encounters—an encounter with our brothers and sisters, an encounter with God's creation, an encounter with God. We do not simply meet the other. In Spanish, we would say we have an *encuentro* with our brothers and sisters. We look eye to eye at the other and come to know the other more deeply beyond the first hellos. We come to know the other's hopes, joys, challenges, sorrows, and frustrations. The encounter is mutual, for we allow ourselves to be encountered as well. An encounter requires time and openness. In the process of encounter, if we are open(ed), we are transformed as well. This book is also about transformation.

As we encounter God, we come to see not only how God sees us (with unrelenting love) but also the great love with which God sees all of God's people and creation. Beloved of God, we are invited to love all God loves, too, and to seek the flourishing of all. Such encounter transforms us and how we see all around us.

Transformation happens through relationship. Yes, the pastoral spiral helps us respond to problems in the world today, both locally and globally, yet it is about so much more. Yes, we need to go about the effort to name problems and find ways to respond. But there is so much more. The process of the pastoral spiral is to make us alive to our world and its people in ways that move and motivate us to do something to improve life and to respond.[1] It helps us position ourselves and our world with people in ways that move us to care and respond in solidarity, to see all of our lives as interlinked. As our lives intermingle and intersect, we are each and all changed and transformed, often in ways we cannot begin to anticipate. Such are the risk and reward of Christian life, and also of the pastoral spiral.

As we look at the world around us, with so many immense possibilities as well as great challenges, we do not do so alone. We do so as a community, and we do this in community. As Christians we hear in our Gospels the promise of the Spirit working with, in, and through us.

> On the evening of that first day of the week, when the doors were locked . . . Jesus came and stood in their midst and said to them, "Peace be with you." When he had said this, he showed them his hands and his side. The disciples rejoiced when they saw the Lord. [Jesus] said to them again, "Peace be with you. As the Father has sent me, so I send you." And when he had said this, he breathed on them and said to them, "Receive the holy Spirit." (John 20:19–23)

And they were sent. So are we. We have what is necessary in abundance. Now, together, we go forth to love and serve.

Notes

[1] I am grateful to Mary Sharon Riley, RC, for the conversation that ensued here as the conclusion was being written. Part of so many conversations throughout the writing and editing, her wisdom, clarity, and conciseness are sheer gift.

Appendix of Worksheets

1. Experience—Choosing a Topic
2. The Five Whys of Experience
3. Who Else Is Needed at the Table?
4. Beginning Social Analysis with the Pastoral Spiral
5. Values
6. Who Is Involved? How Are They Connected?
7. Charting and Organizing
8. Economic Analysis
9. Political Analysis
10. Cultural Analysis
11. Environmental Analysis
12. Religious Analysis—General
13. Institutional Religious Analysis
14. Religious Analysis—Scripture and Theological Resource Gathering
15. Understanding Differences
16. Faith Reflection
17. Planning for Action
18. Setting Priorities
19. Timeline
20. Action Plans—Guiding, Creating, and Organizing
21. Create Models, Experiment, and Turn the Plan into Action

Worksheet #1: Experience—Choosing a Topic

Before any analysis can be done, a topic must be chosen. It is important to determine if the topic is connected to a larger system of issues and whether it is too broad or too sufficiently limited for your work. In order to get started, all individuals and groups must

- Choose a topic.
- Make use of narratives and data.
- Limit the topic.
- Give reasons for the choice.
- Name their experience.
- See who else / what additional information is needed at the table of discussion.

1. Name the issue and briefly explain it. (What is the problem you want/need to address?)

2. Explain its importance in 100 words or less and explain why this topic needs social analysis. Explain the issue so that people understand the basics and have enough detail to know why it's important right now. What is at stake?

3. Is this an issue in which a wrong needs to be stopped, something new needs to be created, or both? Explain.

4. How is this topic connected to other larger issues (e.g., the death penalty is connected to society's struggle with justice and just consequences for crimes)?

5. Is this a local, national, or international issue? (Note that this is helpful later on in connecting your topic to wider issues and even collaborating with other groups.)

6. Is your topic limited enough to be manageable (e.g., water pollution in Lake Michigan is limited, while water or pollution by themselves are not).

7. If you were to offer a brief presentation on this issue today, how would you title it?

8. What initial information have you found on this topic (social media, print media, lectures)?

9. Is there sufficient information to justify choosing this issue to pursue? If yes, explain why.

10. In two to three sentences, explain why you are interested in this topic (e.g., this topic directly impacts me or someone I know; acquaintances are impacted; hearing about this topic stimulated me to learn more).

11. What word best describes this issue for you? For me this is a(n) _____ issue (e.g., justice, rights, compassion, love of neighbor, etc.).

12. Who else is interested in this topic, and what is each person's current involvement in this area? (For example, as a resident of Texas I find the death penalty _____; in my Catholic school we are learning about this issue).

13. Define the basic terms used in this issue (e.g., HIV stands for _____; child trafficking is defined as _____; pollution consists of _____).

14. What resources might you need in order to deal with this issue?

15. What resources do you have for dealing with this issue?

WORKSHEET #2: THE FIVE WHYS OF EXPERIENCE

The following exercise is helpful in personally connecting to the topic at hand.* Each question is meant to uncover layers of reasons for one's interest and feeling about the topic to examine some of the deeper reasons. One person should read this out loud for the group. Then, going question by question, ask people to select one dominant emotion, allowing about thirty seconds between questions.

1. When I reflect on (the situation of) _____
I feel (write down the emotion) _____.
2. Why do I feel this way?
3. And why does that (answer to #2) make me feel this way?
4. And why does that (answer of #2) make me feel this way?
5. And why does that (answer to #4) make me feel this way?
6. And why does that (answer to #5) make me feel this way?

---

*Process adapted from Nancy Sylvester, IHM, Institute for Communal Contemplation and Dialogue, 8531 West McNichols, Detroit, MI 48221; www.engagingimpasse.org.

WORKSHEET #3: WHO ELSE IS NEEDED AT THE TABLE?

After sharing with the whole or in small groups about this topic, take some time to look around and ask who might still be needed for this project.

1. Whose perspective is missing?
2. Whose perspective would add information?
3. What expertise do you feel you still need for this project?
4. Whose experience is it necessary to hear? (For example, if all the people in a group considering immigration reform are from the United States, the stories and experiences of recent immigrants would widen the understanding of a group and offer suggestions for directions.)
5. Keep a journal or log of ongoing and unanswered questions and other needed information.
6. Pray for all involved in this issue. Ask for the grace of openness to know where you are called to work for these next weeks.

WORKSHEET #4:
BEGINNING SOCIAL ANALYSIS WITH THE PASTORAL SPIRAL

Pastoral Spiral

Experience
Anecdotal
Statistical

Social Analysis
Sociological
Economic
Political
Cultural
Environmental
Religious

Action
Sociological
Economic
Political
Environmental
Cultural
Religious

Faith Reflection
Reflectively engaging scripture,
tradition, mission statements, etc.

We begin with some background on the history of the situation and what structures were and are involved.

1. What is the history of this situation? Was there a time without this injustice?

2. When did it begin? Where did this begin? Who was involved?

3. What structures were changed or used for this injustice to grow or flourish?

4. Was a bias at work making this injustice possible? In light of the history of the situation, what bias was at work?

5. Consider each of the biases of education, race, gender, social status/class, citizenship, income, and geography. What biases might you have concerning this issue?

6. What presumptions were or are being made about this issue?

7. Are there some blind spots in our nation on this issue? (Note that bias is a usually a conscious process. Blind spots are unconscious; the holder of spots is not aware of them.)

Worksheet #5: Values

Values and stances ground our work, and our Christian tradition offers some powerful lenses from which to look at issues. Values are also biases, and it is important to know which values give us a leaning or bias in a particular direction. Every analysis involves some bias, but part of the integrity of analysis comes from clearly acknowledging our biases. (It may be helpful to bring the reflections of chapter 2 into consideration as you reflect and answer the questions below.

1. What general values or biases are you bringing to this approach to social analysis?

2. What value or bias are you bringing to this particular issue (e.g.,, dignity of each person vs. dignity dependent on citizenship; profit vs. freedom; human dignity vs. human trafficking)?

3. List your greatest values (e.g., preferential option for the poor [an emphasis that people made poor are usually in greater need and thus need more attention and effort]; the dignity of women and children).

4. What are your faith-based values?

5. Share your values with your group so that you can see the overlap and differing dimensions at work.

6. Keep these value questions at hand throughout the process so that you can both remember and allow the values to guide you in assessing and making decisions on issues.

WORKSHEET #6:
WHO IS INVOLVED? HOW ARE THEY CONNECTED?

Social analysis, as we know, examines the structures that cause or contribute directly or indirectly to issues of injustice, and so we begin by looking at the persons and groups connected to our topic. We first ask some questions revolving around this question: "Who is involved?"

1. Who are the actors in this situation, and what are the roles of each?

2. What groups or organizations do they belong to or are they connected to?

3. What organizations are involved in this situation, directly or indirectly?

4. How are the persons and groups connected, associated, or interconnected? Or not?

5. What, if any, parts of the Earth community are involved?

6. What is *your* involvement or role(s)? What groups do you belong to? What roles do you play?

7. In light of the history of the situation, what are the important relationships?

Note: In the beginning, include every possible link in your brainstorming, for it contributes to obtaining the widest and most detailed picture possible. At the same time, remember to keep it manageable and to work together.

Worksheet #7: Charting and Organizing

There are a variety of ways to organize the lists of actors for an issue. Different methods may be appropriate for different groups or topics. A brief description of each is provided.

#7A: Who's Who, and What Does Each Person Do?
(For *linear thinkers*)

1. Who are the actors in this situation, and what are the roles of each?

2. What groups or organizations do they belong to or are they connected to?

3. What organizations are involved in this situation, directly or indirectly?

4. How are the persons and groups connected, associated, or interconnected? Or not?

5. What, if any, parts of the Earth community are involved?

6. What is *your* involvement or role(s)? What groups do you belong to? What roles do you play?

7. Is there a particular religious lens or charism you bring to this issue (Franciscan parish, Religious of the Sacred Heart, Mercy hospital ministry, Focolare community, Catholic Worker, Sant'Egidio community, etc.)? What lens does this give you?

8. In light of the history of the situation, what are the important relationships?

#7B: WHO'S WHO, AND WHAT DOES EACH PERSON DO?
(FOR *VISUAL THINKERS*)

A more *visual* way of organizing places the issue in the center of the circle and then creates a larger circle around the smaller circle, listing the actors and groups directly involved. The most peripheral groups are in the outermost circles and are less directly involved. Circle or otherwise indicate the roles of various members of the group (e.g., you are a consumer and so you are in relationship with a particular grocery store; you are a citizen and voter and thus have relationship with the state).

These charts are useful in the beginning to see the connections across areas and with larger groups. They are helpful for adding information as you research the areas of politics, economics, culture, religion, environment, and more. They are also helpful in doing faith reflection to see where movement is called for at this time and to look for insights and leverage points. When you later decide to act, they can be useful in assessing where you have acted and in seeing what parts of the structure still need to be engaged and transformed. Make these organizing frameworks visible and accessible to the entire group, as the whole group can make many more connections than one or two persons.

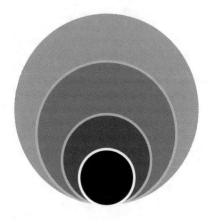

#7C: Who's Who, and What Does Each Person Do?
(For *visual thinkers*)

A *third* way is to create circles or webs of connection like that below. The center circle names the issue and then places the actors in self-contained circles around the topic circle. The most directly connected actors can be larger circles or be placed closest to the issue. Note the interconnections among the actors and link the players together. This may get messy, so have a large sheet available if you choose this approach.

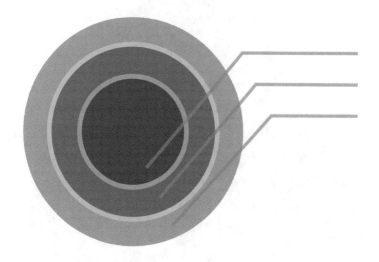

#7D: WHO'S WHO, AND WHAT DOES EACH PERSON DO?
(FOR *VISUAL THINKERS*)

A fourth way, usually best if you have already created some listing, is to find areas of connection and intersection. So, you may have a number of people in a circle who represent state legal concerns. That circle of people can also interconnect with people who work in federal law and perhaps also international law.

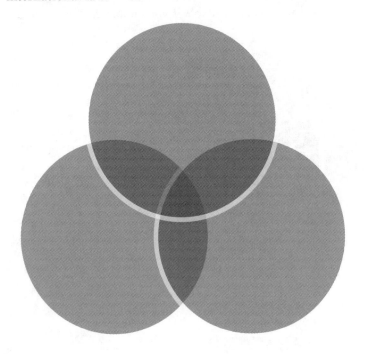

#7E: Who's Who, and What Does Each Person Do?
(Similar to a genealogy chart)

Create a chart listing the roles emerging from the issue, beginning with the directly connected actors followed by supporting connections.

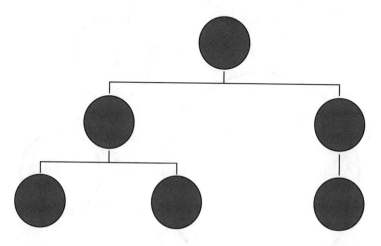

#7F: Who's Who, and What Does Each Person Do?
(For *visual thinkers*)

Create a wheel with spokes. The center of the large wheel identifies the issue, and all the actors connected to the issue emanate out as spokes.

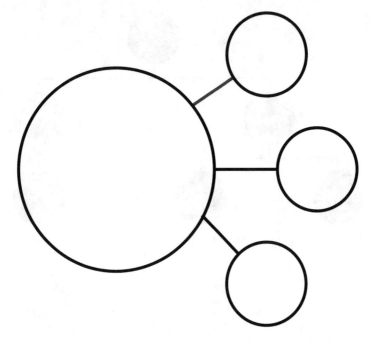

A good use for this particular format is to create charts with each of the systems (culture, politics, economics, environment, religion, etc.) being analyzed. Radiate from the major area all the groups, organizations, and significant persons connected with your topic and notice where the flow goes. A further exercise then would be to see where the major areas (economic, political, cultural, environmental, religious, etc.) intersect or not.

Worksheet #8: Economic Analysis

Economic analysis looks at how resources are allocated and finds links that can illuminate the relationship between the problem to be addressed and economics. For some of these areas you may seek out an expert, but for other areas your own further research is a sufficient starting point.

Throughout, recognizing one's values (and biases) opens the door for clearer discussions within the group as well as among persons with different views. For example, one of our gospel values is a particular sensitivity and concern with the poor and marginalized. Another person's values may lean toward those who have different economic principles. Information and honest communication help all at the table to address the following questions:

1. What is the role of economics in this issue?

2. What are the economic structures and dynamics involved in this issue?

3. What economic systems impact the various groups?

4. What resources can the major actors access?

5. Who benefits?

6. Who is burdened?

7. Who is responsible?

8. How are resources being used to influence or impact this topic?

9. What are the relationships or potential relationships in this area?

10. Where are your relationships in this area?

11. What role does economics play in the history of this issue?

12. Create a list of important documents, articles, websites, books, videos, or other resources. Try to have some resources from ordinary persons as well as experts in the field.

Worksheet #9: Political Analysis

Political analysis looks at the organization of power and politics in the issue at hand. Because issues often have legal and other political ramifications, you should know how politics is being used or how it may be used. Sometimes a law is deemed unjust (e.g., capital punishment), so understanding the law and how it is officially and unofficially legislated and then promulgated is important. It is also important to know how a law came into being. Was it because of a particularly heinous murder? Was it because the culture at the time decided that "an eye for an eye" was a just punishment for a capital crime?

Laws are culturally connected, so knowing who is promoting or dissenting from legislation is also important. This will likely be a factor later on in deciding where or how to commit to action. If you are trying to create legislation—for example, to protect a portion of the environment—then you should see also what precedents have been set elsewhere for such legislation. What power do people for or against this issue leverage within the larger culture of society? Who are the major players, and what do they have at stake in this issue?

Political power is used in many ways. For example, as we have seen lately around the world, persons accessing social media are using the power of media to make a case for a particular stance. The focus of political analysis is to gain information about the structure and dynamics of power, to see where intersections of power and influence converge, and where and how power can be accessed. Address the following questions that apply to your topic:

1. What is the role of politics in this issue? How is politics being used to influence this topic? How might politics be used to influence this topic?

2. What political structures and dynamics are involved or active in this situation/issue?

3. Who has power?

4. What kind of power?

5. What power does each major player have?

6. What power dynamics are at play here?

7. How are they related to each other?

8. How are they related to you?

9. What roles does politics play in the history of this issue?

10. What legislation, if any, concerns this issue?

11. What lobbying groups are involved, and with whom and on behalf of whom?

12. What is the role of social media on this topic in terms of political analysis? Create a list of documents, articles, websites, books, videos, or other resources. Try to have some resources for ordinary persons and experts in the field.

13. Add any new information to your charting of political relationships.

Worksheet #10: Cultural Analysis

Culture has a greater influence on issues than many first think, so understanding and engaging culture are crucial. Two points are important to remember. First, cultural lenses surround issues. For example, recycling bags engages the "throwaway" culture as well as the environmental culture. Issues can involve generational cultures, regional cultures, and more.

Second, with systems in place that affect groups, knowing the relevant culture can help understand the background of an issue. Why did it come into being? Sometimes understanding the culture that has spawned or supported an issue can tell you how you can engage it. Sometimes the culture of a system can shift with education, political pressure, or economic factors. To know a culture is to understand what moves below the surface. The questions that follow aim at understanding cultures and their impact on your issue. Knowledge is power.

1. What is the role of culture in this issue?

2. What are the cultural structures and dynamics involved?

3. What cultural values are the various groups working with or influenced by?

4. How does culture express meaning or value with this issue?

5. How does culture frame the issue?

6. Which cultures play a prominent role?

7. What cultural values and practices influence your thinking and acting?

8. What role does culture play in the history of this issue?

9. Create a list of documents, articles, websites, books, videos, or other resources. Try to have some resources for ordinary persons and experts.

WORKSHEET #11: ENVIRONMENTAL ANALYSIS

Increasingly the environment impacts almost every issue, directly or indirectly—from water shortages to wars to health issues to migration issues and so on. Issues directly related to the environment, such as drought, deforestation, and mining, have clearer connections to the other areas of analysis (economics, politics, culture). Most issues have some impact on the environment and vice versa, even if only indirectly. With environmental issues in particular, see whether you are trying to stop an injustice (illegal logging) or create something new (protect a freshwater source or create safe-use policies).

Answer the following questions. Note that if you are engaging an environmental issue directly you may need to answer the questions more than once. The first time would be appropriate for stopping an injustice, and repeating the questions would help with creating a new method or protection.

1. How is the environment impacted?

2. How is the issue impacted by environment?

3. How is the health of the Earth community (all living creatures) impacted?

4. What is flourishing?

5. What is languishing or dying? What is burdened?

6. What is the state of elements related to air? Water? Land?

7. What is the geography of this issue? (Where is this happening or potentially happening?)

8. What responsibility for the environment does each actor have? How is that responsibility being fulfilled?

9. What group(s), if any, is attentive to the environment's role in this issue? Are environmental groups involved? If so, which group(s)?

10. How is the environment being used for leverage by politics, economics, or culture?

11. Are the environmental connections for this issue local, regional, national, international, or a combination?

12. In what way do the environmental implications affect you or your group?

13. How is beauty being affected by the issue?

14. What role does environment play in the history of this issue?

15. Create a list of documents, articles, websites, books, videos, or other resources. Try to have some resources for ordinary persons and experts in the field.

Worksheet #12: Religious Analysis—General

Religious groups are increasingly involved in the public sphere, and so it is important to make use of their resources and challenges. These also offer important resources for ongoing faith reflection.

Distinguish between religious analysis and faith reflection. Religious analysis seeks information. While information can be a resource for reflection, at this point the focus is on finding out who is saying what on this topic and to gather and organize these resources.

The Roman Catholic social tradition explicitly engages the world, as does scripture. Even as each religious tradition can utilize its own resources, some general questions apply to most organized religions or groups with a faith base.

1. What is the role of religion on this issue?

2. What religious beliefs and values are particularly pertinent?

3. Are there any significant opposing religious beliefs and values in this area? If so, list them.

4. How are religion or religious beliefs and values being used to influence this topic? How might religion be used to influence this topic?

5. What religious structures and dynamics are involved or active in this situation or issue?

6. Who has power?

7. What kind of power?

8. What power does each major player have? What power dynamics are at play here?

9. How are they related to each other?

10. How are they related to you?

11. What roles does religion play in the history of this issue?

12. What lobbying groups are involved, and with whom and on behalf of whom?

13. What is the role of social media in terms of religious analysis?

14. Is there a particular religious lens or charism you bring to this issue (Franciscan parish, Religious of the Sacred Heart, Mercy hospital ministry, Focolare community, Catholic Worker, San Egidio community, or a non-Christian lens—Hinduism, Buddhism, humanism)? What lens does this give you?

15. Create a list of documents, articles, websites, books, videos, or other resources. Try to have some resources for ordinary persons and experts in the field.

Worksheet #13: Institutional Religious Analysis

The following questions, written with the Roman Catholic tradition in mind, can be adapted to various denominations or religious traditions.

1. What does the Roman Catholic Church say publicly about this social issue? Who is speaking?

2. What do public church offices say (i.e., pope, Vatican congregations, USCCB, diocese)?

3. Is this issue being engaged locally, nationally, or globally? Do we have speeches or documents from popes, bishops, Vatican offices, or national church bodies?

4. What are theologians saying? For example, much recent writing has addressed a theology of migration, so this would be a valuable resource on local, regional, national, and international levels.

5. How are dioceses engaged? Parishes? Bishops or bishops' groups? Lay Catholic groups?

6. Who is speaking from the broader church communities (religious orders? Catholic nonprofit groups? advocacy groups such as Bread for the World)?

7. Are there any ecumenical, interfaith, or faithwide statements or efforts in this area?

8. What do religious orders say? What is their involvement?

9. What are religious writers saying? Consider publications such as *America*, *The Tablet* (London), *Commonweal*, *U.S. Catholic* (Catholic examples), and also *Sojourners* and *Christian Century*, two ecumenical publications.

10. What other faith-based groups are involved?

11. To what other concerned groups are we naturally connected by values?

12. Create a list of any quotes you find particularly compelling or significant.

WORKSHEET #14: RELIGIOUS ANALYSIS—
SCRIPTURE AND THEOLOGICAL RESOURCE GATHERING

Religious analysis must include scripture and tradition, for those ground our values and resources for further development. Use your religious tradition for resources concerning your social issue. Remember that sometimes the resources directly engage your topic (document from US-Mexican bishops on migration), and at other times they indirectly engage your topic (scripture and hydraulic drilling). The more information you can offer here, the better.

1. What does scripture say directly about your issue?

2. What does scripture say thematically or indirectly?

3. What does the Catholic social tradition (or a social statement of your denomination) offer directly or indirectly on this issue?

4. In what way, if any, does our liturgical life connect to this social issue (e.g., bread and wine certainly have correlatives to poverty, community, table welcome, the example of Jesus, the care of creation)?

5. What understanding might doctrines such as the Trinity, incarnation, Christology, and so on offer?

6. How might scripture and tradition illuminate topics of creation, community, the paschal mystery, suffering, and redemption that relate to your issue?

7. Assemble relevant sources and resources, including (1) scripture and religious tradition; (2) church documents and teachings; (3) writings by theologians and persons in other disciplines with expertise in the topic and the tradition (or at least engaging both); (4) wider faith community resources (denominational, ecumenical, faithwide contexts); and (5) public statements from religious leaders.

WORKSHEET #15: UNDERSTANDING DIFFERENCES

During the information-gathering phase, you may encounter writers from your own tradition with deep values and convictions who hold a different perspective than you do. This is actually helpful for analysis because you have the opportunity to see with a different light and engage respectfully with a different point of view. This kind of prophetic dialogue can come forth from a respectful sharing of differences and theological lenses. It is always important to be able to attend to diverse opinions with keen attention and a light hold. Some questions that may help you see these divides are as follows:

1. Are there differing theologies on this issue? If so, what are they?

2. What are the key values in each position (overt and subtle)?

3. What common values do the positions hold?

4. Are there any inaccuracies in the positions? If yes, what are they?

5. Where is concern found for the individual, the community, and the Earth?

6. How is concern for the poor, vulnerable, and marginalized brought forth?

WORKSHEET #16: FAITH REFLECTION

While faith reflection is part of all the steps of the pastoral spiral, it has a particular role after experience and social analysis have been completed. Once a group has determined the focus or issue to be examined through the pastoral spiral, all involved in the topic become part of our daily prayer. Since systemic change is about personal and structural transformation, we know that grace is part of it. Praying for God's wisdom and insight assists us as we engage in the pastoral spiral as well as for those involved in the issue in any way. Prayer helps us know God's direction, and it also help us achieve the stance of openness to what we are called to do. The goal is to put ourselves and God's designs for humanity and all creation as one in God. In this way, faith reflection leads us to discernment toward action.

There are a variety of ways to do faith reflection. The suggestions and frameworks below are samples to be adapted to your group. If you have a particular lens or charism (such as members of a Franciscan parish, members of a Catholic Worker community, students in a high school with a particular religious group or congregation focus, or participants in a particular area [high school Peacemakers program, Jesuit Volunteer Corps]), your focus may be quite clear; if so, you are highly encouraged to use materials from this type of spirituality.

Faith reflection is to be both personal and communal, so a few different formats are offered below. Always allow adequate time for silence and creative reflection; never rush to a decision. Three worksheets are included: personal faith reflection, personal reflection through contemplative walking, and communal reflection. Note that the first two forms of personal faith reflection can also be used for communal faith reflection.

WORKSHEET #16A: PERSONAL FAITH REFLECTION

"See I am creating something new; can you perceive it?" (Isa. 43:19)

1. Find a quiet space, preferably in sight of beauty.

2. Choose an image that reflects the issue you are engaging and place that in front of you. Keep the rest of the space uncluttered.

3. Ask for the grace of openness and availability to what God is inviting you.

4. Optional: Take one of the scripture passages you found attractive in the religious analysis step. Read it silently once. Read it out loud a second time.

5. Sit in silence for five minutes.

6. Optional: Jot down briefly any reflections or connections that come with your topic and this passage.

7. Look "lightly" at the materials or notes you have gathered during your social analysis, seeking not more information but a sense of direction for your action. (If it is necessary or helpful, jot a few words or phrases down, but this is not the time for note taking. This is time for attentiveness and openness.)

8. Note any words, phrases, or images that emerge. If they do, jot them down in a notebook.

9. Sit in silence, thanking God for this time and asking for openness throughout each day.

10. Gather your reflections and insights, and when the group meets, bring them to share.

Worksheet #16B: Personal Reflection through Contemplative Walking

This exercise makes use of the wonderful contemplative tradition of a monastic or cloister walk, where religious walk prayerfully and purposefully, though with no "arrival point" in mind except listening and responding to God.

1. Find a quiet space, preferably in sight of beauty.

2. Choose an image that reflects the issue you are engaging and place that in front of you. Keep the rest of the space uncluttered.

3. Ask for the grace of openness and availability to what God is inviting.

4. Look "lightly" at your notes from social analysis and recall the experiences that bring you to this point.

5. Leave all behind (except perhaps a blank sheet of paper and pen you can put in your pocket) and walk in silence and solitude for twenty to thirty minutes, simply asking, with your issue in mind and heart, "I wonder . . . I wonder what it would look like if. . . ." Simply walk with this stance of wondering and allow your religious imagination to move as it chooses. Do not force anything, but simply allow yourself to be open to explore possibilities.

6. As insights come (and they will probably come quietly), jot them down or remember them. Allow further insights to come. Do not rush this process; it is not magic but a form of prayer.

7. Return to your quiet space. Write down what you heard within you.

8. Give thanks for this time.

9. Gather your reflections and insights, and when the group meets, bring them to share.

Worksheet #16C: Community Faith Reflection

I am about to do a new thing;
now it springs forth, do you not perceive it?
I will make a way in the wilderness
and rivers in the desert. (Isa. 43:19)

1. Place chairs in a circle. In the middle of the circle, create a focal space that somehow reflects the topic at hand.

2. Invite each person to bring some image that reflects the topic for them. (Ideally it is an image the person also uses with personal prayer and throughout the gatherings with the group.)

3. Find a scripture quote that particularly names the issue you are engaging.

4. Take some of the quotes from the religious analysis section that would be fitting for some group reflection and put them on a handout for the group. (Consider inviting people to send you their "top three quotes" and use them for more than one such gathering.)

5. Invite people to gather in the space and, with some gentle music in the background, read the scripture passage that relates to the topic.

6. Invite each person to place an image or object in the center of the circle as an offering and focus.

7. Ask for the grace of openness and availability to what God is inviting.

8. Sit together in silence for five minutes.

9. Read out loud the quotes for reflection, inviting different people to read slowly and reflectively.

10. Take twenty minutes of personal time to read, walk with, or journal with the quotes, asking "What are we invited to at this time?" Jot down notes.

11. In a large group (or in smaller groups), invite each other to share what you are hearing, sensing, and seeing as it relates to your issue. Trust that movement is happening, whether you

SOCIAL ANALYSIS FOR THE 21ST CENTURY

get a firm sense of where you are headed next or not. Often it takes more than one time to get a firm direction. Trusting the process is essential, and group members together must remind one another not to jump too quickly (as is often an impulse to be resisted in faith reflection).

12. Ask one person to take notes for the group during this time and after about twenty minutes to share what the person is hearing, seeing, and sensing. Listen to the group's affirmation or lack of it.

13. Sit in silence for five minutes to allow what you are hearing, sensing, and seeing to move in you. An alternative may be to go outside or be in direct view of nature to connect with some beauty for fifteen minutes in silence and then return. Use whatever avenues are available and inviting for the religious imagination to evoke insights. The call is to be attentive personally and communally to where God may be inviting the group to use its gifts to move.

14. Take another fifteen minutes to share. Invite a different person to listen and take notes for the group and then to share what is heard, sensed, seen, and felt. If the movement is present, at some point the connections and insights will become clear and articulate. Movement will flow. If you do not find this to be so, or if this does not remain in the days after the meeting, then the group should return and continue the process.

15. Sit in silence for five minutes.

16. If something has moved the group, write it down, asking people to pray with this and feel their reaction over the next few days in cognitive and emotive ways. Is this resonating with you? Is this the direction? Is something more or something else calling and we have not yet reached it? Does this flow from your deepest values?

17. Decide on the next meeting time. Between meetings you may wish to invite people to email or blog or thread a discussion on what they are finding in the days following the faith reflection gathering.

18. Give thanks for this time together.

Note that if a direction becomes exceedingly clear, the energy in the group may move enough to begin some planning for action. Seeing where this leads can also serve to test the waters of this discernment.

Follow Up on Faith Reflection

First, if the group is not yet sensing the direction, the next meeting can have a similar format, with an invitation to bring in further insights that have emerged from faith reflection. If the group returns and senses that a direction at least is set, the group can move to the action steps, which will further direct the group's movement.

WORKSHEET #17: PLANNING FOR ACTION

Testing the direction of the faith reflection must be done freely. Avoid action that stems from are impatience for results and the willingness to take any movement as long as it is movement and a decision. In addition, flexibility is necessary in order to regularly test the Spirit's direction as you move toward action. We must be free to ask questions such as the following and respond in light of what we hear:

- Does this express the guiding instinct we had?
- How does this action respond to the issue, both systemically and locally?
- Is this a response on behalf of those on the margins of society or a dimension of creation at risk?

If the answer to the questions is yes, you are ready to move to action planning. As a reminder, action is built around five key movements:

- Envision.
- Use social analysis categories for short- and long-term organizing and planning.
- Create models.
- Experiment.
- Get to work.

Once these movements are completed, it is time to assess and revise and to repeat the steps as needed.

WORKSHEET #18: SETTING PRIORITIES

It is now time to return to the categories of social analysis that we used to gather information. With the information we have and a named vision, the group lists what action needs to be done, when, and in what order. The following categories of questions can help develop and shape action. You are encouraged to adapt these or create your own.

As a group, notice which areas (economic, political, cultural, environmental, and religious) generate energy and whether particular needs demand priority.

1. Discuss the following questions:

- Which area(s) [economic, political, cultural, environmental, religious] are most immediately needed to move toward your goal (where you faith reflection led you)?
- How do these areas move you closer to your long-term goals?
- Which areas have short-term goals that lead to the long-term goal?
- Where does the energy of the group members lean?
- Are there time-sensitive events you need to incorporate into your choices. For example, is legislation possible or pending? Is an important parish meeting coming up? Is action within an academic year important?

2. Once you have considered the questions above, depending on the group's size, choose one or two short-term goals to prioritize and designate subgroups for each. You may wish to chart the different areas and see how each connects to the larger goal.

3. Meet regularly to see how your efforts are contributing to the larger goal.

Worksheet #19: Timeline

Once you have chosen a goal, draft a timeline to indicate visually what is needed next. The sample below is simply one way to organize a schedule.

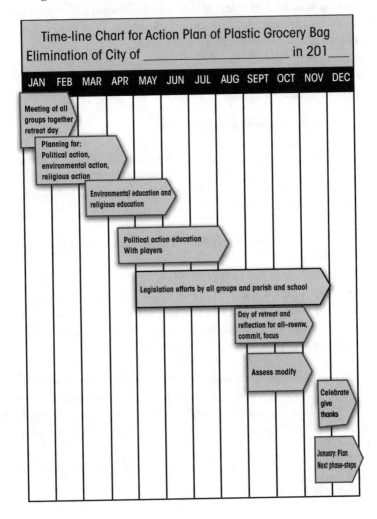

Time-line Chart for Action Plan of Plastic Grocery Bag Elimination of City of _____ in 201____

JAN FEB MAR APR MAY JUN JUL AUG SEPT OCT NOV DEC

Meeting of all groups together retreat day

Planning for: Political action, environmental action, religious action

Environmental education and religious education

Political action education With players

Legislation efforts by all groups and parish and school

Day of retreat and reflection for all—reenw, commit, focus

Assess modify

Celebrate give thanks

January: Plan Next phase-steps

WORKSHEET #20: ACTION PLANS—
GUIDING, CREATING, AND ORGANIZING

In thinking about possible action, the following categories of questions are helpful: *guiding questions*, *creating questions*, and *organizing questions*. Questions in each area of social analysis include the following (please adapt and edit as needed):

Economic Action

Guiding questions
- What role does economics play in your short-term plan? In your long-term plan?
- How is economics connected to the systemic change you seek to bring about?
- What faith values need to impact the economic factors in this issue (e.g., immigration reform must also consider human dignity, solidarity, rights, and responsibilities)?
- Is there a particular form of action that flows from your particular group (for example, a Franciscan- or Jesuit-run parish, an educational ministry, a healing ministry, and so on)?

Creating questions
- If there were a blank slate for economic factors, what kind of system would you create?
- How would you change the economic structures in place to a vision that more closely reflects your faith values?

Organizing questions
- Who is needed for this group?
- What skills are needed?
- Who has expertise?
- What actors are still needed? (This may be in the specific area or you may invite a few persons who imagine be-

yond economics or across disciplines with a good deal of imagination to stimulate your thinking.)

Political Action

Guiding questions
- What role does political action play in your short-term plan? In your long-term plan?
- How is politics connected to the systemic change you seek to create?
- What faith values need to impact politics and law in this issue?
- Is there a particular form of action that flows from your particular group (e.g., a Franciscan- or Jesuit-run parish, an educational ministry, a healing ministry, and so on)?

Creating questions
- If there were a blank slate for political factors, what kind of system would you create that would be different?
- How would you change the political structures in place to achieve a vision that more closely reflects your faith values?

Organizing questions
- Who is needed?
- Who has expertise?
- What actors are still needed?

Cultural Action

Guiding questions
- What role does culture play in your short-term plan? In your long-term plan?
- How is culture connected to the systemic change you seek to bring about?
- What faith values need to impact culture?
- Is there a particular form of action that flows from your particular group (e.g., a Franciscan- or Jesuit-run parish, an educational ministry, a healing ministry, and so on)?

Creating questions
- If there were a blank slate for culture, what kind of system would you create?
- How would you change the cultural structures in place to achieve a vision that more closely reflects your faith values?

Organizing questions
- Who is needed for this group?
- What skills are needed?
- Who has expertise?
- What actors are still needed?

Environmental Action

Guiding questions
- What role does the environment play in your short-term plan? In your long-term plan?
- How is the environment connected to the systemic change you seek to bring about?
- What faith values need to impact environmental efforts in this area?
- Is there a particular form of action that flows from your particular group (e.g., a Franciscan- or Jesuit-run parish, an educational ministry, a healing ministry, and so on)?

Creating questions
- If there were a blank slate for the environment, what would you do to create a workable system?
- How would you change the environmental structures in place to achieve a vision that more closely reflects your faith values?

Organizing questions
- Who is needed for this group?
- What skills are needed?
- Who has expertise?
- What actors are still needed?

Religious Action

Guiding questions
- What role does religion play in your short-term plan? In your long-term plan?
- How is religion connected to the systemic change you seek to bring about?
- What faith values need to impact religious structures?
- Is there a particular form of action that flows from your particular group (e.g., a Franciscan- or Jesuit-run parish, an educational ministry, a healing ministry, and so on)?

Creating questions
- If there were a blank slate for religious factors, what kind of system would you create?
- How would you change the religious structures now in place to achieve a vision that more closely reflects your faith values?

Organizing questions
- Who is needed for this group?
- What skills are needed?
- Who has expertise?
- What actors are still needed?

Worksheet #21: Create Models, Experiment, and Turn the Plan into Action

Create Models

It is now time to try out in miniature scale some of the ideas and plans generated. To do so we

- Group people according to vision and energy.
- Maintain time limits.
- Design what you envision.
- Fill in details for the vision.
- Communicate often with whole group.
- Adjust models as needed for the vision.
- Create models that may be parts of the process or the whole.

Assessment, Revision, and Next Steps

Once you have created, experimented with, and followed certain steps of action, you need to see what is working and what needs modification or improvement. Assessment aided by questions is essential for initial and ongoing efforts. The following questions are intended to continually assess and revise sections of the action and to ask some relevant personal and global questions, including the following:

1. How is your particular area (economic, political, environmental, cultural, religious) being put to action?

2. Are there gaps between what you are trying to do and the results? If so, what is necessary to close the gap?

3. What next step is needed in your area?

4. What major players are involved? Are there others you have not yet considered?

5. How are you affecting the system you are seeking to change?

6. What is happening to the persons (or Earth community) most adversely impacted by the system of injustice that you are addressing?

7. How is your action connected to creating a world marked by justice and peace?

8. Where are you finding God in this process?

9. Is your deepest envisioning present? If not, why? What next step could improve this?

10. Who are you becoming in the midst of this? Do you sense a change?

11. How has this process affected your group or community?

12. What is the possible impact on civil and international life?

Selected Bibliography

Bevans, Stephen B., and Roger P. Schroeder. *Prophetic Dialogue: Reflections on Christian Mission Today*. Maryknoll, NY: Orbis Books, 2011.

Brackley, Dean. *The Call to Discernment in Troubled Times: New Perspectives on the Transformative Wisdom of Ignatius of Loyola*. New York: Crossroad, 2004.

Catechism of the Catholic Church. New York: Doubleday, 1995.

Catholic Biblical Association of America, Confraternity of Christian Doctrine, and Bishops' Committee. *New American Bible*. New York: P. J. Kenedy, 1970.

Cimperman, Maria. *When God's People Have HIV/AIDS: An Approach to Ethics*. Maryknoll, NY: Orbis Books, 2005.

Dorr, Donal. *Option for the Poor: A Hundred Years of Catholic Social Teaching*, rev. ed. Maryknoll, NY: Orbis Books, 1992.

———. *Spirituality and Justice*. Maryknoll, NY: Orbis Books, 1984.

Ellacuria, Ignacio. "The Crucified People." In *Mysterium Liberationis: Fundamental Concepts of Liberation Theology*, ed. Ignatio Ellacuria and Jon Sobrino, [**QY: Give complete page range**]. Maryknoll, NY: Orbis Books, 1993.

Flannery, Austin, ed. *Vatican Council II: More Postconciliar Documents*. English ed. Grand Rapids: William B. Eerdmans, 1982.

Freire, Paulo. *Pedagogy of the Oppressed*, rev. 20th anniv. ed., trans. Myra Bergman Ramos. New York: Continuum, 1997.

Goizueta, Roberto S. "Solidarity." In *New Dictionary of Catholic Spirituality*, ed. Michael Downey, 906. Collegeville, MN: Liturgical Press, 1993.

———. *Caminemos con Jésus: Toward a Hispanic/Latino Theology of Accompaniment*. Maryknoll, NY: Orbis Books, 1995.

Groody, Daniel G. *Globalization, Spirituality, and Justice*. Maryknoll, NY: Orbis Books, 2007.

———, ed. *The Option for the Poor in Christian Theology*. Notre Dame, IN: University of Notre Dame Press, 2007.

Gula, Richard M. *The Call to Holiness: Embracing a Fully Christian Life*. New York: Paulist Press, 2003.

———. *The Good Life: Where Morality and Spirituality Converge*. New York: Paulist Press, 1999.

———. *Moral Discernment*. New York: Paulist Press, 1997.

———. *Reason Informed by Faith: Foundations of Catholic Morality*. New York: Paulist Press, 1989.

Gutiérrez, Gustavo. *A Theology of Liberation: History, Politics, and Salvation*, rev. ed., trans. and ed. Sister Caridad Inda and John Eagleson. Maryknoll, NY: Orbis Books, 1988.

———. *We Drink from Our Own Wells: The Spiritual Journey of a People*, trans. Matthew J. O'Connell. Maryknoll, NY: Orbis Books, 1984.

HarperCollins Study Bible, New Revised Standard Version, ed. Wayne A. Meeks. New York: HarperCollins, 1993.

Himes, Kenneth R. *Christianity and the Political Order: Conflict, Cooptation, and Cooperation*. Maryknoll, NY: Orbis Books, 2013.

Hoppe, Leslie J. *There Shall Be No Poor among You: Poverty in the Bible*. Nashville: Abingdon Press, 2004.

Keane, Philip. *Christian Ethics and Imagination: A Theological Inquiry*. New York: Paulist Press, 1984.

Keenan, James F. "Proposing Cardinal Virtues." *Theological Studies* 56 (1995): 708–29.

———. "Spirituality and Morality: What's the Difference?" In *Method and Catholic Moral Theology: The Ongoing Reconstruction*, ed. Todd A. Salzman, 87–102. Omaha, NE: Creighton University Press, 1999.

———. "Virtue Ethics." In *Christian Ethics: An Introduction*, ed. Bernard Hoose, 89–94. Collegeville, MN: Liturgical Press, 1998.

———. *Virtues for Ordinary Christians*. Franklin, WI: Sheed &Ward, 1999.

———. "The Virtue of Prudence (IIa IIae, qq 47–56)." In *The Ethics of Aquinas*, ed. Stephen J. Pope, 259–71. Washington, DC: Georgetown University Press, 2002.

Lederach, John Paul, *The Moral Imagination: The Art and Soul of Building Peace.* Oxford: Oxford University Press, 2005.

Lohfink, Norbert F. *Option for the Poor: The Basic Principle of Liberation Theology in the Light of the Bible,* ed. Duane L. Christensen, trans. Linda M. Maloney. 2nd ed. North Richland Hills, TX: BIBAL Press, 1995.

Lynch, William F. *Images of Hope: Imagination as Healer of the Hopeless.* Baltimore: Helicon Press, 1965.

McCarthy, Eli Sasaran. *Becoming Nonviolent Peacemakers: A Virtue Ethic for Catholic Social Teaching.* Eugene, OR: Pickwick Publications, 2012.

Myers, Bryan L. *Walking with the Poor: Principles and Practices of Transformational Development,* rev. exp. ed. Maryknoll, NY: Orbis Books, 2011.

O'Keefe, Mark. *Becoming Good, Becoming Holy: On the Relationship of Christian Ethics and Spirituality.* New York: Paulist Press, 1995.

Reid, Barbara E. *Taking Up the Cross: New Testament Interpretations through Latina and Feminist Eyes.* Minneapolis: Fortress Press, 2007.

Scharmer, C. Otto. *Theory U: Leading from the Future as It Emerges.* Cambridge, MA: Society of Organizational Learning, 2007.

Schreiter, Robert J. *The Ministry of Reconciliation: Spirituality and Strategies.* Maryknoll, NY: Orbis Books, 1998.

Sobrino, Jon. *The Principle of Mercy: Taking the Crucified People from the Cross.* Maryknoll, NY: Orbis Books, 1994.

Vatican Council II: The Conciliar and Post Conciliar Documents, new rev. ed., ed. Austin Flannery. Vatican Collection, vol. 1. Grand Rapids: William B. Eerdmans, 1992.

Wijsen, Frans, Peter Henriot, and Rodrigo Mejía, eds. *The Pastoral Circle Revisited: A Critical Quest for Truth and Transformation.* Maryknoll, NY: Orbis Books, 2005.